A MORAL ONTOLOGY FOR A THEISTIC ETHIC

This book develops a moral ontology for a theistic ethic that engages the work of contemporary moral and political philosophers, and reaffirms the relevance of a theistic tradition of God's relation to the world reflected in the fundamental teachings of Judaism, Christianity and Islam. Drawing on recent thought in the non-religious fields of psychology and political and moral philosophy, which build around the concept of human flourishing in community, Frank G. Kirkpatrick argues that a theistic ethic need not be the captive of parochial or sectarian theological camps. He proposes a common or universal ethic that transcends the fashionable ethnocentric 'incommensurate differences' in morality alleged by many post-modern deconstructionists.

In the wake of ethnic religious strife post September 11th 2001, this book argues for a common morality built on the inclusivity of love, community, and justice that can transcend sectarian and parochial boundaries.

D1607935

HEYTHROP STUDIES
IN CONTEMPORARY PHILOSOPHY, RELIGION AND THEOLOGY

Series Editor
Laurence Paul Hemming, Heythrop College, University of London, UK

Series Editorial Advisory Board
John McDade SJ; Peter Vardy; Michael Barnes SJ; James Hanvey SJ;
Philip Endean SJ; Anne Murphy SHCJ

Drawing on renewed willingness amongst theologians and philosophers to enter into critical dialogues with comtemporary issues, this series is characterised by Heythrop's reputation for openness and accessibility in academic engagement. Presenting volumes from a wide international, ecumenical, and disciplinary range of authors, the series explores areas of current theological, philosophical, historical and political interest. The series incorporates a range of titles: accessible texts, cutting-edge research monographs, and edited collections of essays. Appealing to a wide academic and intellectual community interested in philosophical, religious and theological issues, research and debate, the books in this series will also appeal to a theological readership which includes enquiring lay-people, Clergy, members of religious communities, training priests, and anyone engaging broadly in the Catholic tradition and with its many dialogue partners.

Published titles include:
Essays Catholic and Critical – Edited by Philip G. Ziegler and Mark Husbands
Reading Ecclesiastes – Mary E. Mills

Forthcoming titles include:
God as Trinity – James Hanvey

A Moral Ontology for a Theistic Ethic

Gathering the Nations in Love and Justice

FRANK G. KIRKPATRICK
Trinity College, USA

ASHGATE

© Frank G. Kirkpatrick 2003

Published by
Ashgate Publishing Limited
Gower House
Croft Road
Aldershot
Hants GU11 3HR
England

Ashgate Publishing Limited
Suite 420
101 Cherry Street
Burlington
VT 05401-4405
USA

Ashgate website: http://www.ashgate.com

British Library Cataloguing in Publication Data
Kirkpatrick, Frank G.
  A moral ontology for a theistic ethic: gathering the
  nations in love and justice. – (Heythrop studies in
  contemporary philosophy, religion and theology)
  1. Religion and ethics 2. Ontology 3. Theism
  I. Title II. Heythrop College
  210.1

Library of Congress Cataloging-in-Publication Data
Kirkpatrick, Frank G.
  A moral ontology for a theistic ethic: gathering the nations in love and justice / Frank
  G. Kirkpatrick.
      p. cm. – (Heythrop studies in contemporary philosophy, religion, and
    theology)
  Includes bibliographical references.
  ISBN 0-7546-3156-7 (alk. paper) – ISBN 0-7546-3157-5 (pbk.: alk. paper)
  1. Christian ethics. 2. God I. Title II. Series.
BJ1251.K525 2003
241–dc21   2002032690

ISBN 0 7546 3156 7 (Hardback)
ISBN 0 7546 3157 5 (Paperback)
Typeset by MHL Production Services Ltd, Coventry
Printed and bound in Great Britain by MPG Books Ltd, Bodmin, Cornwall

To my ever-growing community of discourse and love:
Liz, Amy, Jeff, Daniel, and Penne

'I will gather all the nations' (Joel 3:2)

'He shall judge between the nations, and shall arbitrate for many peoples; they shall beat their swords into plowshares and their spears into pruning hooks; nation shall not lift up their sword against nation, neither shall they learn war any more.'
(Isaiah 2:2–4)

Contents

Preface

This book is an exploration of some of the ways in which a theistic ethic can find fruitful overlap and common ground with non-religious moral and political philosophy. It grew out of the opportunity afforded me as a Charles A. Dana Research Professor at Trinity College to participate in a series of conversations with colleagues outside the Department of Religion. Most of these persons were in the fields of philosophy and political science. Together we read works by Charles Taylor, John Rawls, communitarians, Kant, and numerous contemporary moral philosophers and philosophers of emotion, psychology, epistemology, and science. As I read and conversed my way through discussions of political liberalism and communitarianism, anti-theory, deconstruction, the nature of the self, analyses of flourishing, object-relations theory, theories of justice, feminism, Marxism, virtue ethics, natural law, and a host of related topics, I became increasingly convinced that many of the themes traditionally incorporated under the rubric of 'theistic' or more narrowly 'Christian' ethics, overlapped or had significant points of commonality with many of these philosophical themes.

I also became convinced that a truly theistic ethic was, in the end, a human ethic. As such it should provide the basis for a great deal more commonality in ethics than is presently considered fashionable by many postmodern deconstructionist moral philosophers. I want to argue that while a complete universal ethic is probably impossible, there is much more universality possible in an ethic for human beings than critics and skeptics want to allow for. This universality, I am convinced, rests ultimately upon the universality of God as the ground for a common human nature and as an historical Agent working to bring about concrete experiences of commonality, especially through the instantiations of love and community.

As an ethicist in the Christian tradition I do believe that Christian ethics has grasped some essential truths about human nature as such. I am convinced however, that these truths are not uniquely or distinctively Christian. They are, as 'truths' common to any ethics rooted in the belief that God makes a difference to the structures and history of the world. Christian ethics as such, of course, makes certain claims about the importance of Jesus Christ to the fulfillment of God's intentions in history, but these claims do not, I think, run counter to the more fundamental ontological foundation for a universal human ethic rooted in the creative intention and actions of God if the latter are construed as leading to the flourishing of the human person in community. Therefore, while I will draw upon a number of Christian theologians in my reading of a theistic ethic, the truth of the latter does not depend upon Christian theology (rather it is the other way around).

Throughout the process of conversation and reading, I wondered why many contemporary theological treatments of ethics seemed devoid of references to the work of philosophers dealing with the same things without the theistic reference. I also wondered why most philosophers seemed ignorant of, or at least indifferent to, the work of some of the best theological ethicists. I decided to attempt a study in which I would integrate and evaluate the best work being done in both arenas.

There was, of course, a limited number of issues I could take up. First among these was the problem of grounding what I call a 'moral ontology'. By that I mean an understanding of the realities of the world that have to be taken account of by any moral theory. One obstacle that had to be dealt with immediately was whether such an ontology is possible at all in light of the postmodern, deconstructionist belief that we simply cannot 'get at' reality except through historically, culturally, and psychologically conditioned and contingent construals that can never truly 'reveal' the underlying ontology of the world (even assuming there is one). As a Christian ethicist, I was convinced that there are certain ontological claims that underlie theistic moral insights. Among these, first and foremost, are the ontological reality of a personal agent God, and God's intentions and actions in the world. I had dealt previously with the philosophical problems involved in defending a belief in the ontological reality of God as an objective, individual, personal Agent whose actions shape the structure of and carry forward divine intentions in the world.[1] Now I wanted to develop the implications of those ontologically structuring and purposeful divine actions for the fulfillment of human beings seeking to respond to them faithfully and responsibly in the midst of their embedded, historically contingent, moral pluralistic, social and personal lives.

This meant that I had to confront the challenges of deconstructionism, relativism, moral pluralism, anti-realism, and anti-theory in contemporary moral philosophy and epistemology. I eventually opted for what I call a moderately realist theory of knowledge, situated within a broadly pragmatic frame. I am convinced that such an epistemology can do justice both to the theistic foundations of a Christian ethic and to the truth of the deconstructionist and pluralist claim that we human beings do construct our interpretations of reality: they do not come implanted in our brains, in a completely foundational fashion, with a built-in conceptual guarantee of their 'mirroring' of the world as it is.

This led me to take up the question of how the Biblical theistic tradition[2] constructed its own interpretation, or construal, of God's presence in the world of human experience and action. After laying out the core of the divine intention as discerned from a critical reading of Scripture (still a basic resource for any Jewish or Christian ethic), I then attempt to show how God's purposes incorporate and ground what moral philosophers like to call human well-being and 'flourishing'. Much of the book is an attempt to flesh out what flourishing means for the full human person understood as a unity of body, mind, and spirit living in a world of political, economic, and social structures. I wanted, in short, to integrate the theistic understanding of flourishing in and through love in deeply personal communal relations with a political understanding of life lived in the impersonal structures of society shaped by the principles of justice.

A second theme emerged clearly at this point: the commonality, at least in some basic and essential respects, of human nature. If God's intention incorporates the entire human race, then no matter how important human diversity and difference are, there must be some 'core' to human flourishing. This had to be established in the face of claims to radical moral pluralism, incommensurate moral claims, and irreducible human differences. Underneath the much heralded 'incommensurability' of moral outlooks, I found a common core to the fulfillment and flourishing of human nature which, while thin in some respects, was quite thick in others, especially as it bears on the ubiquitous human experiences of love, mutuality, and community.

An alternative title of the book might well have been 'to gather the nations', a phrase taken from the Biblical tradition. To me it represents God's intention to gather up all peoples, without annulling their uniquenesses and individualities, into one universal human community (or, more properly, a community of communities), and thus underscores the commonality of human beings that anchors all the diversity and pluralism that we can bear and celebrate.

The key to reconciling commonality and difference lies, I am convinced, in the celebration of diversity and 'otherness' within the mutuality of community. Community became the linchpin for holding together genuine mutuality with a deep appreciation and lively celebration of uniqueness and individuality. A theistic ethics has much to teach moral philosophy (which in liberal political philosophy often focuses not on the substance but on the *forms* of sociality) about the *content* of mutuality, love, and relationship within community. At the same time, it has much to learn from the field of psychology, especially object-relations theory, about how relationships with others constitute the psychological health of persons. There is also interesting work in the field of emotionality that can be drawn upon by a theistic ethic of flourishing for people struggling to be whole persons.

The work on flourishing that is emerging from moral philosophy has many rich contributions to make to Christian understandings of the role and nature of altruism, trust, love, other-regardingness, and reciprocity. At the same time, a Christian ethic can enrich these contributions by insights drawn from its theistic moral ontology in which God's love and action constitute essential markers for human fulfillment and without which it cannot be attained.

There is also much to be learned from a conversation between theistic ethics and the moral wisdom of feminism and contemporary reinterpretations of Marxism, some of which echoes theistic themes of relationality even while ignoring ontological claims about the divine reality who creates and sustains the conditions of relationality. (Much of the suspicion in this particular dialogue centers on outdated and inadequate views of God found among the secular conversationalists.)

There is also much in the natural law tradition and in virtue ethics which supports the theistic ethic I am developing and which, by their very foundation, links up with philosophical ethics rooted in an understanding of the human person. I argue that natural law ethics has been misappropriated in some respects and that its congruence with non-theistic ethics is stronger than many secular critics have allowed. In the development of this congruence, Christian ethics has to face the issue of whether some of its traditional insistence on radical self-giving (agape), to the exclusion of self-interest, is necessary. I suggest that it is not and that there are ways, within a philosophy of community, to reconcile self-interest with altruistic self-giving to others through what I call, drawing upon the philosophy of John Macmurray, the logic of mutual heterocentrism.

Ultimately, a theistic ethics must face the question of the relation between its theologically grounded understanding of community and political philosophy's understanding of society. A theistic ethics has much to learn from political philosophy about life in societies in which love and mutuality are capable, at best, only of approximation, never of full instantiation. All communities are societies, but not all societies are communities, in the sense used by most Jewish and Christian ethicists. But the structures of society, especially those having to do with justice, are an indispensable foundation for communities of mutuality. Therefore, a clearer articulation of the relation between society and community than is normally found in Christian ethical theory in particular is called for.

No matter how clear theists are in their own minds about construing the ontological reality of God and God's intentions, no matter how precisely they draw out the moral implications of these intentions for ethically responsible living, there always remain ontological gaps between God's intentions and our grasp of them; between our conceptual grasp of them and our actions in pursuit of them; and between our ideals and our achievements. This is where the work of contemporary political philosophers in both the liberal and communitarian traditions, needs to be integrated into a Christian social ethic.

I would like to acknowledge the support of a number of people in the development of this book. Dr. Jan Cohn, Dean of the Faculty at Trinity College, who appointed me as Charles A. Dana Research Professor for the years 1993–95 deserves special mention. During that time I had the opportunity to read voluminously in the fields of moral and political philosophy. I also want to thank a number of colleagues whose conversations in various 'reading groups' or 'collaborative studies' proved invaluable in helping me think through many of the ideas that were eventually incorporated into this book: Richard Lee, Miller Brown, Mel Woody, John Gilroy, and Larry Vogel, professional philosophers all. A special note of gratitude is given to my friend and colleague Maurice Wade, of Trinity's Philosophy Department, without whose intellectual enthusiasm and continual invitations to new reading and dialogue this work might never have seen the light of day. Thanks are also due to a number of people outside Trinity College. Above all to James W. Jones, whose personal friendship and scholarly work deeply informed this study; Richard Tombaugh, whose reading of an early draft helped improve it; Jack Costello, whose unflagging support for my various endeavors and whose reading of the manuscript contributed to its culmination; Lee Wallace, a 'non-professional' but thoroughly scholarly companion; Michael Fielding of the John Macmurray Fellowship in the UK, at whose invitation I was given the opportunity to deliver to that organization in June of 1995 a version of Chapter 9 of the present book; and, of course, to the usual cast of characters at home: my wife Liz, and my two (now grown) children, Amy and Daniel, whose very being and love always have made community more than a naive ideal for me.

Notes

1 Frank G. Kirkpatrick, *Together Bound: God, History and the Religious Community*, (New York: Oxford University Press, 1994).
2 There are, of course, many theistic traditions, including Judaism, Christianity, Islam, many African Religions, and so forth. Because I am most familiar with the Christian tradition, and to a slightly lesser extent with Judaism, I have restricted my analysis primarily to those two religious outlooks. This in no way suggests that my treatment of theistic ethics would not also apply to Islam, but I am not a scholar of Islam and would hesitate to suggest points of contact between its theism and that of Judaism and Christianity that I cannot support by my own scholarship in the area. When I use the word 'theism' therefore, it can be taken, for the purposes of this book only, to refer to the main themes found in the Biblical traditions of Judaism, and given my own expertise, especially in Christianity.

Introduction

Theistic ethics and non-theistic moral philosophy rarely seem to draw from the riches of the other. Moral philosophers are not generally inclined to take the claims of theism seriously and find little of interest in religious ethics. At the same time, many theological ethicists, while borrowing selectively, often fail to consider the full resources of secular[1] moral philosophy. I want to show that the divide can be crossed more fruitfully than is often appreciated and that theistic ethics has much to learn from its secular counterpart, without abandoning its theistic foundation. That foundation commits theistic ethics to certain core beliefs about the authority for moral action. That authority is different, in certain crucial respects, from the authorities to which non-theistic ethics tends to look. By the same token, if secular moral philosophy could overcome its often uncritical rejection of theism, it would find an openness in theistic ethics to many of its favorite themes, such as historicity, the significance of the 'Other', pluralism, and varieties of human flourishing. But despite different foundations there is much common ground between these moral outlooks.

In the process of developing this common ground, in particular around understandings of love and community as decisive elements in human flourishing, it is important not to reduce theistic ethics to a pale reflection of a generalized humanist ethic. While there are crucial differences between theistic and secular ethics, I am convinced that many of these are not irreducible. In this respect I take a stance rather different from that of Stanley Hauerwas who can write, from a Christian perspective, a book entitled *Against the Nations*. My stance, also from what I take is a theistic perspective (informed by Christian ethics), is somewhat more embracing of the secular than his. There is a place in Christian ethics both to stand against the secular world and a place from which to embrace that world, albeit critically and on the basis of particular and distinct theistic ontological claims. I want to be faithful to what I take to be the core claims of a theistic ontology regarding some things that are real and will not go away regardless of the contingent narratives of their role in the shaping of historical experiences.

It might be objected, particularly by Christian ethicists, that in focusing upon flourishing or human well-being, I have not done justice to the fullness of what Christians take to be the victorious, renewed life of a person 'in Christ'. I do not deny the charge. There is more about the fullness of human life that Christians might want to say with respect to how the grace and power of God in Christ impact human life than can be captured in words like 'flourishing' and 'well-being' which are taken primarily from the secular vocabulary of moral philosophy. Whether *all* that the Christian believes constitutes the Christ-filled life can even be captured in words is probably doubtful. But my task is not to point toward what cannot be said but toward what is being said by non-Christian, non-theistic moral philosophers about the possibilities life has to offer for the most flourishing, exciting, and fulfilling life imaginable for human persons. Surely such a life would not be at odds with what the Christian life entails, though it may fall short of it in some crucial ways. But if God created human life to be fulfilled in and through the created order, then flourishing lives in that order must significantly overlap or have multiple points of commonality with lives formed by Christian and other theistically grounded ethical forces. A Christian ethic is not ultimately incongruent with a fully developed human ethic, in both of which human flourishing is the primary end. Both religious and secular moral philosophies are grounded on the same reality: the life of persons is most enriched in loving, mutual relationships. Any true renderings of that reality must necessarily cohere with each other.

The Authorities for Christian Ethics

If Christian theology and liturgy are taken seriously, they seem committed to the following authorities for determining the appropriate course of Christian lives: the authority of their own personal experience of a divine and gracious presence in their lives, the authority of the Bible (the narrative record of that presence in the lives of others before them), the authority of the religious tradition to which they belong (the historical teachings and practices of the religious community that has continued to experience that presence), and the authority of their creeds and their liturgies in which they express their convictions about reality. On the basis of these authorities, theists would seem to be committed to a basic belief in a supreme, powerful, and decisive reality other than human beings from whose will and actions the way in which their lives are led (morality) must gain direction and guidance. That reality is, of course, God.

But the very existence of this God, along with the validity of any claims made about God, including those having to do with a moral response to God's intentions, are subject today to enormous skepticism within the philosophical community, and, increasingly, in the religious community as well. As this skepticism has found its way into some segments of the Christian community, other Christians have pulled up the drawbridges and retreated into a modern version of fideism in which all rational assault against Christian belief is repelled by claims of Biblical inerrancy, revealed truth, and the impregnable barriers of a tradition-bound constructed narrative unique to a particular Christian people.

One of the most compelling objections to a theistic ethic is that set forth by a number of moral philosophers espousing what is sometimes called 'anti-theory', or postmodern, deconstructed ethics. Their arguments are important because they cut through to the deepest problems in moral reflection and raise, in a variety of different ways, many questions about the universality of ethics for the peoples of all nations and communities.

In the following sections, I want to set forth the principal claims of this postmodern ethic and then to provide what I believe is a Christian response to it based on a view of God that departs significantly from the classical view of an immutable, utterly transcendent, and non-historically involved deity, a view the critics assume is necessarily tied to all forms of theistic ethics in the Jewish and Christian traditions.

Situating the Constraining Points of this Ethic

What sets this approach to ethics apart from most studies in moral philosophy, and even in theological ethics, is the centrality of God's purpose as enacted through divine agency in history. Of course, all theological ethics make reference to the will of God. But often God's will is believed to be found only in the structures and dynamics of human nature. What I have attempted is to locate that will in the *actions* of God as construed through the narratives of Scripture and in the life-stories of people who believe themselves to be the recipients of divine grace. I want to press to the limit the notion of God as an Agent who manifests a purpose in and through God's actions in the lives of historically contingent human persons. It is only in and through those historical actions that one can infer what God is up to concretely over and above what one can know of God simply through the unchanging structures of nature. And it is only in and through a correct discernment of God's purpose that persons can have a meaningful basis for knowing what to do responsibly (morally) in response to what God has done and what one believes God is intending for human beings.

I believe that a credible case can be made for the rational cogency of the idea of an acting, historically engaged, Being with sufficient power (as well as the moral use of that power) to be worshipped as God. That was the burden of my previous book *Together Bound: God, History, and the Religious Community*.[2] However, the rational cogency of an idea is not the same as the proof that such an idea, in fact, corresponds to something real. It is even more difficult, perhaps, to make the case for correspondence if one draws primarily from the 'evidence' of the Biblical narrative and the life-experiences of persons who constitute the ongoing community that is informed by that narrative.

Not only is the question of the privileging of that narrative over other narratives a problem, but also internal to the Biblical narrative are problems about what kind of consistent, non-contradictory picture of God one can draw from it. I do not intend to solve all these problems in this study. My argument should be seen clearly within the limits that surround it. I am trying to present a case for a theistic moral ontology that faithfully reflects the core of what most theists most of the time have believed to be the case about God and God's relation to history. For the Christian, for example, there is a normative quality to Irenaeus' notion that the Church (the community of believers) believes "these points [of doctrine] just as if she had but one soul, and one and the same heart, and she proclaims them, and teaches them, and hands them down, with perfect harmony, as if she possessed only one mouth."[3] While there is certainly much dispute about the exact range and detail of "these points of doctrine", I believe a theistic moral ontology must take as fundamental to its construal of the Biblical account a belief in a creator God who acts in history to further God's intentions.

I intend to position my argument primarily within the Christian tradition, but not bound absolutely to the specific language or thought forms of all its historic creeds and doctrines. I also want to place myself in continuity with the intent of the Biblical witness to God's saving action, but not to a fundamentalist, literalist understanding of it. And I want to position myself to a very large extent within the philosophical community, committed to its principles of coherence, consistency, and adequate verification of truth-claims within a generally pragmatic and moderately realist epistemology. These locating points may not always square easily with each other, but my argument is predicated upon the hypothesis that a theist can be rationally reflective about as well as experientially committed to the reality of a saving power bearing down on her with such force that she is compelled to respond (through ethical reflection and moral action) to that power's intentions for her life and for the world. I want to take seriously the witness of others who have experienced the actions of this saving power (and represented those experiences in the narratives of the Bible). I want to take seriously the constraints of human rationality on what we can think intelligibly and meaningfully. And I want to take seriously the reality of a 'world' beyond myself that sets limits to what can be successfully proposed in thought and acted upon in practice. That world provides the minimal foundation for some universal elements (that extend to all persons) that a theistic ethic must reflect.

The Attack on Universal Ethics

The universal dimension in an ethical philosophy has come under severe criticisms of late. These are based on reality of historical change in the development of social and personal ethics, the historical contingency and conditions of ethical practice, the fact of moral pluralism, the suspicion of reason as a neutral, objective means of accessing truth, a questioning of moral 'systems' and moral 'theories' as capable of grounding an ethic or of resolving its dilemmas without ambiguity or neglect of unique moral particularities, a sensitivity to the inescapability of moral conflict (both between and within individuals), a questioning of unchanging moral absolutes, and an unexplored assumption that God is no longer relevant to the development of any mature ethics in the postmodern world.

I believe a case can be made that historical development is an integral part of a Christian ethic, that moral diversity (of a particular kind) is essential for this development and for its fullest possible historical expression, and, most importantly, that God is an historical personal agent whose own values and intentions for the created order are the foundation of theistic ethics. Nevertheless, these divine intentions do not constitute an 'authoritarian, external, abstract, or remote' source of moral action. The view of God on which I rely is at odds with much of the theological tradition that has grown up around the Christian faith, especially as it became expressed in the thought forms of Greek and medieval philosophy. Nevertheless, I believe it is close to the view of God that is present, albeit often at a low level of consciousness or reflection, in most active Christian persons who mean what they say when they recite their creeds, utter their prayers, participate in their liturgies, and read and interpret their Bibles as a record of divine actions in history.

A divine personal agent, actively involved in the history of the world, stands at the foundation of the Biblical construal of ethics. This God (and not the God of classical theology) can underwrite moral diversity, the reality of historical particularities and moral conflicts, the differences between individual persons as they affect moral decisions, and the importance, as well as the limits of, moral theory. At the same time, it is this God that provides the continuities and commonalities that keep diversity from breaking off into divisiveness, and pluralisms from degenerating into moral relativism. This God holds together both diversity and unity by God's intentions for and actions on behalf of a universal community[4] of flourishing fulfilled persons, each of whom experiences the bounty of God's grace in unique and particular ways appropriate to his or her uniquely created individuality but within a framework of human flourishing that, at its core, is common to all persons and expressed ultimately in community.

The Essential Claims of a Theistic Moral Ontology

Most secular moral philosophers tend to pigeon-hole Christian ethics (when they bother to treat it at all) into a box reserved for outmoded, ahistorical, absolutist, inflexible moral theories that are grounded in an unintelligible or at least unpersuasive belief in a transcendent reality.

The foundation of any theistic response to this pigeon-holing has to confront head-on the ontological nature of the reality of God and the metaphysical claims about it. Ultimately, I believe, there is no adequate response to the attack on the ethics of the Biblical tradition that does not directly deal with the issue of the reality of God. But even acknowledging the reality of God is not enough to adequately ground Christian ethics. We must go further and identify *which* God is meant by both the theists and the anti-theists. Different metaphysical principles implicate different conceptions of God. This means that the theistic response to the deconstructionist, relativistic claims against it must accept and deploy specific ontological and metaphysical principles that are bold enough (in the face of persistent philosophical skepticism) to assert the following:[5]

1. Theistic ethics is grounded in the ontological reality of a personal supreme divine Agent. Without asserting some metaphysical theory that accounts for God's ontological reality, theistic ethics cannot get off the ground; however, the grounding of this metaphysics need not entail the traditional or classical notions of God as non-temporal, impassable, unable to act in history, and ontologically transcendent of all that is finite and historical. There is more than one metaphysical system or set of ontological claims. A Biblically based ethic is committed to only one of them or at least to only those that are committed to the following claim.

2. God reveals God's reality through divine historical actions. These include the act of creating the essential conditions of life itself as well as further acts that sustain these conditions; a non-acting God, no matter how dressed up in the metaphysical finery of conceptual abstraction, is of no help in establishing and undergirding a theistic ethic.

3. The inference drawn from Scripture is that the divine Agent intends to fulfill, nourish, enhance, and bring to completion all that God has created. Human persons may not be the only objects of God's intention, but they do seem to have a particular importance in the created order because, unlike other created beings, they are able to respond to divine actions in a moral manner. This does not mean that

their fulfillment must conflict with the divine intention for the fulfillment of the rest of the cosmic order.

4. To be fulfilled in accord with the divine intention requires that human life be lived in some ways rather than others. There will be some ways of living that simply are not compatible with what God intends for human flourishing.

5. Morality is the response persons make to what they construe as the divine intention for human fulfillment. This means that a Christian ethic has a teleological orientation (though this does not eliminate the need for moral principles, rules-of-thumb, personal virtues, and so on).

6. The basis for human values, therefore, is their conformity to values that a more powerful agent ontologically grounds, *provided that persons want at some deep level to live in accord with the kind of life those divine values promise (that is, a life of flourishing and exquisite well-being)*; this means that God has so determined the structures of reality that human fulfillment must conform to those structures, no matter how many variations in ways of life there are that are compatible with that conformity. Some degree of diversity in the expression of humanly fulfilling ways of life need not conflict with universal, underlying structures of reality common to all life that is in basic conformity with God's values.

7. It also demands that human beings retain the freedom to reject the way(s) of life God intends, even when such rejection may lead to ultimate disappointment. God cannot impose his fulfillment on persons who choose to reject it.

8. The ontological claim underlying this kind of theistic ethic is that fulfilling life, ultimately, can only be lived *in and through a universal human community bound together by God's love for it and the members' love for each other as empowered by God's love for them*. Mutual community is the singular locus that creates and reconciles diversity, particularity, fulfillment, and universality; the conditions of human community set the limits to diversity but at the same time provide the basis for its expression since no community can be fulfilling to its members unless it nourishes their particularities as individuals.

9. Because of the historical nature of human life, Christian ethics cannot be practiced except through particular, historical communities responding to what they take to be God's will to create a universal community. Theists cannot make adequate moral judgments completely outside the context of communal life lived in conformity with God's will. It cannot be stressed strongly enough that the origin of Christian ethics in particular is in the life and work of Christians living together in community. It is their concrete experience of life together formed through common commitments and practices that provides the content of theological reflection, which, in turn, gives rise to the idea of a God who grounds their lives and the ethics by which they live them.

Each of these claims will need fleshing out. But binding them together is a set of convictions that reality has been structured in a certain way by the historically decisive acts of a particular individual that we call God. The realities of God and the world that God has created cannot be ignored either in practice or in theory if one is to do theistic ethics, especially in dialogue with secular ethics. It will not be enough to sidestep the ontological claims they require. This fact is what makes a theistic ethic so difficult to fit into much of what now passes as postmodern ethics. Ontological claims are deeply suspect, as are any claims that one's beliefs are rooted in a reality beyond one's own particular, historically conditioned, limited perspective.

It can, in fact, be argued that epistemological relativism lies behind the suspicion of any moral claims that intend to have universal reach. We have reached a time in philosophy when claims to knowledge, certainty, and objectivity have little or no credibility among many postmodern philosophers. These philosophers are deeply wary of any claim to knowledge that is absolute and non-relative to and not conditioned by the particular personal and cultural context of the knower. It is because so many philosophers are now convinced that ideas cannot be shown to reflect any absolute reality absolutely, that they are reluctant to believe that we can establish an overarching, universal, all-inclusive ethical system, the ontological foundation for which could be rationally articulated and defended. The quandary of postmodern epistemology is that it cannot guarantee that any systems of thought, any ideas, concepts, or theories, represent anything other than the (limited, contextual, perspectival) mental world of the thinker or her 'community' of like-believers. The old notion of ideas 'representing', or mirroring faithfully, an 'external' world is no longer considered credible by many contemporary philosophers.

Because I believe God is an historical agent, I want to treat the idea of God as one would the idea of any reality that is experienced in and through the particular moments of one's own or others' history. That means to treat it pragmatically. A pragmatic treatment asks the question "What historical difference does God make?" And this question makes sense only if God is an historical Agent.[6]

Conversing With Philosophers

It might be asked why a Christian ethics, for example, should not be developed solely on the basis of Christian sources, perhaps even exclusively on the basis of the Bible and the experiences of Christians, both present and in the past. Why bother to 'dialogue' with philosophers who have little or no interest in religion (especially in its theistic foundation) and with some theologians, who often seem more occupied with spinning arcane and abstruse conceptual webs than with straightforward expressions of the actions of God in lives of persons and communities?

I believe that the experiences of persons, especially as inscribed in narrative form, are the ground of reflection. But experience without reflection is stagnant, uncreative, and incapable of providing direction to our lives. And once we enter the world of reflection (without necessarily giving it undue pride of place or overestimating its importance), we need to learn as much as we can about the dynamics and structure of rational thinking. Besides its utility value as a guide to more informed practice, thinking is both a gift of God and an intrinsic delight (at least on many if not all occasions).

While few people have literally been persuaded away from or into moral or religious convictions by logical/rational argument alone, the mature and sober Christian wants her grasp of Christian belief to be as solid, comprehensive, and valid as possible. Careful reflection on reflection is one way to achieve that. Even Christians need the sobering fresh water of a critical exposure of unclear thinking, incoherence, and contradiction in what they believe and assert. They have no reason to fear that Christian belief cannot stand up to the most critical of examinations because one of their core beliefs is that reality is ultimately God's reality. As such, it must be coherent with itself. Therefore, our cognitive grasp of reality (while shot through with ambiguities, incompleteness, and limitation) is grounded in that reality in a way that is congruent with God's work of creation and maintenance of reality.

The Spectrum of Christian Ethics

Finally, I need to say a bit more about where this study ought to be placed within the theological spectrum of Christian ethics proper. Given the conviction that God is the source of the moral order and that human moral action is (or ought to be) our response to God's actions as together they seek the fulfillment, well-being, and flourishing of all persons, I believe that what counts fundamentally and essentially as the flourishing of all persons is common to them all. In this sense, I agree with the natural law insistence that there is an objective good for all persons. On the other hand, I believe, with the 'liberals', that the discernment and working out of this good can take a variety of forms depending upon the historical and personal circumstances in which individuals find themselves. Thus, if labels are necessary (and in a way this work is a challenge to those who want to label positions with old categories), I am conservative in believing that there is an objectivity and universality to certain things that constitute human fulfillment. I am liberal in believing that there are a variety of ways (political, sociological, psychological, and historical) in which those things can be expressed or lived out consistent with the core of human flourishing. I am conservative in believing that there is a divine personal agent whose intentions and actions establish the goals, conditions, and boundaries for appropriate human moral action, extreme defiance of which will inevitably lead to human frustration and something less than full flourishing. I am liberal in believing that our understanding of these goals, conditions, and boundaries must be informed by those disciplines which study nature as it is (that is, the social and empirical sciences). I am conservative in believing that there is still some 'core' to that reality despite the multiple construals and narratives of it imagined by different communities and individuals.

The bridge between my conservative and liberal stances is my conviction that God created one world and one human race. We must conserve by all rational means possible the cogency of the notion of God's objective reality. And we must open ourselves by all rational means possible to learning about the intricacies and contents of the world that God has made and which we have, partially, re-created and transformed. The rational defense of a notion of God as a personal, creative, and active being may not convince all rational persons or be commensurable with all rational 'takes' on reality. But that does not mean that we believe in God for no rational reason or that a case for the rationality of belief in God cannot be made. I am committed to a natural theology but I stress the 'theos' of it as much as I do the 'nature' from which it draws some of its richest insights.

This study can situate itself fairly comfortably within a Thomist moral tradition, at least if that tradition holds (as Jean Porter claims it does) that "our moral evaluation of actions will necessarily be determined in part by our empirically-grounded knowledge of what it is to be human."[7] Unlike purely secular accounts of what it is to be human, however, the Christian ethicist must have recourse to the *practice* of the Christian virtues in the context of specific, faith-formed and historically situated communities. There is no need to set in opposition (as some virtue ethicists such as Stanley Hauerwas and Alasdair MacIntyre tend to do in their more extreme rhetorical flourishes) the claims that:

1   the practice of being human is always worked out in specific communities with specific narratives and places within history
2   the grounding of these practices is in the will and actions of God and
3   there is, therefore, a general practice and objective good for all human persons that, better than all other rivals, is most conducive to human well-being, flourishing, and ultimate fulfillment.

There is no reason to believe that an objective study of the human being in all her historical, empirical reality will yield a view of what it is to be human that is intrinsically at odds with what a Biblical theist believes God has intended for full humanness. There may be wrong empirical views of what counts as the full flourishing of human persons (for example, ones that discount the centrality of mutual love, or the need for a dependence upon the power of God), but this does not mean that empirical, or even political views, *per se*, have nothing true to say to Christian understandings of the human person.

In the end I think the division between a purely theological ethic and a purely humanistic moral philosophy is often too starkly drawn. This study is predicated on the assumption that there are no true insights from the natural order that do not inform and enrich the insights of the theologian. While I agree with Hauerwas and MacIntyre that the theological truth is to be found only where it is being lived out in particular, historically contingent communities, I disagree with their rhetorically exaggerated claims that the 'world' has nothing to offer to the self-understanding of such communities. They have drawn conceptual lines where none are necessary, *except as tactical maneuvers to keep Christians from a too-easy identification of their deepest insights with false or ersatz forms of sociality*. One can argue cogently and forcefully, as they do, against the liberal individualism of contemporary culture or against a false universalism that reduces persons to autonomous free-floating units of rational choice-making without denying that a deeper understanding of the natural order might well yield truths about human nature that cohere with the Biblical vision of the one God's creation of a single, unitary world within which persons sharing a common human nature struggle to find fulfillment.

Put simply, if the Biblical vision of human life in relation with God is true, its truth cannot, in the end, be hidden from those who study nature with an open mind for the truths it contains. One of those truths, in fact the central truth, I am convinced, is that in practice, human beings discover that their fulfillment, well-being, and flourishing can only occur maximally when they live in communities characterized by mutual love, trust, compassion, and until the Kingdom comes, in societies of justice.

On Hauerwas

In this respect, I need to situate my work in relation to Stanley Hauerwas' work in particular. I've subtitled my book *To Gather the Nations* while he has entitled one of his *Against the Nations*. I do not want to suggest that there are no differences between us, but I do think they can be exaggerated (in large part because Hauerwas has a tendency to exaggerate and to oversimplify his own claims for the sake of polemic).

Hauerwas' diatribes against much of what passes as Christian ethics rest on his profound suspicion of what he takes to be the liberal, enlightenment agenda rooted in the goal of freeing the self from entanglements with others so that it can pursue its personal vision of the good without undue interference. He is also suspicious of any Christian ethic that simply echoes or provides grounding for an understanding of human life that is not distinctly Christian, and worked out in the context of specific, particular Christian communities. He wants to avoid vague, universalistic appeals to 'community,' 'justice,' and 'love,' if they are not particularized in the life forms and virtues of specifically Christian lives lived in specifically Christian communities informed by a specifically Christian 'story' arising from the specific life and teaching of the specific individual, Jesus.

Nevertheless, Hauerwas insists that what makes Christian life in community possible is a conviction that it rests on *the* truth. "The only reason for being a Christian ... is because Christian convictions are true."[8]

I believe that Hauerwas' caution regarding the liberal agenda can be defended without falling into his almost Manichean dualism between the Christian and the 'worldling'. Hauerwas himself admits that he is not world-denying but "aggressively world affirming".[9] Nor has he an interest "in legitimating and/or recommending a withdrawal of Christians or the church from social or political affairs."[10] What then is the fuss all about?

Hauerwas is right that some persons will catch hold of a true vision of the reality of God's work in the world by living in a particular kind of community that more fulfillingly than others embodies God's intention. But this fact does not subvert the claim that ultimately that intention can be lived by all persons (if they catch the vision of it through the power of those who witness it) and that will fulfill them more completely than any other competing visions, including the liberal, demo-cratic one as long as it is untempered by Christian insight.

When Hauerwas differentiates Christians from the world,[11] he sometimes means simply to castigate the liberal culture of individualism (and its various corollaries, all of which center human hope solely in human effort and imagination, to the exclusion of divine action and inspiration).[12] When he is being more traditionally theological the world is the object of God's love which God has redeemed and to which the church (as the community of those who testify to that redemption) offers its witness and its service. The truth about the world may be found in the life of a distinct Christian community that the world at large now little recognizes or appreciates. But that does not make this truth exclusively parochial.

To live the truth, one must have a grasp of what truth it is that one is living. If all Hauerwas intends to say is that it is not enough just to think the truth, that one must live it as well, then the point is trivial and does not need the exaggerated division between church and world he suggests.

If Hauerwas really means it when he insists that all persons live in some kind of social union or another, then all persons will live, until the Kingdom comes, in nations or groups that aspire to be something like nations. Ultimately, therefore, the outcome of the Christian ethic ought to be a gathering of all nations (and the people who constitute them) into the one kingdom of God. One assumes that once in the kingdom those lines of distinction that constitute invidious or destructive differences between nations will disappear in a common brotherhood or fellowship.

For Hauerwas, the effort to speak a non-Christian language is not worth it[13] because it fails to take account of the fact that all ethics are done (when done rightly) from below, within and through the language of particular, historically situated faith communities, not from above in the language and thought-forms of human beings as such or in general. Moral convictions are inherently "historical and community-dependent".[14] Nevertheless, Hauerwas cannot let go of the fundamental Christian claim that what is true for Christians (since it derives from a God who is the God of all persons) is ultimately true for all.

Hauerwas, therefore, admits that the life of the Christian community is linked to a universal truth rooted in the one reality of God. It is not a truth exclusively *for* Christians, though they may be the only ones presently living it. Christians, he admits, cannot "give up claims of universality, but ... the basis of our universalism comes by first being initiated into a particular story and community." And the Christian's confidence in God's lordship leads to a trust that "the truth 'will out' " at the eschaton.[15]

So there is a universalism in Hauerwas, located precisely where one would expect it and where I have also located it: in the intention and actions of the one God of history. It would be better to understand his tendentious and provocative attacks, therefore, as attacks upon what he sometimes calls a 'false universalism', as it is embodied in the liberal, rationalistic, enlightenment project which places the value of individual self-sufficiency at its center. The details of this view we will examine in a subsequent chapter.

But the suspicion of the liberal project does not mean that the Christian theologian/ethicist should not be informed by its insights into human nature that point to and support (often without knowing that they are doing so) the Christian understanding of true life as life in communities characterized by compassion, trust, mutual love, and service to others. Hauerwas has raised a red flag where none is needed. And his deepest insights into truth often belie his more provocative and tendentious rhetoric. In this sense, I believe, he and I are not finally at odds with each other.

Notes

1 I use the word 'secular' simply as a counter to an ethic grounded on some 'religious' foundation. It should carry no other meaning that would extend the concept of secularity to a single set of ontological commitments beyond those that reject religious ontological claims.

2 Frank Kirkpatrick, *Together Bound: God, History, and the Religious Community*, (New York: Oxford University Press, 1994).

3 Irenaeus, 'Against Heresies,' in *The Apostolic Fathers With Justin Martyr and Irenaeus*, American edition, arranged by A. Cleveland Coxe, in *The Ante-Nicene Fathers*, eds. Alexander Roberts and James Donaldson, Volume I (Grand Rapids: Wm. B. Eerdmans, 1885), Book One, Chapter X, Section 2, p. 331.

4 I am using the word 'community' here more loosely than in my recent book *The Ethics of Community*, (Oxford: Blackwell, 2001), in which I distinguish between community proper (a direct personal relationship characterized by mutual love among a limited number of persons) and society (an association of indirect, more formal relationships of justice among a large number of people). Since the distinction between community and society has not reached a high degree of precision in most moral literature, I will revert to the somewhat profligate and vague use of the terms in this book.

5 For another statement of these principles see my *The Ethics of Community* pp. 4–6.

6 For a much fuller defense of the notion of God as an historical agent, see my *Together Bound: God, History, and the Religious Community*.

7 Jean Porter, *The Recovery of Virtue: The Relevance of Aquinas for Christian Ethics*, (Louisville: Westminster/John Know Press, 1990), p. 145.

8 Stanley Hauerwas, *A Community of Character*, (Notre Dame: University of Notre Dame Press, 1981), p. 1.

9 Stanley Hauerwas, *Against the Nations*, (Minneapolis: Winston Press, 1985), p. 7.

10 *Ibid.*, p. 1.

11 Hauerwas, *A Community of Character*, p. 91.

12 *Ibid.*, p. 109.

13 Hauerwas, *Against the Nations*, p. 38.

14 *Ibid.*, p. 41.

15 Hauerwas, *A Community of Character*, p. 101.

Chapter 1

The Challenge of Relativism and Deconstruction to Theistic Ethics

If one were to peruse the numerous books and articles currently being published by scholars in the field of philosophical ethics, the following assumptions and claims would present an immediate challenge to anyone committed to an ethic grounded in some notion of God as the Agent whose intentions for all of creation unify the historical stream within which each human agent acts and responds to the acts of others.

1. Moral disagreement and diversity are widespread; the same person at different times of her life, different persons, different communities of persons, the same community at different stages of its history – all express somewhat different moral values (or at least the ordering or prioritizing of values). People who agree on some values radically disagree on others.

2. This disagreement and diversity mean that there is no universal human consensus as to basic moral principles or values (except at the 'thinnest,' most general, and abstract level); this lack of consensus leads to a deep suspicion of the validity and worth of traditional moral *theories* that, by their very nature, assume the universalization of moral principles, that is, the application of the same principles to all persons regardless of fundamental differences between individuals and the cultures that shape them. The differences between moralities and moral theories are so great that most moral philosophers refer to them as 'incommensurable'. This means that there is no single standard of measurement by which they can be compared with each other. Incommensurability also means that the only moral standards we have are local, particular, and restricted to the specific historically contingent community of which we are part. There are no common, underlying universal moral principles that bind all these historically contingent communities and their moralities together.

3. There is no universal agreement as to whether there is such a thing as human nature in general (the ostensible basis for a universal ethic), or if there is, what its constitutive elements are; even should such agreement be reached it is unclear to many whether it is so inchoate and unformed as to provide a necessary or sufficient basis for a 'thick' ethic applicable to all persons.

4. Agreement that all human decisions and thought patterns are decisively shaped by particular, non-universalizable, historically-contingent, psychological, and cultural influences, causes, and frameworks; this leads to profound epistemological skepticism that is wide-spread, and fundamental. It even applies to ideas that once

were allegedly believed by some to 'represent' or 'mirror' the external world but now must be understood as, at best, pragmatically useful tools for negotiating one's way around in the world and as reflections simply of the thinker's conditioned reality.

5. Moral decisions often occur only in the context of genuine dilemmas and uncertainties; what moral philosophers call 'quandaries'. None of the available moral options is absolutely immoral but is, instead, a choice between competing and incommensurable moral goods; equally valid moral choices may tragically conflict with each other and there is no 'higher' moral ground on which to resolve the conflict in favor of one choice or to ameliorate the tragedy of having to make it.

6. Morality must be peculiarly sensitive to the 'otherness' or uniqueness of different persons: it is a failure of moral theory to lump all persons indiscriminately under a general moral principle (of the 'generalized Other') that pays no attention to their differentiating and unique characteristics; the more attention is paid to unique persons in particular situations the less universal an ethic covering them can be; the more universal it is, the less capable it is of speaking to specific situations for uniquely different persons.

7. One dimension of concern for the otherness and diversity of persons in different historical/cultural/moral contexts is a particular sensitivity to historical change in the development and manifestation of moral values; the fact of historical change, both between individuals and between groups in different historical periods, undercuts any claim of an ethic to be universalizable to all persons and historical epochs without qualification.

8. Instead of developing universal moral norms, the focus of moral concern should be the nurture, care, well-being, and flourishing of distinct, particular, and other human beings, albeit most especially those within one's own particular, historically constructed community; but there are many different, equally moral, ways of life that cannot be reduced to a single morality covered by a single moral theory.

9. Morality, to be authentic and truly human, must enhance individual autonomy: there is a deep suspicion and distrust of a 'heteronomous' ethic, that is, one that 'imposes' a moral obligation on the individual by and from a source 'external' to him or her and unswayed by human choice.

10. As a consequence of assumption 9, there are no persuasive arguments for, and many against, belief in an external source that can ground a universal human ethic, especially a theistic one that is transcendent of any direct involvement in the historical experience of persons.

11. Finally, there is the view that because of the relativity of moral values and differences between individuals, as well as the need to sustain their moral autonomy, one should be extremely 'tolerant' of diverse moral views. If one cannot appeal to an absolute standard of morality, binding upon all persons, then one can

hardly 'blame' (a morally pejorative word) people in other moral communities for acting in accordance with a moral code that is not the same as one's own. Tolerance is a way to avoid making invidious judgments against other people's morality when we have no absolute vantage point from which to deliver such moral judgments.

All together these 11 assumptions make up a strong rejection of traditional religious, especially theistic, ethics. As traditionally understood these ethics relied upon a belief that the source of ethics was an external (heteronomous), transcendent authority whose absolute, unchanging will determined a moral code of conduct that was binding on all persons (whether they had conscious access to the terms of that code or not and regardless of their place in history or their membership in particular cultural/ethnic communities). This ethic was taken to be unchanging, absolute, and not particularly sensitive to the historically-contingent differences between individuals, between individuals and groups, between groups and groups, and between one historical epoch and another. This ethic was grounded in a non-relativistic belief in the reality of an objective and absolute God, a belief which could in principle be formulated as part of a wider, more comprehensive metaphysical scheme reflecting the essentials of the reality (that is, the cosmos) this God had created and continues to sustain.

Boiled down to its essentials, the attack on this version of theistic ethics faults its inability to reflect historical change, individual and community differences, and its naiveté regarding the fact that theory/reflection has no neutral, context-free access to 'the truth' about reality as such. The attack on a theistic ethic assumes that it is only by rejecting 'totalizing' reason as having the power to represent objectively an unchanging absolute truth (whether in metaphysics or morals), that one can create room for moral autonomy, the ability to think and choose freely without coercion by an external heteronomous source that 'necessarily' restricts and conditions one's thoughts and decisions.

The Contextuality of a Theistic Response

I want to respond to this attack on theistic ethics on the basis of its general, basic, and ongoing core convictions about God, human nature, and life lived in response and relation to all these. These core convictions provide the boundaries, the framework, and the general norms for my response.

I accept the critics' claim that we all think from within frameworks and contexts. I do not claim to speak from an 'external' and allegedly neutral viewpoint, a "view from nowhere" as Thomas Nagel puts it. I am fully aware of the historically conditioned nature of thought and language, and of my own (and my various communities') subjective expressions, ideas, orientation, and 'take' on the reality they reflect.

Unlike the postmodern deconstructionists, however, I do not believe that we are exhaustively understood as prisoners of our historically conditioned, parochial or subjectively biased language games. I am convinced, and will argue the point at some length, that we have the ability to get a well-justified, warranted purchase on non-relativistic, non-subjective truth and validity, at least within limits. This purchase makes possible at the very least a minimal, moderately, or critical realist defense of beliefs about the objective reality both of the world and also, I will argue, of God and of God's involvement in the world, and especially in human history. As a result of that involvement (from the original act of creation on through specific divine acts of liberation, grace, deliverance, empowerment, and so on), God has provided human beings the basis for an ethics of response that is itself objective, non-relativistic, and 'true' (within limits). But there is nothing in this moderate realist approach that should undermine the confidence of theists in their fundamental convictions, even though claims to 'absolute' certainty of belief, or access to truth beyond all limits and conditions, are not tenable. The epistemological options are not exhausted by a naive correspondence theory of truth or by a completely subjectivistic, relativistic conversation about what one should do even in the absence of theory and truth. How these options apply to belief in God will be examined in due course.

The Fear of Heteronomy and the Virtue of Autonomy

Perhaps the central point of contact between the complex ruminations of moral philosophers and the intuitions of theists who have been profoundly shaped by a predominantly Western or European culture is the suspicion, even fear, of what is called 'heteronomy'. 'Hetero' means 'other'. In the moral context it means an external authority other than, outside of, and beyond the individual self that has some degree of power in determining the choices that the self makes. The opposite of heteronomy is autonomy: the autonomous self exercises free, self-determining power in the making of personal choices.

A 'heteronomous' source of ethics, (in the critics' view) is a law, or command, emanating from an external authority (for example, God, or the state) that stands 'over against' the self coercing its choices by threat or reward.

In the moral realm, most persons have come to distrust what they take to be heteronomous moral laws. Such laws are seen as having been 'imposed' on them without their approval. If they have had no hand in creating these moral obligations, or to which they have not given their full and free consent, except grudgingly or under threat, they can only regard them as alien to their moral autonomy. A morality that is imposed without consent is, for many people, no morality at all.

In many cases, this fear of heteronomy is based on the actual experiences of people living under alien laws: laws that many people have justifiably experienced as coercive, inhumane, stultifying, and repressive. The heteronomy of law imposed upon persons of color or women in America prior to the Civil Rights acts of the 1960s and the gender equity acts of the present is experienced by its victims as oppressive: as an imposition by force of someone else's morality. 'Get your morality off my back!' has become a battlecry for some individuals who feel discriminated against by a majoritarian morality that keeps them from enjoying the full exercise of what they take to be their inalienable rights to uncoerced, freely chosen behavior.

In the end, this kind of non-consensual imposition can be maintained only by force: not the force of moral authority, rational persuasion, or conscience, but the force of coercive political power. It is the authority of compulsion: the power to bring unpleasant consequences on those who choose to disobey it.

Through the work of psychologists, among others, this experience of heteronomous morality has been observed to result in psychologically unhealthy persons. People who live out of fear of someone else's power, especially when it is decked out in the finery of allegedly absolute and universal moral laws, ultimately find themselves living a lie: living in trepidation out of fear of others, and not joyfully for themselves. As a result they feel conflicted, inauthentic, and alienated from their deepest selves.

To regain a sense of human authenticity and wholeness, it is argued, people have to take morality back from its external, authoritarian keepers who have beaten them with it into demeaning submission. Morality must be returned to the only source from which I can claim it as reflective of my interests and needs: I must be the author of my own morality or at least give my free and full consent to a morality (when it is proposed to me by others) in order for it to represent *my* interests, rather than the interests of someone other than myself, whom I have no reason to believe has my interests at heart.

Obviously, according to its secular critics, one of the most glaring examples of a heteronomous source of morality has been the traditional God of Judaism, Islam, and Christianity. This God is taken to be external, objective, absolute, heteronomous, law-commanding, sovereign, powerful, coercive, and authoritarian. His (and God usually is given the masculine pronoun as a symbol of this kind of heteronomy) power determines the content and enforcement of morality. As the ultimate determiner of the destiny of all persons, God can impose his will (in the form of moral law) upon persons and know that if they disobey, some kind of divine punishment will be meted out. The oppressive character of this fact is not mitigated by the promise of eternal happiness as reward for moral obedience.

In a world in which the reality of God is itself in dispute, the authority of a divinely authored heteronomous moral law has been rendered virtually nil for many people. And if not even the power of God can instill obedience to heteronomous law, how can the power of lesser beings (ones whom we know are as corrupt, fallible, and limited as we are) evoke in us anything more than grudging respect for the exercise of coercive power to compel obedience?

The Power of Self-interest

It has become virtually uncontested among political philosophers that all persons seek power for the purpose of protecting or expanding their individual self-interest. This 'truth' explains and justifies most of the political and governmental structures of modern, Western, European societies. It is the underlying truth of modern economic theory. Christian ethicist Reinhold Niebuhr even argued that the power of organized groups of people is simply the means by which individuals can more effectively secure their private interests. Groups can be more effective purveyors of power on behalf of their members than can the separate individuals whose common interests constitute the *raison d'être* of the group.

Placing self-interest at the center of our understanding of the human person and her relations with others has become a hallmark especially of the sciences of human behavior. Self-interest is even alleged to be found at the lowest biological level, the gene. In what has been called the 'selfish gene theory' by authors such as Richard Dawkins, "reproducing itself is all the gene cares about," even if it means sacrificing the interests of the organism in which it occurs. This selfish gene theory has remarkable (and not coincidental) parallels with much of contemporary economic, behavioral, and biological theories about the nature of the human person. The common vision they all share is that "in essence, human beings are economic beings. They are out to pursue self-interest, to satisfy wants, to maximize utility, or preference, or profit, or reinforcement, or reproductive fitness. They are greedy, insatiable in the pursuit of want satisfaction. ... In the last analysis, what is right is what survives."[1]

This view of power and interest reveals a striking understanding of the human person. Whether couched in theological language (sin or depravity arising from egocentric pride) or in secular language (acquisitive self-interest), the human person is regarded essentially as incapable of placing the interests of others ahead of his/her own. When there does exist cooperative action with others, it is either because such cooperation promises a more effective way of accomplishing self-interest, or because the competing self-interests of others need to be regulated by coercive, external laws that require common obedience if the self-interests of the majority of competing individuals are to be realized.

Given the presumption of self-interest it is not surprising that a heteronomous ethic will be seen as serving the interests of the 'Other' whose ethic it is. (Even the traditional view of God, as we shall see, could not make much sense of God's imposition of morality on human persons except that it must have advanced God's interests to do so. The notion that God was also vulnerable to and affected by the ethic that God imposed upon God's creation was simply not 'on the table' for discussion.)

The idea that a heteronomous ethic can be mutually fulfilling for both the giver and the receiver, let alone be primarily for the sake of the receiver, has not been given due attention in most moral theories. But it is precisely this notion of an *other-centered heteronomous ethic* that I want to pursue. I want to argue that the Biblical picture of God's relation to human beings is of a *heterocentric heteronomous* ethic. This is an ethic that emanates from an 'Other' (God) but intends the well-being of *its* other (us), even to the point of a willingness to sacrifice something of itself for the sake of the other. (Christians will read this as referring to their belief that God gave up His only son so that the other might live.) There is nothing in the fact of heteronomy *as such* that requires a violation or diminution in the integrity and fulfillment of the self on whom the heteronomous morality is placed. In the God-human relationship, the otherness of each partner in the relation is a form of heteronomy but is one whose *specific nature* is such as to intend the enhancement and fulfillment of the deepest needs of the human person. And this view stands in clear tension with the primacy of self-interest.

The Problem of Estrangement

The fear of heteronomy stands in curious tension with an equally great fear among many people: the fear of being alone. Many fear isolation, alienation, and estrangement from others. We want to overcome alienation but we do not want alien morals laid upon us. We want to enter into relationships with others but we do not want others to determine the content of those relationships without our consent. We want autonomy and self-reliance but we also want to live interdependently in community with others. We fear restrictions on our freedom but are willing to limit it for the sake of a beloved if it will ease her pain. And we do not know how to reconcile these tensions. The theistic ontological claim is that in the presence of, and by the grace of, a loving personal God who 'restricts' God's freedom in order to serve us, we find both the seeds of true freedom, dignity, and self-worth, as well as the basis for serving others ourselves. The 'Other' who is God is ultimately not an alien other but a loving Other who overcomes our alienation and fills us with all that is necessary for a completely satisfying life (even though this form of satisfaction may be quite different from what we now falsely take to be satisfaction in our alienated state).

One of the oddities of much contemporary moral philosophy in the deconstructionist mode is that while it fears a heteronomous ethic, it criticizes traditional religious ethical theories on the ground that they are not appropriately sensitive to the particularities of distinct and individual 'others'. This criticism is part of a rejection of the universalizing tendency believed to be present in all ethical theory. It has been assumed by many ethical theories, exemplified perhaps in the moral philosophy of Immanuel Kant, that the only true ethic is one that is equally and universally applicable to all persons understood not in their unique particularities but as 'generalized' rational beings stripped of all individuating characteristics. Christian ethics has often been assumed to meet this criterion of a true ethic. No exceptions can be made for a particular person in a particular situation if those exceptions would jeopardize the application of a universal maxim or general moral rule. To permit such exceptions is to leave nothing of what we mean by ethics: an ethics for me that is not also an ethics for you is simply a cover for letting me do what I want to do provided that I can get away with it.

The purpose of ethical theory has traditionally been understood to specify just what qualifications can be permitted in the application of universal moral laws. If we are not going to say that I can kill someone just because I feel like doing it, we need to specify the exact conditions under which the taking of human life will be morally justified. Ethical theories may differ on what those conditions are, but all theories have to clarify the conditions that are relevant for it. (One theory may say killing is morally permissible only in self-defense: another may say killing is morally permissible in the defense of someone else's life; and still a third may hold that killing is never morally permissible.) But every moral theory has to have some sense of moral principles, rules, or laws that are applicable to all persons unless clear and explicit restrictions are indicated. And those restrictions must not themselves be so idiosyncratic as to apply to some individuals rather than to classes or types of individuals. Exceptions to moral rules are not based on individuals but on offices or functions that have themselves been previously justified by appeal to moral principle (for example, a society is morally justified in protecting itself from armed and dangerous criminals, therefore, a police force is morally justified, and anyone who legitimately serves as a member of that force is morally justified in carrying out the functions of that force, such as killing under specific conditions, whereas as a private person he would not be so justified).

The problem with this whole way of understanding moral theory, according to its critics, is that the uniqueness of individual situations and persons is overridden or ignored. There always seem to be, at least intuitively, circumstances which call into question the application of all universal, exceptionless, moral laws. If I am morally obligated to save the life of someone who is drowning, provided I am in a position to do so (I can swim and I am standing at the side of the pool in which someone is calling for help), I am not to make my decision based on the personality of the endangered person. We might regard my act of rescue as especially meritorious if the person I jump in to save is the same person who sexually abused my daughter some years previously. I will have acted *against* my inclination or desire, and in so doing will have risen to the heights of moral duty as defined by a universal moral rule. My moral duty to save the drowning person is not qualified by who he is. Giving moral priority to a member of one's immediate family is rarely, if ever, justified in Western ethical theory, though it may reflect tribal, customary, or even psychologically understandable practices.[2]

The Attack on Moral Theory and Moral Absolutism

Among the most important of the attacks on traditional religious ethics is that which has been put forward by a variety of persons generally categorized as postmodernists: they include anti-theorists, deconstructionists, and anti-foundational epistemologists who are convinced that it is not possible to obtain a neutral, unbiased, and objective standpoint from which to secure an uncontested truth or knowledge of reality, including moral reality. While there are important and often subtle differences in the forms of attack on traditional theistic ethical theory, for the sake of convenience (and without distorting the essential thrust of their argument), I will call them in general deconstructionists or postmodernists.

Before we examine their attack, it is important to note that virtually all the critics of traditional moral theory *assume* that a theistic basis for morality is no longer (and probably never was) tenable. It will turn out, I believe, that most of the problems that contemporary critics find in moral theory, epistemological realism, and ethical objectivity derive ultimately from what they believe is the impossibility of cognitive access to a divine ground for ethics. This impossibility assumes the radical 'Otherness' of a classical transcendent God. An alternative view of God, namely one who is a distinct living, willing, acting agent who can be known in and through that agent's actions (as they constitute a decisive part of history), is rarely considered seriously. When this alternative view of God is missing from moral reflection, ethics winds up being grounded either in the cognitive mystery of an utterly transcendent unknown or on realities that, by virtue of not being divine, are contingent, limited, conditioned, contextualized, and non-absolute. All of these limiting characteristics, as we shall see, are attributable to the various substitutes for divinely grounded ethics presented by the contemporary critics.

Moral Disagreement and Diversity

One of the hallmarks of contemporary moral reflection is the 'fact' of radical moral diversity. It is simply taken for granted (especially from anthropological data) that different cultures practice different morals reflected in different ethical 'theories'. It is also assumed that the differences between moral practices are so great that they cannot be reconciled by some kind of 'supra-ethic' or universal moral theory applicable to all persons without qualification. As Stuart Hampshire has observed, human beings are not so constructed "that they have just one overriding concern or end, one overriding interest, or even a few overriding desires and interests. They find themselves trying to reconcile, and to assign priorities to, widely different and diverging and changing concerns and interests, both within the single life of an individual, and within a single society."[3] And the moral intuitions that underlie these different moral practices are 'irreducibly plural'.

The link between moral diversity and moral pluralism is clear. Pluralism is simply the recognition that there are many moralities and moral theories underlying them. Critics also point to the fact that there is an absence of moral theory in many cases where there are vibrant moral practices. The human condition is such that a variety of different moralities is appropriate to its cultural diversity. A moral pluralist is one who recognizes that "good lives require the realization of *radically different* [my emphasis] types of values, both moral and nonmoral, and that many of these values are conflicting and cannot be realized together."[4] In the context of value pluralism, there is no one overriding value that can reconcile all the other values or even subordinate them in a consistent and coherent hierarchical ranking scheme.

Pluralism is supported by the fact, according to its proponents, that the basic goods people strive for, in order to achieve what they take to be necessary for their well-being or flourishing, are quite different from one context, theory, person, and group, to others.[5] These contexts are 'mutually autonomous'[6] and there is no hope that different moral ideals will 'converge' into a single, unifying ethical theory.[7] In short, different moral principles, ideals, and theories are 'incommensurate'; they have no common yardstick, criterion, or standard by which they can be ranked, judged, or evaluated with respect to each other.

The fear, of course, is that if such a universal or monolithic standard could be found, it would become the heteronomous source on which an absolutist ethic would be erected and then imperially imposed on unwilling subjects, restricting the autonomous freedom of individuals (or cultures) to determine their morality as they see fit, according to their own lights and circumstances.

There might, at best, be 'thin' moral commonalities, moral principles that are so abstract and vague that they can stretch across multiple individuals and cultures without determining in any rigorous and detailed way the specific content of their otherwise very different moralities (the 'thick' moralities of particular cultures, replete with specific rules, injunctions, mores, customs, laws, and principles). 'Be fair' might be a thin moral principle that all persons would recognize as a standard for their behavior. But 'being fair' may mean, in practice, very different things from one culture to another.

Context is Everything: Ethnocentric Thinking and Valuing – Richard Rorty

In short, pluralists claim, context is everything. What counts as fair is determined by each specific moral community and its unique traditions, values, folkways, customs, and the conceptual framework within which its leading ideas are framed and articulated. It is not determined by an abstract, impersonal, non-contextual principle of transcendental reason that rises above all conditioning particularities and judges them from an impersonal and impartial distance.

The indispensability of context has led a number of moral philosophers to maintain that it is impossible for individuals to erect an epistemological standpoint *outside, above, or independent of* some particular (and therefore limited) vantage point. And the vantage point from which individuals think is determined by the communal context in which they exist and from which they receive the criteria and standards of meaningful thought. This context is shaped by many things over which the individual has little control and for which he is not always epistemologically responsible. We are, even as thinkers, very much the products of our psychologies, traditions, cognitive frameworks, and cultural biases.

One irony that is often missed in this argument is that while rejecting the imposition of heteronomous authority from God, many pluralists wind up substituting the imposition of the heteronomous authority of culture, psychology, and even genes: all in the name of preserving moral autonomy from an overweening heteronomous God.

Richard Rorty has probably done the most among contemporary philosophers to drive home the claim that all thinking is context-bound. He has done this by attacking what is sometimes called the foundationalist or objectivist view that assumes "that we must step outside our community long enough to examine it in the light of something which transcends it, namely, that which it has in common with every other actual and possible human community."[8] Those who are committed to this attempt to 'step outside community' have to assume that there is a universal and unimpeachable foundation for knowledge: a foundation equally accessible to all rational thinkers simply by virtue of reason itself, uncontaminated and unqualified by the limited vantage point of each thinker's peculiar, historically contingent situation or psychological history.

In Rorty's view epistemological foundationalists are committed to what he wants to attack: the correspondence theory of truth. This theory holds that true beliefs 'correspond' to, reflect accurately, and truly represent in thought, a non-cognitive reality that is independent of the thinker and her cultural/cognitive context. The external reality represented in thought stands as a check on the truth or falsity of belief.

In contrast to this foundationalist or representational view of knowledge, Rorty holds that truth cannot be separated from the interests of the community in which truth-seeking takes place. Truth ultimately, he argues, is what is "good for *us* to believe." In line with the American pragmatist tradition, Rorty wants to abandon the correspondence view of truth and in its place put the view that "the consensus of a community rather than a relation to a nonhuman reality is taken as central."[9] There is, for Rorty, no community that is larger, more basic, or more objective, than the 'us' that exists here in this particular, cultural, historically contingent community of thinkers. There is no point at which the contextualized or situated 'us' disappears entirely to be replaced by an ahistorical, trans-cultural, trans-communal, contextless 'us' thinking from the standpoint of pure objective thought. We might try to enlarge our community of conversation to include other persons, Rorty concedes, but we cannot transcend limited human communities in some form.[10] For Rorty there is no 'world' out there to which a cognitive idea can conform. The 'world' is "either a vacuous notion of the ineffable cause" of our sensations or that which we are not presently questioning.[11]

Rorty maintains that his position is best characterized as an 'ethnocentric' one. One's *ethnos* "comprises those who share enough of one's beliefs, as they have been shaped and conditioned by the intellectual tradition that stands behind that group, to make fruitful conversation possible."[12] Those beliefs that, in the ethnos's cognitive and practical experience, seem well justified but clearly not beyond correction in the future, are given the honorific 'true'. Different cultures will have different references for the word 'true', as well as different procedures for assigning meaning to the terms of discourse that constitute knowledge for them.

This ethnocentric focus reflects the shared ways of doing things, including intellectual and scientific work, within a particular community. There is no way to justify the knowledge-superiority of one community over another without begging the question of whether its criteria of truth are somehow more 'objective' or 'truer' than the criteria and procedures of other groups. We cannot escape the context of the group through an objective cognitive door that leads us out beyond it to a non-relative vantage point from which to look back and compare all groups by a single standard of cognitive measurement. "We should say that we must, in practice, privilege our own group, even though there is no noncircular justification for doing so [because the criteria of justification are determined by the group itself]."[13]

The differences between one linguistic community and another (language being the only distinguishing characteristic between conceptual frameworks) are unbridgeable by translation. Donald Davidson, on whose work Rorty draws, holds that "[n]either a fixed stock of meanings, nor a theory-neutral reality, can provide ... a ground for comparison of conceptual schemes ... something conceived as common to incommensurable schemes."[14] We cannot even say intelligibly that schemes are different or similar because there is no uninterpreted reality by reference to which we can base assertions of similarity or difference.

The Ethical Implications of Rorty's Ethnocentric Stance

It should be clear that Rorty's epistemological ethnocentrism plays itself out in an ethical position that is equally ethnocentric. If all is context, then the moral self is also a completely contextual, historically-situated figure. The human self is "created by the use of a vocabulary."[15] There is no moral foundation 'out there' nor any 'human nature' as such to which moral behavior must conform in order to be truly moral. In Rorty's ethnocentric frame, the world has been collapsed into the construction of the community's linguistic practices and so has the self.

There occurs at this point what Frank Farrell calls a double dissolution:

"the dissolving of the world as that to which our practices must accommodate themselves in order to get matters right, and the dissolving of the self-relating subject into a mere construction of social practices and linguistic codes. ... [T]here is no further support for our practices beyond the fact that we support them."[16]

If the self has no identity independent of the social context that creates it, then it is not surprising that the highest moral value for Rorty is 'solidarity', commitment to the ongoing conversation of and within the community to which one belongs. Even an enlarged community "would feel no need for a foundation more solid than reciprocal loyalty."[17]

But this loyalty is a fragile, heroic, even sentimental thing, because in the end what really matters "is our loyalty to other human beings clinging together against the dark, not our hope of getting things right."[18] There is no moral law, no divine reality, no universal rationality, no human nature on which to build a trans-ethnic morality. At best we can develop an "ability to sympathize with the pain of others."[19] But if others do not share this sympathy there is no common court in which I can appeal to nonfeasible rational principles in order to persuade them into sharing a common sympathy with me. In a stark statement of this conclusion, Rorty confesses that "[t]here is no neutral, common ground to which an experienced Nazi philosopher and I can repair in order to argue out our differences."[20]

The Deconstruction of Meaning

Closely related to the suspicion that there is no common ground on which to erect a universal morality or metaphysics is the attack on the cognitive and moral constructions of Western religion and philosophy. This attack is known, appropriately, as deconstruction. It challenges the whole of what it calls the Enlightenment's project to pursue truth by objective reason into all areas of life. The project is based upon what the deconstructionists take to be a fatally flawed belief: the belief that reason has a privileged access to the nature of reality, including moral truth. For the deconstructionists (the earliest of whom were French scholars interested in language) enlightenment values and epistemological assumptions are now obsolete. The ontological link between thought, words, and reality has been irretrievably broken. All forms of meaning are nothing more than human constructions, inventions, creations, shaped by specific interests and particular historical circumstances. Reason simply cannot comprehend the specificity of these constructions nor reduce them to a common denominator. There is, according to Jean-François Lyotard, an "'abyss of heterogeneity' that opens up beneath every ... attempt to comprehend history in rational, purposive, or humanly intelligible terms."[21]

For the deconstructionist there is no final or absolute distinction between truth and untruth, reality and illusion. There is no ultimate truth behind the constructions of reason. 'False' appearances go 'all the way down'. What stands between us and others is socially constructed language and we can never use language (of which there are many varieties) to pierce the veil that hides whatever is 'behind' language, even assuming that language intends to 'represent' something other than itself. The focus on the centrality of language is the 'linguistic turn' that has led so many literary critics to embrace deconstruction and to find meaning solely in the text, not in the intentions of its author or in the extra-textual realities behind or to which the text 'points'.

Some of the more extreme deconstructionists claim that all forms of thought, all 'realities' formerly identified as having a substantial identity (for example, God, or the human person) are now to be seen as the invention of language. We have simply constructed our realities in and through the medium of words. Deconstruction intends "to show that the cathedral of the modern intellect is but a mirage in cloud-cuckooland. Neither language nor human self-awareness conceals any thread of reference to things as they are."[22]

Jacques Derrida, one of the gurus of deconstruction, has said that philosophers should understand that they are not writing 'about' anything: philosophy is simply writing, not a verbal reflection of things as they are. (It is clear why Rorty draws so heavily on Derrida in this regard.) The meaning of the words written is to be determined entirely by the linguistic framework in which they appear. The limits of language are the limits of one's world. There is no 'transcendental signified', no 'real' object of reference transcending the language of reference. There is no 'logos' or reason permeating reality to which our words or concepts have direct, or even indirect, access. "Meaning ... is the endless *displacement* of one sign by its successor. Derrida proclaims boldly: 'From the moment that there is meaning there are nothing but signs.'"[23] And, therefore, there are no criteria for judgment.[24]

This is especially true of texts that purport to be about history. A new 'historicism' has replaced an older view that historical texts reveal historical realities 'as they were'. Instead, we are left with only interpreted texts that are themselves as much historicized as the events they claim to represent. In the process of interpretation, we have to give up any belief in 'extra-historical' realities as well as belief in any historical realities that can be known without an interpretive screen shaped by the cognitive biases of a particular intellectual culture. We have, at best, "only a contingent interpretation of the contingencies of history".[25] There is no correspondence between historical claims and a 'real' history 'out there'. We have no privileged access to some meta-narrative that explains all history.[26]

In the wake of deconstruction, when our creative construction of God is deconstructed, the echoes of God's death "can be heard in the disappearance of the self, the end of history, and the closure of the book,"[27] the book being the Bible. The record of divine action is deconstructed into something less than a meta-narrative of history.

The 'religious' deconstructionists seem particularly focused on deconstructing the view of God as 'Other'. Their target is the notion of an ontologically transcendent, ahistorical God, characterized as omnipotent, omniscient, immutable, ineffable, eternal, and omnipresent. As such God has no way to establish a genuine relationship with what is Other-than-God without diminishing or contaminating God's transcendent otherness or abrogating the authentic otherness and freedom of the other by swallowing it up into Godself. The only relationship is a negative one, a non-relationship, a denial of the Other-than-God. God's otherness cancels out anything which is Other-than-God. But as wholly other, God stands over us "as the shadow of death",[28] canceling us out, depriving us of our ontological authenticity. The ontological infinity of God has no room for the finitude of the human being.

The point of this brief dip in the rhetorical waters of deconstructionism, as they swirl around the problem of God, is to highlight the problem of relationship between authentic others. Like the deconstructionists, I, too, want to question the *radical* otherness of God when it is articulated through the dualist view in which God's otherness is made so absolute, radical, and ontological that relationships with human persons are rendered problematic. But unlike the deconstructionists, I think that questioning dualism can lead to an understanding of God as 'an' Other with whom all human beings can stand in the deepest kind of personal and ontological relationship and whose 'otherness' is not so radical as to negate the possibility of God's presence in a history that God and human beings co-create by their mutually implicating intentional acts. Otherness is essential to relationship, but it does not take the kind of conceptual and linguistic mystifications of deconstructionism to argue that God's being is preserved both as unique and as relational simultaneously.

As in the case of Rorty's contextualism, however, it will be necessary to go beyond the boundaries of ethnocentrism in order to ground a metaphysics of relationship in something more than a language and a conceptuality that are *nothing but* the contingent products of time, place, and culture. Like some deconstructionists, I will put a heavy premium upon a pragmatic approach to this grounding, but unlike them, I believe that we can signify more intelligibly that which is other than ourselves, has a reality of its own, and stands in genuine relation to us.

Otherness

The fact of otherness, the reality of continual interpretation and re-interpretation, and of contextuality, all stand at the heart of deconstruction's 'take' on ethics. When an ethic seeks to universalize its rules or maxims, it becomes insensitive and inapplicable to the radical otherness of particular historical persons. As John Caputo puts it, deconstruction requires that we "wade into the difficulty of factical life without the guardrails of metaphysics or ethics."[29] We must live with a quasi-ethics that denies that there is an "ahistorical 'human nature'" or any other kind of metaethical, metaphysical, transcendent, or absolute 'ground' for ethics.[30] We must act in 'aporetic' or uncertain situations making judgments without absolute proof that they are right in every respect and beyond the shadow of doubt or qualification.

In this refusal to bind decisions to a formal set of moral rules as determined by an abstract moral theory, the stress is on the uniqueness of the situation and of the particular, irreplaceable others who stand in it. The otherness of the Other must be respected and not reduced by impersonal, absolute moral rules to a sameness that smothers uniqueness. The issue that is posed to a non-deconstructionist ethic, therefore, is how to preserve singularity and otherness without sliding off into sheer relativism or, at the other end of the moral spectrum, embracing a totalitarian absolutism that permits no exceptions.

A theistic ethic grounded in the Bible holds that God, a unique and singular personal Agent, can and does create a world in which human fulfillment can come about only through a respect for the unique and singular personhood of all other persons. In this created state, human fulfillment can occur in no other way than through a personal relationship with God and with the other persons God has also created, but that precisely because it can only occur in *this* way means that all ethical acts must respect the uniqueness and singularity of all persons. And this can occur only if relationality and mutuality (of the kind that the deconstructionist often calls for), presuppose *relevant* personal differences. Only a divine personal agent who loves what is genuinely other can create the conditions in which mutuality in and through a community of agapic love[31] enhances particularity without destroying it. And only such a divine being can undergird and affirm the uniqueness of individuals and the necessity of community without turning into a heteronomous coercive Other bearing other persons down, as distinct from bearing down on them as the loving reality to which they are called to respond in love.

Anti-theory in Ethics

A movement in moral philosophy known as anti-theory, encapsulates many of the themes just discussed. Anti-theorists attack moral theory on the ground that such theory "consists of an abstract principle or set of principles that all agents are expected to use to guide their own moral behavior and thought as well as to evaluate the moral behavior and thought of others."[32] Moral theory consists of general rules that apply to specific cases. It codifies moral practice according to rational criteria of evaluation. It overrides and supersedes local, traditional, context-bound moral behaviors and norms. It tries to stand above practice, looking down on it from a transcendent perspective in order to regulate and evaluate it. But all theory arises from and reflects particular contextual circumstances and thus is bound in chains of interpretation.

We can see in this understanding and rejection of theory clear echoes of the deconstructionist themes of contextuality, particularism, value pluralism and the denial of a transcendent, objective point of view.

The anti-theorist maintains that "the norms of actual moral practices are vague in order to permit context to play a role in determining their applications."[33] Abstract, normative principles simply cannot take into account all the particular, idiosyncratic, culturally-specific background constraints that are in play in any given moral situation.

Ethical theory is also confronted by the fact of 'irremovable' moral conflicts or dilemmas between moral obligations that moral agents feel to be equally binding. The rationalist demand that there be only one morally correct action simply cannot be satisfied. The classical example of Antigone comes to mind. She was morally obligated by the norms of the State to which she belonged not to bury the body of an enemy soldier. But she was equally obligated by familial moral duty to bury the body of her slain brother. Unfortunately, her brother was one of the enemy. There was no overarching moral theory to which she could appeal to resolve her dilemma.

It will not do to insist that the norms that create moral dilemmas are not really moral (being 'only' conventional): clearly the existential anguish of Antigone has had resonance down through the ages precisely because we *feel* that she is torn between equally compelling moral claims that cannot be resolved by appeal to moral theory.

Finally, there is the argument of the anti-theorists that rationalist normative theory cannot reconcile many of the moral virtues that ideally co-exist in each person. A moral virtue is a disposition or character-orientation toward acting in accord with moral principles. If my character is oriented or disposed toward honesty, I will be disposed toward telling the truth. But there are clearly circumstances that call upon conflicting moral virtues, such as a disposition both to shelter innocent persons from harm and to be truthful. The virtue of truth-telling and the virtue of providing shelter will conflict when a known killer asks me whether his intended victims are hiding in my home. The resolution of this conflict between virtues cannot be achieved simply by appeal to a general moral rule, as provided by rationalist moral theory.

Immanuel Kant's moral theory is usually taken as a paradigm case revealing the dilemmas of moral theory. Kant insists that morality requires that I be willing to universalize whatever principle (maxim) I act upon without regard to the consequences of my act. But what maxim would resolve my dilemma in the face of the terrorist's question? As long as lying or sheltering are not qualified by circumstances (lie only to people who threaten harm or shelter only persons who are innocent), there is no way to decide which maxim (never lie, always shelter) should override the other. But if we start down the path of maxim qualification, we are already into the contextualization of ethics, which is precisely what a Kantian moral theory hoped to extricate us from.

If there are problems determining moral behavior for an individual or within a single culture by reference to moral theory, there are even larger problems as one seeks a moral theory that would cover more than one human community. Like politics, all morality is, according to anti-theory, local or ethnocentric. And there is no theory that can bridge the gap between one locality and another. If rational moral theory requires a universal set of true ethical norms comparable to the truths of science, then few philosophers hold out any hope for it.[34]

Even if there are some continuities that extend across the range of human experience, these will "radically underdetermine the ethical options even in a given social situation."[35] There are simply too many different forms that restraints on such things as killing and lying take in different cultures; too many different and various forms of human excellence that cannot be harmonized with each other for there to be consensus on an objective moral theory applicable to all persons everywhere and at all times.

Ethical theories must be in some consonance with the facts of human nature, and those facts are always subject to empirical inquiry that may reveal multiple, conflicting, and contingent historical and social origins of moral practice, as well as the multifarious forms of their expression. But if moral theory has to await the results of such empirical studies, then, anti-theorists ask, how do we account for the fact that people behaved morally, and *knew* they were acting morally, *prior to* the existence of such theories? If ethical theory is up the same tree as Hegel's owl of Minerva, then it cannot fly until the end of the day (when all the evidence is finally in). But surely we have been moral and have known that we were moral long before the sunset of completed fact-gathering. And this fact itself cannot be explained by moral theory and even suggests that moral theory (in the rationalist, universalistic sense) is not necessary for local or ethnocentric moral life.[36]

In many cases people act morally simply because of who they are. "Occasion by occasion, one knows what to do (if one does) not by applying universal principles but by being a certain kind of person: one who sees situations in a certain distinctive way."[37] The role of intuition, perception, insight, imagination, and feeling are more important than theory or rational moral knowledge.

Living morally is more basic than thinking ethically. "The moral life is ... not a habit of reflective *thought*, but a habit of *affection* and *conduct*."[38] These habits of behavior are learned from within the context of our particular 'ethnocentric' moral community, and do not require a set of abstract moral ideals to inform them.[39] In fact, some anti-theorists have argued that we have no "pressing need for satisfactory total explanations of our conduct and of our way of life."[40]

Rational moral theory, in the minds of its critics, threatens to annul or override all that is rich, thick, and detailed in the actual lives of moral persons who flourish in different ways in different cultures. Anti-theory is hostile to the notion of a common underlying human nature, to a single point of reference for moral evaluation, and to a single heteronomous source of moral wisdom or truth.

The God Who Will Not Go Away

It is ironic, but important, to note that many of the anti-theorists seem to acknowledge (usually parenthetically and with a curious sympathy toward it) that only a theistically-based moral theory would escape from their attack. This acknowledgment suggests that a theistic moral theory is, in principle, a viable alternative to anti-theory. The only reason it is not recognized by non-theists is because the metaphysical ground for theism is regarded as incoherent and unintelligible.

Annette Baier, who declares herself a 'secular moralist', admits that "religious thinkers were the ones who really *did* have a theory, in the strict sense – a representation of God's creation."[41] She admits that from the unity of world-and-God moral guidelines could be extracted but such a unity is, alas she laments, not available to a postmodernist rational thinker.[42]

There is a continuing lament among many moral philosophers (but no willingness to revise their assumptions) about the loss of God. They seem to acknowledge that if one could overcome the hurdle of believing in a divine being with a universal purpose, a universalistic ethic would make sense. G.E.M. Anscombe, for example, has argued that the concepts of moral obligation "are survivals outside the framework of thought that made them really intelligible, namely the belief in divine law."[43]

But these secular ethicists are not willing to concede the possible truth of the theistic account even though they might on occasion acknowledge its intelligibility in principle. Nevertheless, Bernard Williams says cavalierly "we know that it could not be true ... since if we understand anything about the world at all, we understand that it is not run like that."[44]

There are other critics, such as Quentin Skinner, who reject the religious account on psychological grounds. He is convinced that to believe in God is "grossly irrational" and anyone who affirms a belief in God "must be suffering from some serious form of psychological blockage or self-deceit. This is why modern unbelievers have little inclination to acknowledge that theism offers its adherents 'a fully adequate moral source.' "[45]

I believe that the deconstructionist anti-theorists have an extremely narrow (and increasingly outdated) view of God and are therefore caught in an unnecessary dilemma. I hope to show that they need not drop their concern for the human construction of ethics in communal contexts, nor must they insist that God has no role to play in this construction. But it will require a very different notion of God from the one they assume theists hold. They treat theism with the same casual scrutiny that they routinely condemn in others when all other topics, besides that of God, are under consideration. But despite their rejection of what they uncritically take to be the 'official' theistic view of God, when they are honest they admit something is lost when God disappears from the agenda.

This is not to say that the loss of God is an unmixed blessing for secular thinkers. David Wiggins has said that "we moderns" feel envy regarding the "almost unattainable conviction that there exists a God whose purpose ordains certain specific duties for all men ..."[46] Even Richard Rorty laments the loss of a theory in which reality and justice are held together in a single religious view in which a "surrogate parent ... unlike any real parent, embodied love, power, and justice in equal measure."[47]

He admits that his rejection of both God and a common human nature seems to shatter, even tragically, the vision of "an ultimate community which will have transcended the distinction between the natural and the social, which will exhibit a solidarity that is not parochial because it is the expression of an ahistorical human nature."[48]

Charles Taylor's Tentative Opening to Theism

Charles Taylor, clearly working within the arena of secular moral philosophy, has been a conspicuous exception to the anti-theistic stance of most moral philosophers. He has been bold enough to claim that we cannot hope to realize our fullest human possibilities in the absence of God.

In his *Sources of the Self: The Making of the Modern Identity*[49] Taylor has argued that belief in God offers the most illusion-free source of morality. At the very least, he suggests, someone who accuses religious believers of "psychological blockage" (Skinner) reveals "an astonishing selective narrowness of spirit".[50]

Taylor's own view is that "a certain theistic perspective" is justified. The greatest spiritual aspirations of humankind do not inevitably lead to destruction or self-deception. He is openly sympathetic to Judaeo-Christian theism's "central promise of a divine affirmation of the human, more total than humans can ever attain unaided."[51] One purpose of my study is to show ways in which this divine affirmation of the human is entailed by a theistic ethic and coheres with many of the insights (carefully separated from their anti-theistic surroundings) of secular moral philosophy.

The fundamental obstacle to taking seriously a theistic ground of ethics is what anti-theists take to be the ontological status of God and the metaphysical credibility/

intelligibility of believing in God and having that belief be true. If the idea of God can be shown to be a faithful reflection or 'representation' of a living Personal Agent whose acts in history, including the experiences of one's own personal life, are the basis for constructing that idea, then incredibility of belief in God will have been seriously qualified, if not entirely removed. What is needed, I believe, is an understanding of God, drawn from the living experience of human persons in community responding to what they take to be God's purposes in and for the world. The God to whose purposes they think they are responding is experienced by them as a Personal Agent (not an absolutely transcendent reality) whose acts reveal the divine purpose. As such, the knowledge of God is empirically based and pragmatically verified. And if the overriding intention of God is for the flourishing of individual human persons in their unique particularities, provided that flourishing takes place in the context of mutually loving communities, then the concerns of the anti-theorists and deconstructionists for particularity, community, context, and the historically mutable, can all be met. It need not be the case, as Rorty implies, that the only way for human flourishing in community to occur is through the impossible dream of a non-parochial community built on an ahistorical human nature. There is nothing ahistorical about human beings building and sustaining contingent and fragile communities in the 'warp and woof' of history. There may well turn out to be in history some commonalties that do transcend parochialism and some expressions of human nature that are contextually determined. It is not an either/or choice. But there is nothing that necessarily precludes an historically-acting divine agent from acting in and through the historical experiences of persons and communities in the world to bring about the greatest degree of flourishing for all. And if theory really reflects the reality and overarching unity of such a divine intention (as distinct from an abstract, purely formal, universal 'principle' or 'law'), then even moral theory, appropriately qualified, can be rescued from the dustbin into which anti-theory has attempted to discard it.

On Coherence as a Test of Moral Theory

One part of that rescue operation would be to re-examine what many ethicists have come to regard as the only viable justification of moral theory: the test of internal conceptual coherence. But there is also a wider view of coherence, one in which the beliefs or intuitions within morality must cohere with beliefs about a whole range of different realities, such as those of psychology, sociology, anthropology, genetics, and so on. This kind of coherence is not just internal to the moral set but also external, linked to the world outside it.

In the external test of coherence, as developed by James Griffin,[52] our moral beliefs must prove themselves to be 'reliable' guides to action, with strong predictive and explanatory power. This means, Griffin insists, that though the contextualists are right that we cannot step outside any and all conceptual frameworks, "parts of that framework [that we happen to be in] are responsive to, are corrected by, a reality independent of it."[53]

No morality can afford to be at odds with the realities of the world in which moral action takes place. This does not mean that we have a privileged access, unaffected by the conceptual frameworks in which we are enmeshed, to those realities. But the moral intuitions and beliefs that we act upon must mutually support each other and be supported by, shown to be reliable with respect to, and able to help us find our way around in, the world in which we live and act.

If this view of coherence as a test of moral truth is persuasive, then the theist needs only to add the 'fact' of God. Not just of God as a principle of meaning, or as a ground of being, but as an ontologically real, acting, decisive, personal 'Other' whose concrete actions in the world make a difference to the realization of human intentions. If God's acts are facts, and if the divine intention behind those acts both unifies them and allows us to see (albeit as through a glass darkly) where history is going (assuming God has some decisive, though not absolutely unilateral control over it), then our moral beliefs, in taking account of what constitutes and supports reliable beliefs, must take account of God's intentions and actions. But if we are to take account of God, we need an epistemology that makes belief in God credible and coherent, if not absolutely certain. We need, in short, a new epistemology that does not run from the attacks of the contextualists and anti-theorists, but does hold out for the reality of God in the same way as it holds out for the reality of other persons. It is to that epistemology that we now turn.

Notes

1 Barry Schwartz, *The Battle for Human Nature*, (New York: W.W. Norton, 1986), pp. 148–149.

2 For an illuminating discussion of partiality in ethics as it relates to universality, see Marilyn Friedman, *What Are Friends For?*, (Ithaca: Cornell University Press, 1993), especially Part I: Partiality and Impartiality.

3 Stuart Hampshire, *Morality and Conflict*, (Cambridge: Harvard University Press, 1983), p. 20.

4 John Kekes, *The Morality of Pluralism*, (Princeton: Princeton University Press, 1993), p. 11.

5 See Michael Walzer, *Spheres of Justice*, (New York: Basic Books, 1983), p. 8. See also Terrance McConnell, 'Metaethical Principles, Meta-Prescriptions, and Moral Theories', *American Philosophical Quarterly*, 22, 4, October 1985, p. 299.

6 Zygmunt Bauman, *Postmodern Ethics*, (Oxford: Blackwell, 1993), p. 4.

7 Bernard Williams, *Ethics and the Limits of Philosophy*, (Cambridge: Harvard University Press, 1985), p. 152.

8 Richard Rorty, 'Solidarity or Objectivity?', in *Objectivity, Relativism, and Truth*, (Cambridge: Cambridge University Press, 1991), p. 23.

9 *Ibid.* See also footnote 1, same page.

10 *Ibid.*, p. 38.

11 Frank B. Farrell, *Subjectivity, Realism, and Postmodernism – the Recovery of the World*, (Cambridge: Cambridge University Press, 1994), p. 119. Farrell's book is an intriguing study of Rorty and Donald Davidson (on whom Rorty draws continually). Farrell claims that Rorty actually misreads Davidson, especially on the question of whether the world "remains a criterion [of belief] in the sense of being that to which our beliefs attempt holistically to accommodate themselves. ... Rorty will not allow the world to be any sort of criterion at all for belief; it collapses into that for which it was supposed to be providing the standard. For Rorty the world is just a shadow of our discourse while for

Davidson language can be meaningful because of the shadow cast upon it by the 'antics' of what is real'' (p. 120).

12 Rorty, 'Solidarity or Objectivity?', p. 30.

13 *Ibid.*, 29.

14 All these references come from Donald Davidson, 'On the Very Idea of a Conceptual Scheme', in *Inquiries into Truth and Interpretation*, (Oxford: Clarendon Press, 1984), pp. 186–222.

15 Farrell, *Subjectivity, Realism and Postmodernism*, p. 143.

16 *Ibid.*

17 *Ibid.*, p. 45.

18 Richard Rorty, *Consequences of Pragmatism*, (Minneapolis: University of Minnesota Press, 1982), p. 166.

19 Richard Rorty, 'Trotsky and the Wild Orchids', *Common Knowledge* 1, 1 Spring 1992, p. 148.

20 *Ibid.*, 149.

21 Quoted in Christopher Norris, *What's Wrong with Postmodernism?*, (Baltimore: Johns Hopkins Press, 1990), pp. 7–8.

22 *Ibid.*

23 *Ibid.*

24 Quoted in John C. Caputo, *Against Ethics*, (Bloomington: Indiana University Press, 1993), p. 98. Lyotard has said, "Absolutely, I judge. But if I am asked by what criteria I judge, I will have no answer to give ... we judge without criteria."

25 William Dean, *History Making History*, (Albany: State University of New York Press, 1988), p. 18.

26 Norris, *What's Wrong with Postmodernism?*, p. 28.

27 Mark C. Taylor, *Erring: A Postmodern A/theology*, (Chicago: University of Chicago Press, 1984), pp. 7–8.

28 *Ibid.* p. 23.

29 Caputo, *Against Ethics*, p. 102.

30 *Ibid.*, p. 103.

31 This term refers to the Biblical notion of a love that is other-regarding, that loves the other for his or her own sake, not primarily because the other can serve the interests of the self. It will be explicated more fully in Chapter 5.

32 Robert B. Louden, *Morality and Moral Theory*, (New York: Oxford University Press, 1992), p. 88.

33 Stanley G. Clarke, 'Anti-Theory in Ethics', *American Philosophical Quarterly*, 24, 3, July 1987, p. 238.

34 Bernard Williams, *Ethics and the Limits of Philosophy*, pp. 151–152.

35 *Ibid.*, p. 153.

36 See Cheryl Noble, 'Normative Ethical Theories', in Stanley G. Clarke and Evan Simpson, eds., *Anti-Theory in Ethics and Moral Conservatism*, (Albany: State University of New York Press, 1989), pp. 49–64.

37 John McDowell, 'Virtue and Reason', in Clarke and Simpson, *Anti-Theory in Ethics and Moral Conservatism*, p. 105.

38 Michael Oakeshott, 'The Tower of Babel', in Clarke and Simpson, *Anti-Theory in Ethics and Moral Conservatism*, p. 187.

39 *Ibid.*, p. 189.

40 Stuart Hampshire, 'Morality and Conflict', in Clarke and Simpson, *Anti-Theory in Ethics and Moral Conservatism*, p. 163.

41 Annette Baier, 'Doing Without Moral Theory?', in Clarke and Simpson, *Anti-Theory in Ethics and Moral Conservatism*, p. 34.

42 *Ibid.*, p. 35.
43 Quoted in J.L. Mackie, 'The Subjectivity of Values', in Geoffrey Sayre-McCord, ed., *Essays on Moral Realism*, (Ithaca: Cornell University Press, 1988), p. 116.
44 Bernard Williams, *Ethics and the Limits of Philosophy*, p. 32.
45 Quentin Skinner, 'Who Are "We"? Ambiguities of the Modern Self', *Inquiry*, 34, 1992, p. 148.
46 David Wiggins, 'Truth, Invention, and the Meaning of Life', in Geoffrey Sayre-McCord, ed., *Essays on Moral Realism* (Ithaca and London: Cornell University Press, 1988), p. 129.
47 Rorty, 'Trotsky and the Wild Orchids', p. 147.
48 Rorty, 'Solidarity or Objectivity', p. 22.
49 Charles Taylor, *Sources of the Self: The Making of the Modern Identity*, (Cambridge: Harvard University Press, 1989).
50 Charles Taylor, 'Comments and Replies', *Inquiry*, 34, 1992, p. 241.
51 Charles Taylor, *Sources of the Self*, pp. 518, 521.
52 See James Griffin, 'How We Do Ethics Now', in A. Phillips Griffiths, *Ethics* (Royal Institute of Philosophy Supplement: 35, Cambridge University Press, 1993), pp. 159–177.
53 *Ibid.*, p. 172.

Chapter 2

Knowledge as Relational

In the wake of the deep skepticism directed at ontological or metaphysical claims that we examined in the previous chapter, how can a theistic ethics proceed? It is obvious that it cannot simply ignore attacks on the possibility of objective truth, nor can it accept uncritically its complete reduction to the situated context of the truth-claimant. No matter how nuanced one's understanding of faith is, all theistic ethical theories rest ultimately upon the objective irreducible reality of God as other than the human person, no matter how related they are to each other.

The deconstructionist argument that no assertions are context-free would be deeply troubling if God could only be known independently of the historical, communal, and psychological situation of the one who believes truths about God. There are some truths that are essential to any coherent theistic ethic (even of a contextual kind) and that represent the core convictions of the religious traditions covered by theism. Whether we can know them only by a disengaged, abstract cognitive grasp of the 'idea' of God, or whether we can know them only in and through an intersubjective engagement with God's acts in history and in our own lives, is the basic question.

The Nature and Function of God

For theists in the Biblical tradition God has God's own distinct integrity and existence. This is the core conviction of theistic moral ontology. God is real, independently of the human imagination and its ideas about God. God's objective reality is not dependent upon our cognitive or experiential grasp of it. God is not a figment or construction of the human imagination. We might create our ideas *about* God, but we do not create God, just as we do not create our lovers, no matter how much and in what imaginative ways we might create myths and images of them.

Without reducing God to mere functionality (to the role that God is taken to play in one's view of reality), it must be true that people believe in whatever they take God to be because they expect God to do or be something that 'makes a difference', who decisively influences their lives and the world. It is God's reality, and not just my idea of God, that makes this difference. (This fact, of course, does not deny the powerful psychological effect belief in God can have on one's psyche. Nevertheless, theists want more than psychological effectiveness: they want a God whose actual existence makes a difference.)

In principle almost anything can serve the function of being a God for someone. As Paul Tillich has noted, anything *can* be taken as answering one's ultimate concern for meaning and fulfillment. But only some things can *truly* answer it.[1] Not all objects taken to serve the God-function turn out, in the end, to be successful in meeting people's basic needs. It is simply not true that people can believe whatever they want and find, in practice, that what they believe will prove reliable, fruitful, or helpful in achieving the purposes for which they thought the belief would be a useful guide.

Someone may take the human love between herself and her family as the absolutely reliable, never-failing source of comfort and meaning in her life, only to discover that when this human love dies or is betrayed, she still finds meaning and consolation for her life in something deeper, more reliable and abiding (and therefore discovers a new and more trustworthy 'ultimate reality'). If there is something that exists in its own right, something that objectively has the appropriate attributes that theists have traditionally ascribed to God, then that something is not what it is simply and solely because we form ideas about it.

Epistemological Accuracy and Reliability

The question for religious epistemology, therefore, is whether human beings are in a position to form reasonably accurate ideas about a reality, with its own ontological authenticity, 'external' to them, who does perform the God-function satisfactorily. A 'reasonably accurate' idea need not necessarily require the *bête noire* of postmodern deconstruction, namely a naive correspondence theory of truth in which ideas 'mirror' reality in a completely objective manner, free from interpretation or interaction with it.

Accuracy of thought may be far better understood as reliability in the guidance of action than as an objective mental picturing or 'photograph' of reality as it is in itself. Reflection need not mean 'picture-taking' separated from an ongoing relational interaction between the knower/doer and the world in which her actions are guided by systematic disciplined reflection on the world.

I want to suggest that a credible theistic ethics can meet the challenge of postmodern deconstruction through an epistemology that is essentially relational, engaged, world-embedded, and founded on the primacy of the self as agent-in-relation, not on the primacy of the self as thinker-in-detachment-or-abstraction. Only a fully relational or interactional epistemology can do justice to what I believe is the conviction that God is a Personal Agent actively involved in the world God has created and in the lives of the people with whom God has entered into active and personal relationship. But a relational epistemology rests on the stubborn objective reality of the 'Other', the partner in engagement, the related-to, what the deconstructionists reject as the 'transcendental signified'. It accepts the reality of that which is not myself, even while also accepting many of the limits on our theoretical knowledge of that Other that have been articulated by deconstructionism. At the heart of this relational understanding of our knowledge of the Other is the reliability of our ideas with respect to our action in relation to it.

A naive correspondence theory requires us somehow to 'see' the correspondence between my belief and the object to which it refers apart from the cognitive framework within which the belief is formed. It assumes that ideas arise and can be checked for validity in the absence of direct engagement with the world to which ideas presumably correspond. It 'solves' the problem of knowledge solely from within the cognitive act itself. The contextualists and the deconstructionists are, I think, right that I can't step outside my engaged relationships with the world in order to occupy a vantage point from which I could 'see' the correspondence between the world and my beliefs about it independent of my active engagement with it.

The contextual origin of belief does not require me to abandon my trust that if I continue to act upon a conviction that, say, water from the tap is safe to drink, this conviction will be justified by 'reality' and not just by my conception of it. Rationality is grounded ultimately in the reality of relationality between the knower and the Other that is known. I must have a practical relationship or engagement with the water, in order for me to know the 'truth' of the reliability of my belief about it relative to the actions I am taking with respect to it.

The problem with the pure contextualist approach is that in some of its more extreme forms, it tends to abandon entirely any rational justification for the belief that there *is* a 'world out there' in which our beliefs, intentions, and actions take place. But of course, it can't really abandon *in practice* the tacit knowledge that there is a world beyond the self, because even at its conversational best, contextualism presupposes a particular, but very real, context for our thinking and acting. And contexts are quite real and always more than cognitive, independent of any particular individual who happens to occupy one of them. Contexts are 'there' in the sense that they impose constraints on what any given individual within them can think meaningfully and, more importantly, on what she can *do* successfully. And there is also something beyond the context that determines whether or not ideas can be reliably counted on to guide us through our interaction with something other than ourselves and our conversational group.

There is something stubbornly 'there' that constrains our actions and interactions, that conditions the success or failure of our intentions as we try to enact them. Something 'out there' (the world in its facticity) blocks or frustrates some of my intentions. There are real, objective obstacles or impediments that prevent them from being successfully enacted. These obstructions are not usually figments of the imagination. No matter how tightly constrained or 'fictional' the context of ideas in which I think, that context cannot override the practical success or failure of an intention in a world 'beyond' that context, an intention that is normally guided by some set of ideas or convictions about the world. (The philosopher Charles Pierce even defined existence as "that mode of being that lies in opposition."[2])

It would be an interesting thought-experiment to imagine how or why we would come to consider problematic the existence of something if nothing stood between us and the realization of whatever desires or intentions popped into our minds with regard to it. If I could succeed at doing anything I wanted without the least bit of opposition from something 'other' than and external to my desire, why would I need even to raise the question of the existence of anything other than myself, let alone the question of what 'things' are real and what are illusory? There would be no reason to run any kind of practical test of a belief because all beliefs would turn out, necessarily, to lead to successful action. We devise theories of knowledge precisely because not all ideas 'work' against a reality which will not yield to some of them.

Any philosophy that moves to deny the reality of this world of experienced constraints has committed a fundamental fallacy. The denial itself presupposes the possibility of making truth-claims (that is, that no 'external' world exists). Making truth-claims meaningful presupposes some point of reference from which the truth or falsity of the claim can be determined. But if the only point of reference is internal to thinking, or to a conversation among 'credentialed' ethnocentric thinkers who 'choose' the criteria of justification, then the truth or falsity of beliefs, with respect to the world in which actions based on those beliefs takes place, cannot be determined.

The problem with views of the self-enclosure of thinking (that prescind from the externalities beyond the self) is that thinking becomes entirely self-referential. Thinking begins from itself, as it were, and has only itself to refer to. The realm of thought, for the disengaged reflective ego, creates its own internal criteria of truth and meaning for the ideas it contains. Then the gap between thinking and the world which is the object of thinking can only be crossed by thinking. And then the problems we discussed in the last chapter begin. How can thinking cross the gap between itself and 'not-thinking' in order to know whether it corresponds to what is on the other side? As ethnocentrically self-enclosed, thinking can never achieve a not-thinking place from which it can determine its own truth about a world external to thinking itself.

Frank Farrell has pointed out that the mind withdrawn from the world into its own self-presence is, in effect, a worldless mind virtually without content (other than that which it manufactures for itself in the form of free-floating ideas). It may well be true that such a mind is the holy grail of those seeking complete moral autonomy because it is a truly autonomous mind (inasmuch as it permits no intrusions from a heteronomous externality, such as the world, let alone God). But if, Farrell argues, you try to take this self-relating moment as autonomous, "you end with a dark interior where nothing means anything, where we are not setting ourselves in relation to things in any way at all. If you then try to take the relation to the world as an independent moment that can be added on later ... you end up with no genuine relation to the world. The self is not differentiating itself from and relating itself to any other, and without that active involvement in the self's directedness toward the world, no connection is accomplished."[3] What Farrell calls the 'recovery of the world' is not possible if we begin with the self as primarily and essentially thinker.

The Primacy of Relationality

So we must start with a self situated in a world just as the contextualists demand. But its situation is not (or not entirely) of the self's own making. As long as the self's situation is in part determined by its agency, and as long as action must take into account realities other than the agent herself, those realities constitute the 'external' world relevant to the agent/thinker. If we start the problem of epistemology, not with the thinker, but with the already-engaged and world-directed, relational agent, we get a different way into the problems of knowledge and avoid the dead-ends of extreme deconstruction and radical relativism.

The late Scottish philosopher John Macmurray has made an extremely significant point of Kant's insight that ultimately, if moral action is to be justified, it must assume the primacy of practical, not theoretical reason.[4] Morality presupposes freedom and freedom presumes that our theoretical knowledge of the world cannot be absolute. Theory views the world as completely determined through causal law but we know, practically in our moral action, that we are free. The problem with Kant, Macmurray argues, is that he provides us with freedom through action in practice, but no way of understanding it theoretically. A free act would be one that violates or is an unintelligible exception to the sway of causal explanation that constitutes theoretical knowledge of the world.

The Primacy of Action

One way around this problem, according to Macmurray, is to begin our reflections on knowledge not from the primacy and standpoint of thinking but from the primacy and standpoint of acting. Thinking can direct its gaze upon any number of things. It can start its reflection by reference to ideas or it can begin with something more basic and inclusive than thinking. That something, Macmurray proposes, is the *activity* of the self that thinks. Thinking can then be understood as a particular kind of action but not the only action. Action is a doing that includes the act of thinking but is not exhausted by it. Begin then, says Macmurray, with the immediate and primary experience of being agents embedded in a world of relationality and interconnection with others. Thinking then takes its place as one act among others in a person who is primarily agent in relation.

The primacy of action is the knife that slices the Gordian knot that hopelessly entangles reflection that begins with itself as basic and primary. A self that thinking considers essentially to be a thinker cannot be brought over into a world in which thinking is not the primary or exclusive activity of the self. The primacy of thinking may yield more than one set of coherent ideas. But unless there are many different worlds, coherence cannot tell us accurately what the single world is like in which we act on the ideas contained within the set.

Prior to reflection we 'know' experientially that there is a distinction between acts, some of which are more reflective, others of which are more practical or directly world-engaging. In this sense we 'know' ourselves to be essentially agents who can choose a variety of actions depending on the context and the purpose we have adopted with respect to the world in which we exist. I can choose to reflect both on my purposes and on the world in which they are to be enacted in order to make their enactment more effective.

If we know ourselves primarily as agents in and through our relational interaction with others, then we have a basic concept of the self that, paradoxically, makes a self known only in concepts a less inclusive self than one that is known through its actions, of which concept-making is only one, albeit a crucial one. We have, in short, an epistemology that is profoundly relational, interactional, and world-engaging.

Epistemological Pragmatism

Approaching knowledge from the standpoint of the primacy of the self as an interactional agent, we can establish a non-conceptual basis for determining when ideas are true. That basis is essentially a functional or pragmatic one. Acts of thinking 'serve' more inclusive purposes: they function more or less successfully in guiding or contributing to 'successful' action in the world.

We must not be misled by false meanings of the word 'successful'. What counts as 'successful' action is not to be understood as synonymous with narrow self-interest, and in a theistic context can only be understood by reference to conformity with God's purposes (since these determine what will ultimately 'succeed' given God's determinative power). The problem with calling an epistemology 'pragmatic' is that it often connotes a short-term, selfish, or narrowly materialistic sense of success. But this is precisely where a theistic context helps to broaden and deepen the notion of 'successful' action. Rorty is right when he notes that within a pragmatist framework "one is debating what purposes are worth bothering to fulfill, which are more worthwhile than others."[5]

In a theistic context, success can only be ultimately understood against the background of God's overarching, universal, world-encompassing intentions. If God's creative intention is inclusive of the universe, then no actions that fail to take the world into account (as God takes it into account as its creator, sustainer, and redeemer) can ultimately succeed. At the same time, pragmatism need not connote a frozen, static, or purely passive world simply waiting inertly to be acted upon and providing only passive resistance to action. If action is always inter-action, always relational, then it makes a difference to the world. Our actions to some extent and in various ways, change the world. We have to factor in this reciprocal, inter-dependent nature of a world in which agents act as we develop the full meaning of a pragmatic epistemology. The virtue of pragmatism is that it forces us to take account of the reality of the world in which our ideas are to be enacted.

Even for some deconstructionist philosophers such as Donald Davidson, on whom Rorty draws in support of his extreme contextualism, the world "remains a criterion [of belief] in the sense of being that to which our beliefs attempt holistically to accommodate themselves."[6] And Rorty himself, who will not allow the world to be a criterion for belief at all (because we can't get an unambiguous, non-contextual, non-relative conceptual purchase on it), also seems to accept, *in practice*, that the world is 'out there' and *causes* many, if not all, of our beliefs. Pragmatists, of whom he counts himself one, accept the "brute, inhuman, causal stubbornness" of the world's objects.[7]

Through experience we discover that our original or primary knowledge of the 'Other' who is 'there' is practical. It is part of my lived engagement and interaction with what is other than myself. My lived relationship with the world is the presupposition and occasion for a reflective act that, for a time, disengages the self from that relationship. But it is only a partial disengagement, undertaken for reflective purposes. And as such, it continues to presume the very engagement from which it is a temporary withdrawal.

This suggests that we can develop a more detailed itinerary of the journey of thought into the world in a way that does justice to some of the fundamental insights of the postmodern deconstructionists without sacrificing the reality of a world that is larger than our thoughts and in which we are situated as active, intending agents. And this fact constitutes the basis for what we might call a *moderate or critical epistemological realism.*

Moderate or Critical Realism

Moderate realism is an epistemological position that situates knowing in a pre-existing world of persons, objects and events with which the thinker is already practically engaged through interaction. It is contextual in that it acknowledges that all ideas arise in some delimited context of the self-as-agent's practical encounter with the world. No one engages the world exhaustively in its entirety at all times and places simultaneously: we engage it selectively and with respect to some specific intentions at particular times and places: in short, we engage the world contextually, contingently and historically. (This fact suggests that our primary engagement with God will also be in and through our personal experiences and reciprocal historical actions, not in and through timeless abstract conceptual knowledge.)

As situated in the world, our thinking is influenced and to a large degree constrained by the communal, cultural context within which we form our intentions and ideas. And it is clear that theoretical *knowledge* presupposes a practical *acknowledgement* of the 'otherness' of the other(s) with whom we are in practical relation. Otherness, including the otherness of God, is clearly preserved by an epistemology that begins with the primacy of action since action is always interaction in relation to objective Others.

Relationality

At the heart of moderate or critical realism's epistemology is *relationality*, interconnectedness, a direct engagement of an agent with the world. This claim tracks very closely with what some philosophers are calling the 'new meta-physics.'[8] Like the postmodern deconstructionists, the new metaphysicians reject much in the Enlightenment's 'old' metaphysics centered on the disengaged reflective ego. In the new metaphysics the *"primordial reality is man's relation with the world. ... The relation is meaningful, but neither man nor the world is meaningful apart from the relation."*[9] The relationality at the core of the new metaphysics echoes the truth of Macmurray's insistence on the primacy of the self as agent precisely because agency presupposes relationality within a world that is the context for action.

As Charles Sherover has put it,

> I am, from the first, in a world of other persons and of things that are developmentally interrelated ... the thinking act [is] a social activity that continually engages with others ... [Therefore] ... what is presupposed in every act of consciousness is its intrinsic involvement in and reference to what has variously been termed inter-subjectivity or community.[10]

But, and this is the crucial qualifier, if there is a larger, more inclusive world in which we as agents are only a part, then there are 'real things' (structures, events, persons, institutions) that 'objectively' constrain the success of our intentions and limit the reliability of our ideas in guiding those intentions to completion. The Other must be the object of negotiation if we want to act successfully. Charles Taylor has said, "what is real is what you have to deal with, what won't go away just because it doesn't fit with your prejudices."[11] For the theist, of course, the most decisive of those real things is God. Our knowledge of God will therefore be profoundly intersubjective and relational, taking place in the historical interaction between divine action and human response.

This having been said, it must also be clearly stated that the objective reality of God does not entail the epistemological claim that God can be known fully or with conceptual certainty. It does entail that when we act, at least with respect to some, if not all of our actions, we must take God's reality 'into account'; we must negotiate with that reality in some way: it stands objectively as an obstruction or facilitator of our intentions. But our knowledge of its objective reality is not originally or primarily conceptual: it is experiential and practical. There must be a strong pragmatic dimension to our knowledge of God: our ideas about God (especially about God's intentions) can only be inferred by a interpretive reading of history and experience and proved by acting upon what we take to be the divine intentions we discover there. Our actions will, at some point, either 'fit' with or 'conform' to the grain of reality as God has created it.[12] This pragmatic testing of our interpretation of God's intentions may take a lifetime for an individual, or more likely, the lifetime of the human race, or may, for many, remain forever incomplete or open-ended.

A moderate realism does not entail that our knowledge of God is complete or exhaustive. What we know about God will depend upon the context in which we encounter God's reality. My knowledge of things is always limited and contextual, relative to my successful functioning with respect to them. After 30 years of marriage I 'know' much about my wife, but not everything. What I know has proven itself reliable over and over again, but that knowledge does not entail that I have an *exhaustive* knowledge of all that she is, was, or will be.[13] There is no reason not to assume that my knowledge of God is not similarly limited and contextual, relative to my historical, experiential engagement with God. I may only need to know what God needs me to know: namely what God intends with respect to me and my world, what God's character is, and how to conform my intentions to God's purposes in order that I might achieve the fulfillment of my being. Beyond that knowledge, it is not clear what 'use' I would have for other details of God's 'inner life' or anything else about God that escapes my conceptual grasp.

And beyond my contextual knowledge of God, it is not clear that I can claim any certainty for its eternal validity. Dewey was right to suggest the futility of the quest for cognitive certainty. Especially given God's freedom to act, the character of God's future actions cannot be predetermined by us, no matter how reliable our construals of God's actions have proven in the past. At the same time, part of the religious knowledge that theists claim is that God has bound Godself to a consistent and reliable overarching intention for humankind that God promises will not substantially change. But reliance upon another agent's promise and character is not the same as reliance upon a reality that one knows, in theory, cannot ever change. In relying upon God's promises, I am relying upon that which is known and verified only in the ongoing historical relationship I have with God.

Moderate realism denies the absolute autonomy of pure subjectivity. Subjectivity is ultimately constrained by a world beyond it. But the opposite of subjectivity is not a non-engaged, non-relative objectivity. Our beliefs, in Frank Farrell's words, must "accommodate themselves to, or 'track', the contours of the world, and that even with the full exercise of our abilities we might fall short of grasping what is the case. ... Reality is not the child of our abilities for organizing, meaning, and evidence gathering, but is an independent measure of how good those abilities get to be."[14] The subjective side is determined by our interests or reasons for engagement with the world at any particular time and place. They 'light up' (in David Wiggins' phrase) the world in a certain fashion and make certain features of it emerge rather than others. As Wiggins puts it, "the size and mesh of a net determine not what fish are in the sea but which ones we shall catch."[15] We do not need to believe that the world in its entirety conforms to all our rationally constructed beliefs because the world extends far beyond them. As Thomas Nagel argues, the world reaches beyond our capacity to understand it, yet our pursuit of an objective understanding of reality is the only way to expand our knowledge of what there is beyond the way it appears to us.[16] The net of understanding is subjectively woven in and through a particular context, but it can catch real fish. It may not catch all the fish there are, and it may not catch anything other than fish, but it does catch fish and if one fishes in order to eat, one will be fed. The net, in short, proves (pragmatically) reliable in action for fulfilling our intentions in particular relevant contexts.

Rational Reliance

The view I am defending here is closely related to what James Ross has called 'rational reliance'. Much of our knowledge of the world relies upon persons and institutions that we believe we have good reason to trust since they have not let us down in our previous practice. Few of us know, in the strict epistemological sense, what black holes are, but we trust those astronomers who are well-placed to know what they are to give us the essential information we need for any tasks that might have to take account of black holes. Most of us "cannot get into the position of competent evaluation of the most important channels of belief ... without matured talent at that 'way', whether it be how to play the piano, construct arguments, live justly and humanely, or live a fulfilled life."[17]

This is clearly a form of pragmatism in which beliefs are intended to help us adapt to the environment in which we live and act. Irrational belief is "out of touch with the conditions of environment ... Sanity requires a reasonable match between desire and reality."[18] And it is not irrational to trust those in a position to know when their knowledge (and not ours) can help us make that match more reliable. This would apply to those religious people whose encounters with God have proven reliable to the fulfillment of their lives and who, therefore, can be guides for others.

The philosopher of science Roy Bhaskar has made the claim that truth is not, despite the deconstructionists, just what we make of it in accordance with prevailing consensus-beliefs. Those beliefs may, in fact, "encounter real obstacles".[19] He does not deny that knowledge is a social construct but its objects "exist and act independently of" the knower. He insists that "if science is to be possible the world must consist of enduring and transfactually active mechanisms."[20] The 'mechanisms' to which Bhaskar refers are those "independently existing and active things" that any intentional agent confronts in her field of action as she attempts to carry out her intentions. Science is the conceptual vehicle for enabling the task of acting in furtherance of our intentions to be successfully completed. If the world did not have the structure it has, science would not be possible.

There are many different ways of getting around those obstacles, one of which is to rethink the map or reweave the net through which we have tried to create action-guiding and reliable ideas that will facilitate our practical engagement with the world. But ultimately the only way around the obstacles is by acting on ideas that we have reason to believe (due to previous practical experience, our own or others') will prove reliable in practice. And there is no sense in denying that these ideas are developed in specific intellectual or cognitive contexts that do not transcend historically specific net-weaving, map-making, and idea-linking in general. Knowing is always an activity that "completes itself in the real"[21] but the real is always *encountered* relative to the context of the knower/agent. (The real is not exhausted by this encounter nor is it the product of the encounter.) And this, of course, does not foreclose the possibility that some things have a permanent, relatively unchanging reality from context to context. One of those realities, for a theist, is the loving action and purpose of God.

William Alston has recently argued, with respect to sense experience, "the practice of forming beliefs about the immediate physical environment on the basis of sensory experience *works*. It is a *successful practice*."[22] But all justification of belief takes place in a context in which other beliefs are fixed and not subject to skepticism. "Contextualism meshes with the pragmatist insistence that the need for justification arises only when there is some special reason to question a belief."[23] Alston's observation squares with our claim that the reason to question a belief presupposes some frustration or obstruction in the attempt to carry out our intentions practically: and if our action is successful then all those beliefs that continue to prove reliable in action do not need questioning in that context. You cannot, in the famous image, replace all the planks on the raft of philosophical thought at once: some have to remain in place in order to give you a place to repair the others. But this epistemological position only makes sense on the assumption that action is primary and that thinking is one kind of act relative to other, more inclusive kinds of action that are not essentially cognitive. We want the raft to sail to some destination and we stop to repair it (with the aid of our conceptual tools), at least in part, only when we discover that it is sailing less successfully than it should or could.

The Metaphorical Character of Knowledge

Some have argued that epistemological realism is undermined by the irreducibly metaphorical character of our knowledge. As contextual, my language about the objects I know, including God, will employ a particular vocabulary and set of metaphors. You, in another context, might employ a different vocabulary and metaphorical set. The reality of God may be such that no single human vocabulary, or even the totality of vocabularies, can exhaust all of what God is. Rorty accuses his opponents of searching for one final, absolutely objective vocabulary. But a moderate realist has no need to search for such a vocabulary or metaphysics. Realism of a moderate sort can accept a plurality of vocabularies since it is not committed to the extreme claims that vocabularies 'create' objective realities or that they exhaustively represent the realities that exist. A vocabulary, like a conceptual map or net, may be more or less useful in helping us find our way around in a relationship with the Other, but it need not be taken as a 'photograph' of the Other independent of that relationship.

George Lakoff and Mark Johnson, who address the question of metaphors, have carefully threaded their way through the two extremes of absolute objectivism and absolute subjectivism by an epistemology that is fully supportive of the moderate realism that I am defending because it is essentially *relational or interactional*. At the heart of their work is the assumption that 'human purposes' determine what will count as ways of knowing. Our concepts and metaphors arise out of our experience or engagement with the world. "The kind of conceptual system we have is a product of the kind of beings we are and the way we interact with our physical and cultural environments."[24] Even if cultures influence our ways of thinking and perceiving, "each culture must provide a more or less successful way of dealing with the environment, both adapting to it and changing it."[25]

Truth is not lost in this contextual, relational approach to knowledge. Truth matters, they contend, "because it has survival value and allows us to function in the world." But we only need a contextual understanding of the world ("sufficient for our needs"[26]) for truth to matter reliably. But this means that our concepts or categories are not necessarily true (or do not need to be claimed as true) of the objects in themselves. They are, rather, "interactional properties, based on the human perceptual apparatus, human conceptions of function ... that make sense only relative to human functioning."[27] (This observation suggests a clear link with our earlier notion that God must serve some deep human function, such as empowering complete human flourishing, in order to be meaningful.[28])

Our understanding of a situation must only be 'close enough' for our purposes, not objectively certain in some absolute sense. Truth "is relative to our conceptual system, which is grounded in, and constantly tested by, our experiences and those of other members of our culture in our daily interactions with other people and with our physical and cultural environment."[29]

But as conceptual-system-relative, our ideas (or metaphors) always hide something about reality just as the conceptual net lets some fish (and non-fish) slip through. The objectivist is right to insist that there are real things "which constrain both how we interact with them and how we comprehend them."[30] The subjectivist is right to insist that it is our *personal* intentions and interests that determine where and for what reason we interact with (selective) parts of the world. But in the end, Lakoff and Johnson reaffirm our commitment to a moderate realism that locates an authentic epistemology not in thought alone but in the self as a relational, engaged, and world-directed agent.

In a more explicitly theological context, Janet Martin Soskice has argued that religious metaphors must have a "reality depiction" component directed towards "a cosmos-transcending absolute being".[31] She rightly rejects attempts to make the referent of religious language be simply the experience or creative imagination of the theologian. There must be some being in whom we trust, who is the referent of our experience of radical faith.

Soskice is particularly and rightly critical of attempts to deny the reality depiction element in religious metaphor by substituting for it "the world we create in and by our language and our story so that what is 'out there,' apart from our imagination ... is as unknowable as ... our fingerprints, had we never been conceived."[32] But Soskice insists, in line with the argument of Lakoff and Johnson, that the cognitive model of the divine is action-guiding "in virtue of its claim to be reality depicting, namely, this is how it is with our relationship to God."[33]

Nor does Soskice deny that a reality depicting model is always a social and context-relative construction. The context of our inquiry will give us "epistemic access to important causal features of the world".[34] But this access does not require the metaphors that express it to "mirror the world in an unrevisable fashion. Its terms are seen as representing reality without claiming to be representationally privileged."[35] Revisability is essential for any account of the world "that aims to adapt itself to the world"[36] because speakers may be wrong in their references.

If this is taken as a form of epistemological relativ*ism*, then so is any knowledge of any object external to ourselves with which we are in some way engaged or in interactive relation. But this kind of relativism is not vicious or extreme, nor does it depend solely upon my subjective desires and constructions. It does not mean that my ideas about any object are true regardless of what the object's own reality is. I cannot think anything I want of my wife and by so thinking make her conform to my intentions or desires. At some level she has a stubborn facticity, her own unique 'otherness', over-against me, limiting and constraining what I think about and intend toward her.

These principles of knowledge would also be true of God existing in God's own right and sustaining the conditions for our successful action: God's otherness, facticity, or over-againstness, sets limits on what I can reliably think about God if I am to use my thoughts as guides to successful interaction with God *provided that God is the kind of Being with whom one can interact in the world*. If God is a free Personal Agent, and responds to loving intentions with reciprocal love, and I have come to believe that God is indifferent or incapable of loving, and I act upon this (erroneous) belief, I may find that I never experience God's love toward me. In short, acting upon a false view of God will frustrate some of my intentions about what to expect of a God-relationship. Acting on a true, that is, reliable, view of God will contribute to my fulfillment as a person created by God for well-being. For the theistic realist, this means that she "may simply be wrong" in her various beliefs and if so, her "whole structure of belief is gravely flawed ... This possibility of being in error is the risk such a realist takes."[37] But it is the price one must pay in order to give intelligibility and meaning to religious claims about the reality of God and God's affect on the world. Soskice concludes that "the realist position ... depends upon the belief that God is causally related to the world, at its origin or perhaps [I would say, necessarily] even in specific events and experiences within human history.''[38]

Construals

Closely related to the use of metaphors is the reliance upon construals in a moderate epistemology. Julian Hartt has said that theology is a way of 'construing' the world.[39] A construal is a way of cognitively 'taking' the world, of seeing it in the light of a particular perspective. It is, literally, a construction of the world in thought. (And naturally, the object of deconstructionist attacks when it forgets its creative, interpretive, and constructed basis and claims to be a mirror of the world.) As a construal, it involves a subjective interpretation of a selective portion of the world, shaped by imagination, metaphors, tradition, and communal practice. A construal is not determined solely by the rational cognitive faculties employing purely logical criteria. A construal is ultimately determined by its practical reliability in and for action. It is an interpretation of (that part of) the world in which the construer is herself an embedded, engaged, interactional agent.

As such, a construal needs verification in and through continuing active engagement with the objects-in-the-world of which it is a construal. The idea of God ought not be an exception to this pragmatic moderately realist epistemological principle.

At the heart of the Biblical theological construal is the interpretation that the world is under the sway of divine intentions. And to construe the world in that way is to intend to "relate to all things in a manner appropriate to their *relations* to God.''[40] Ethics then becomes the actions informed by this construal so that they conform to the appropriate relations human beings have to God, and, through those relations, to all other parts of the created order.

Emotions

A crucial element in every construal is the emotional dimension of engagement with the world. Construals do not arise solely from a detached cognitive awareness of the Other. The significance of the emotional dimension of human life has been, of course, central to the insights of religion generally. But emotions, despite rationalism's frequent suspicion of them, can prove to be highly reliable guides to action. In this sense, they can even be understood as objectively valid. John Macmurray, for instance, has argued that there is such a thing as "emotional reason.''[41] Reason in the broadest sense, he argues, is "the capacity to behave consciously in terms of the nature of what is not ourselves ... the capacity ... to behave objectively.''[42]

This is perfectly congruent with the moderate epistemology we outlined in the previous chapter. Reason helps us interact successfully with the world. Clearly the truth and falsity of our thoughts lie "in a relation between them and the things to which they refer.''[43] But our feelings also refer to what is outside themselves, to some object to which they are an emotional response. I feel trepidation upon encountering a mother bear on the trail I am walking. My fear is related to the bear and her potential behavior toward me. (If I immediately become convinced that the bear is an apparition, my fear disappears.) In this sense my fear can be either "rational or irrational in precisely the same way as thoughts, through the correctness or incorrectness of their reference to reality."[44] In this case, if the reality is an angry bear ready to attack me, then my fear is thoroughly rational, completely well-founded because of the nature of the object my feelings are a response to. (If the object on the trail is a kitten, and I have an emotional reaction to it similar to what I have toward the bear, then it could be said that I have an irrational fear since, as far as we know, kittens cannot threaten our life in the same way bears do.)

Now the upshot of Macmurray's observations is that if reason is ultimately instrumental in aiding our successful active engagement with the world (by proving reliable as a guide to action), then thought is related to action through emotion. Our first and immediate relation to the world of others is emotional. It is our emotions that orient us toward that world in certain ways (for example, fear, love, trust, hope, and so on). Thinking helps our emotions direct our actions more reliably toward the world, but it does not necessarily supersede or precede them.

In a moral context, Macmurray argues that love is the "fundamental positive emotion characteristic of human beings."[45] But love can be directed truly or falsely. I can love another person for what he does for me (thus exploit him instrumentally), and wind up being in less than a completely *mutual* relationship with him. But a less than mutual relationship is incapable of fulfilling me (or so I will argue). But if I love him only because of his utility, my love is irrational because it will result in my being less than completely fulfilled in relation to him.

Our feelings for and about God, therefore, play an important role in our knowledge of God. We cannot enter into relationship with God on the basis of thought alone. If we treat God as a non-personal object, as merely an idea or concept, or simply as a theoretical explanation of metaphysical realities, we will fail to experience the fullness of a relationship with God. God can be known only in and through our relationship with God and that relationship can be fulfilling only if emotions are at its very core. Whether what we feel for God is 'rational' will depend on the objective nature of God in relation to us and on whether our feelings lead us to fulfilling relations with God. There can be both correct and incorrect feelings for God just as there are reliable and unreliable ideas about God. The proof is in the ongoing mutuality of the relationship, not in the abstractions of logic.

The feeling that we are in the presence of a power bearing down on us is one of our most decisive clues to a knowledge of God and cannot be divorced from it. We exist in our religious communities in large part not because we first share a set of common ideas, but because we share a common experience or feeling about the powers that bear down on us. And at the heart of Biblical ethics is an *experience of love in relation to God*, an experience that is decidedly emotional/feeling-directed toward God. It is from that emotional attachment to God-in-relation-to-us that ethics will spring as the ongoing response to the dynamics of the relationship. Ethics does not derive primarily from thought but from emotion-laden experience.

Emotions can, of course, distort our relationship with reality, but so can ideas. The question is whether emotions can also open up and lead us toward truer relations with reality. And clearly they can when they bring us more reliably into encounter with the reality to which they are directed. In the end, emotions and thought exist in a dialectical tension with each other. Each can serve as a counterbalance for the other. My fear of what I take to be a bear can be allayed by a quick mental calculation of what I remember about bears (for example, that they are normally not angry early in the morning, that if it is a male bear it is less dangerous than a female who has been separated from her cubs, and so on). Or my cognitive calculations can be overridden by a long-term successful relationship with the object (for example, I took her to be a callous, vindictive person given the stories I heard about her, but as I acted upon my loving feelings toward her, I found out she was warm and loving in return). Ultimately, both emotions and thoughts have to be 'proven' by their reliability in establishing and sustaining ongoing, fulfilling relations with objects in our contextual field of action.

Wittgenstein once said that "the way to solve the problem you see in life is to live in a way that will make what is problematic disappear."[46] In theological terms, if we experience some ultimate frustration in fulfilling our intentions, and if one reason for that frustration is that our actions are not in conformity with the reality of God's intentions, then the only way to resolve the problem is by living in such a way, namely living in conformity with God's intentions and actions, that the frustrations disappear in practice. And if God's intentions are the ground of morality, then a theistic morality is grounded in a moderate epistemological realism that takes the reality of God as that which has to be encountered, negotiated and dealt with, struggled against, or conformed to, if what we value is to be realized.

Notes

1 See Paul Tillich, *Dynamics of Faith,* (New York: Harper Torchbooks, 1957), pp. 8–12. (In his theology, only 'Being-itself', not any particular being, can provide the answer to the question of being.)
2 As quoted in John Patrick Diggins, *The Promise of Pragmatism*, (Chicago and London: The University of Chicago Press, 1994), p. 168. "Ideas must be proven ... 'by some permanency'."
3 Frank B. Farrell, *Subjectivity, Realism, and Postmodernism – the Recovery of the World*, pp. 54–55.
4 See John Macmurray, *The Self as Agent*, Introduction by Stanley M. Harrison (New Jersey and London: Humanities Press International, 1957), Chapters II and III.
5 Richard Rorty, *Objectivity, Relativism, and Truth*, (Cambridge: Harvard University Press, 1985), p. 110.
6 Farrell, *Subjectivity, Realism, and Postmodernism*, p. 120.
7 Rorty, *Objectivity, Relativism, and Truth*, p. 83.
8 See the essays in Robert C. Neville, ed. *New Essays in Metaphysics*, (Albany: State University of New York Press, 1987).
9 Nicholas Capaldi, 'Copernican Metaphysics', in Neville, ed., *New Essays in Metaphysics*, p. 46.
10 Charles M. Sherover, 'Toward Experiential Metaphysics: Radical Temporalism', in Neville, *New Essays in Metaphysics*, pp. 80–81.
11 Charles Taylor, *Sources of the Self*, p. 59.
12 See Robert Johann, *The Pragmatic Meaning of God*, (Milwaukee: Marquette University

Press, 1966), in which he draws both upon John Dewey and John Macmurray in constructing a claim that knowledge of God is discovered and validated in the actions that work toward community. If God's intention is universal community, we can only 'creatively interact' with God and each other in order to 'prove' that this intention both defines our being and determines the goal of all (ultimately successful) action.

13 This is especially true because she is a free intentional agent whose freedom entails her ability to act contrary to my best predictions, even if she chooses to use her freedom to act in ways that are completely consistent with the character she has displayed to date.

14 Farrell, *Subjectivity, Realism and Postmodernism*, p. 149.

15 *Ibid.*, p. 160.

16 Thomas Nagel, *The View From Nowhere*, (New York: Oxford University Press, 1986), p. 26.

17 James F. Ross, 'Rational Reliance', *Journal of the American Academy of Religion*, LXII/3, Fall 1994, p. 774.

18 *Ibid.*, p. 777.

19 Quoted in Christopher Norris, *What's Wrong With Postmodernism?*, p. 111.

20 Roy Bhaskar, *A Realist Theory of Science,* (Atlantic Highlands, NJ: Humanities Press, 1978), p. 20.

21 Edward Pols, *Radical Realism*, (Ithaca: Cornell University Press, 1992), p. 155.

22 William P. Alston, *Epistemic Justification*, (Ithaca: Cornell University Press, 1989), p. 325. In a more recent book, *A Realist Conception of Truth*, (Ithaca and London: Cornell University Press, 1996), Alston has defended realism vigorously against its critics. Realism claims that *"all* our beliefs owe their truth value to the fact that they are related in a certain way to a reality beyond themselves" (p. 8). At the conclusion of this book Alston makes the striking observation that opponents of realism are deeply fearful of 'vulnerability'. If our beliefs can be liable to falsity, then we are acknowledging that we are, in a certain way, out of control of things. Alston, who is a Christian theist, sees in this fear of "vulnerability to the outside world, this 'subjection' to stubborn, unyielding facts beyond our thought, experience, and discourse ... [a] ... special case of *the* original sin, insisting on human autonomy and control and refusing to be subservient to that on which our being and our fate depends, which for the Christian is God" (p. 264). I think Alston is absolutely right about that.

23 *Ibid.*, p. 348.

24 George Lakoff and Mark Johnson, *Metaphors We Live By*, (Chicago: University of Chicago Press, 1980), p. 119.

25 *Ibid.*, p. 146.

26 *Ibid.*, p. 160.

27 *Ibid.*, pp. 163–164.

28 To repeat a point made earlier, the existence of God could turn out to be meaningless to some people without it thereby ceasing to be real.

29 Lakoff and Johnson, *Metaphors We Live By*, p. 193.

30 *Ibid.*, p. 226.

31 Janet Martin Soskice, *Metaphor and Religious Language*, (Oxford: Clarendon Press, 1985), p. 106.

32 *Ibid.*, p. 109.

33 *Ibid.*, p. 112.

34 *Ibid.*, quoting philosopher Richard Boyd, p. 131.

35 *Ibid.*, p. 132.

36 *Ibid.*, p. 133.

37 *Ibid.*, p. 139.

38 *Ibid.*, p. 140.

39 As quoted in James Gustafson, *Ethics From a Theocentric Perspective: Theology and Ethics*, p. 158. Gustafson does not necessarily share the theistic perspective.

40 *Ibid.*

41 See especially John Macmurray, 'Reason in the Emotional Life', in *Reason and Emotion*, (New York: Barnes and Noble, 1962), pp. 13–65.

42 *Ibid.*, p. 19.

43 *Ibid.*, p. 24.

44 *Ibid.*, p. 25.

45 *Ibid.*, p. 31.

46 As quoted in Richard J. Bernstein, *Beyond Objectivism and Relativism*, (Philadelphia: University of Pennsylvania Press, 1983), p. xv.

Chapter 3

God as the Personal 'Other' Acting in History

God as an 'Other'

Theistic ethics is grounded in the ontological reality of God and the world as God created it. Its truth will be grounded in a correct metaphysics reflecting that ontology. James M. Gustafson has observed that the first task of a theological ethicist is to develop a coherent interpretation of God.[1] I think Gustafson is absolutely correct even though I disagree with parts of his particular construal of how God is to be understood. But until we get our conception of God straight, it will be impossible to build an adequate theocentric ethics.

There are many deconstructionists who tacitly acknowledge that if there was a God, God's will would be inescapable and would serve as the foundation for a clear and consistent ethics. But of course they deny the existence of God, usually because it seems so self-evident to them that God, on rational grounds, simply could not exist because belief in God is primitive, superstitious, archaic, and irrational.[2] I accept one aspect of the critics' charge: namely that belief in God should be subject to the same epistemological criteria that apply to belief in any 'object' external to the knower. Belief in God will, therefore, be cognitively less than absolutely certain and will be subject to the same pragmatic test of reliability in action as are other beliefs in external objects. This test will not result in any and all ideas of God as being equally valid. Within the context of a relational/interactive epistemology, only the idea of a relational/interactive God, a God who is capable of having intentions and the ability to act upon them in a world that is the field for the realization of the fulfilled human life, would be credible. In short, I want to ground theistic ethics in the *person* of God, in the will, intentions, and actions, of this particular Divine Agent. Ethics will then be human beings' response to what they discern God is up to in the world. A Biblically-based ethics will be the attempt to conform human life to God's intentions (as reflected both in the ontological structures of reality and in God's actions in history) and to act in accordance with the grain of that reality, not against it.

The Biblical Construal of God

The ethics I want to develop is rooted in what I take to be the view of God found in the Biblical narratives of Judaism and Christianity. As a person writing from within a particular context, I am aware that I will inevitably be doing a selective retrieval of the Biblical tradition's recital of its experiences of relationship with what it has construed as the divine power bearing down on its people. Even as a Christian ethicist, I am already situated within one context that will pick at one strand of the tradition rather than all of them simultaneously. I would claim that that strand is one that weaves itself throughout the whole of the tradition and, in some decisive way, links all the other strands.

The strand of Biblical theism that I want to work from is that which is convinced that God acts graciously upon and for the world. That conviction is found inscribed and articulated not only in the pages of the Biblical narrative, but, equally important, in the personal language of prayer and liturgy among Jewish and Christian worshippers throughout the centuries and in the ongoing narratives of their present relations with God. Throughout the Bible, God is always referred to as an acting, engaged, and personal being. Verbs are always associated with God because God is known by what God does: God creates, speaks, urges, commands, inspires, heals, threatens, rewards, loves, aches for, and sends among other things prophets, floods, signs, warnings, Jesus, miracles. In short, the controlling metaphors and language of the tradition are that of God as a personally engaged and relational Agent who *does things* for others.

The Problem of Radical Transcendence

It is also true that there is another strand within the tradition that is in tension with that of God understood as Personal Agent. This second strand begins with the intellectual attempt to point to God as that which absolutely and utterly transcends the finite world of action. In this second strand (usually called the dualist or classical view of God), philosophical/metaphysical reflection has led to a conviction that God cannot be brought within the categories of human conceptuality without diminishing God's radical otherness. The 'ontological' transcendence of God makes it impossible for the human mind to attribute any particular characteristics to God because all such attributes are derived from human experience which is ontologically (that is, qualitatively) different from divine experience. But the concept of this ineffable, wholly other, dualist, transcendent God is in deep tension with the concept of God as a relational, interactive, Personal Agent working in time, space, nature, and history.

Attributing intentions and actions to a totally transcendent 'something' that is not 'a' being but 'being-itself' or the 'wholly other' is logically incoherent. Even when it is attempted it is acknowledged to be paradoxical, irreducibly metaphorical, mysterious, a matter only a 'faith' not bound by the canons of rational intelligibility can allegedly affirm, if not understand.

Radical transcendence fatally compromises God's relationality. As transcendent of the very ontological structures within which action and relationships occur, God could not be said to be 'in relationship' with or to act upon what is 'other' than Godself. To be in relationship to what is Other than God qualifies and limits God's absoluteness. Any two beings in relation to each other limit and qualify each other because of the very meaning of 'relationship'. The one is not the other and cannot be the other. This is especially true if they are persons. Persons are distinct beings, differentiated from each other, whose relationship with each other presupposes that differentiation and distinction. God, therefore, cannot *be* the persons with whom

God is in relation, nor could God become them or override their freedom and intentionality without eradicating their personhood which requires freedom and intentionality.

Interventions and Actions

A totally transcendent 'being' cannot act. To act is to enter into the structures of reality in such a way as to make something happen that would not have happened without that intervention. Action does not require a suspension of natural 'laws', but it does require an intervention into them. Whenever a human agent acts, she interrupts or intervenes in a causal sequence of occurrences that, in the absence of her intervening action, would have produced a result different in some respect from that which comes about as a result of her action. When I decide to blink my eyelid rapidly, I am intervening into the biological or physiological 'laws' that normally cause my eyelid to blink according to a particular organic regularity. My intervention into that organic regularity has the effect of making the eyelid blink faster or slower than it normally would without the intervention. In so intervening, I am not violating the laws of nature, but I am utilizing and deploying them in accordance with my overarching intention. But at no point is my action capable of successful completion in the total absence of the structures of organic, physical reality. Action supervenes on nature, but cannot occur in its absence.

Intentional action is the most inclusive category for understanding reality. Every other category removes some element from intentional action. 'Nature' is the world without action. A law of nature describes what happens regularly provided no agent interferes. An organism behaves in a particular way in the absence of an intentional, directing power. A machine has no function until it used by somebody for some purpose. It has even been suggested by some philosophers that the whole causal infrastructure, the 'world' of causal law, is capable of being thought coherently only by eliminating the presence of intentional action and agents.

Personal agents are, in a sense, the 'north pole' of human thought. Once you have reached that notion, every other concept is less inclusive than or an abstraction from the category of personal agent. What you are left with, depending upon how much you abstract out, is the organic world (which has biological movement as well as materiality) or the mechanical world (which has only mechanical or material parts without even organic relations). But for each of these 'lower' (that is, less inclusive) levels to exist on its own, is to remove from it the presence of an intentional, guiding, purposive power that reaches down through them and deploys them, as an infrastructure, for the carrying out of intentions. The action of the agent, in short, is the encompassing, inclusive field in which the less inclusive dimensions are contained as parts to a whole.

If God and human agents occupy the same ontological field of action (which they must if they are related to each other), what is true of human actions would be true of divine actions: a divine act may utilize, supervene upon, interrupt, or intervene in the organic and physical structures of nature in order to bring about the fulfillment of a divine intention but it cannot occur in the absence of nature or a field of action. In each divine action God is intervening in the structures of finite reality (which God has also created and maintains), just as any agent intervenes in them in carrying out a free act. It is this kind of active, world-engaging involvement that is denied to a totally transcendent God because it diminishes God's radical otherness.

It is often alleged that divine actions must be miraculous. But a miracle presumes a *violation* of natural law, not an intervention into it by an agent's intentional act. If a divine act is miraculous, then so are all human acts because, *as actions*, they are not predetermined by causal law even though they need not necessarily contravene causal law.[3]

Therefore, if a Biblical ethics is a response to the actions of a divine Being establishing relationships with human creatures, it can only be a response to a personal, non-ontologically transcendent agent. It should be clear, however, that I am using the phrase 'non-ontologically transcendent' in this context in a particular way. *All* agents are transcendent *relative to* other beings, including the non-agent, non-personal structures of reality in which they are embedded, but in which they can intervene when they act. Whenever a personal agent chooses to exploit or deploy the causal infrastructures, she 'transcends' them in the sense that her action is not entirely determined by them. Her freedom and her intentionality enable her to interrupt the regular course of events (as it would take place in the absence of her actions). But, as I have suggested, her actions are not ontologically transcendent in the radically dualist sense. They occur *within* the structures of reality: they are in time and in space and presuppose a real distinction between the agent and that upon which the agent acts. Agency presumes differentiation and differentiation presumes 'otherness', and otherness presumes transcendence of a sort, but not the kind of radical, ontological transcendence attributed to God in the classical dualist view.

The problem that gives rise to the radical sense of transcendence and to which it is a response is the problem of Otherness. As long as God is confronted by an 'other', God's supremacy, power, and absoluteness seem to be compromised. Otherness entails mutual limitation. Asserting God's *ontological transcendence* permits the dualist to get rid of the problem of otherness by denying that God has anything to do with, or is in any way similar to, what is other than God. It is no wonder that on the ontologically transcendent notion of God, God is never able to be described except in negatives: God is *not* whatever finite reality (the ontological 'other than' God) is.

The other way of overcoming the problem that otherness poses to God is monism. In a monist view of God, God is All-that-is. God is the Whole and there is nothing but God (and therefore no 'others' who might pose a problematic 'relation' with God). Monism, in effect, denies otherness any reality at all. In monism, there is no 'real' other. What we take to be other than God is ultimately unreal, an illusion. On a monist view, relationship and action are no problem because they have no reality. There is no 'other' with whom God is in relationship (there is only God, the single absolute One without a second). And there is no action for God to perform because there is nothing to act upon and no reason to act upon oneself.

Personal Otherness

A relational, interactive epistemology ultimately affirms the reality of otherness. As such it finds ultimacy not in absolute transcendence or in undifferentiated oneness, but in the power and decisiveness that occur in relationships between ontologically distinct but interrelated beings. In a theistic ethic, ultimacy resides in the power of the actions of an overwhelming, powerful, but loving Personal Agent whose intentions and actions are decisive for the fulfillment of all other personal agents. The supreme power is the power of an agent: the supreme decisiveness is the decisiveness of that agent's actions as they determine the primordial structures of reality and the final outcome of the historical interventions into those structures. (Of course, if this agent's intentions permit some freedom of action on the part of other agents, then the first agent's power to 'determine' the outcome of history will be qualified to some degree.) This is theism in its Biblical if not classical theological form. It is not a theology of a God beyond the God of theism (Tillich), nor of a totally transcendent, non-relational, infinite, absolute reality (the dualist classical view), or of the 'one without a second' of undifferentiated monism. It is a theism of an acting, relating, historically-engaged Personal Agent whose intentions and actions are decisive for the fulfillment of all beings.

It might be objected that this view of God is too limited, too anthropomorphic, too primitive to reflect the stark, overwhelming majesty, infinity and absoluteness of God. And so it is, from the point of view of classical dualist assumptions, or from the perspective of an undifferentiated monism. But we cannot think coherently from within all these perspectives simultaneously. That is part of what being a contextualized thinker means. And these perspectives are, at the level of their root metaphors or basic principles, incommensurate. This leaves the individual theist in the position of having to choose one of them rather than all of them all at once.[4] But it is precisely at this point that the theist has to take seriously the other elements in her contextual situation. She must give due regard to the language and thought-forms of the basic narrative (the Bible) on which her tradition is based. She must acknowledge the significance of the liturgical language in which her corporate worship is expressed and the language of those who communicate with God through prayer. And she must listen to the voices of those who comprise the common religious community of which she is a part. And in all these instances, the motif that stands out is that of persons who claim to stand in some life-affirming relation to a supreme, loving Person whose acts of love and grace bearing down on them have been experienced as providing the fulfillment of their being.

The north pole of theological thought is God as the Personal Agent whose creative, sustaining, empowering, and loving acts decisively affect the destinies of human beings and the course of their mutual history. Within the context of Christian or Jewish community, God is ultimately construed as that Person who has acted in history, whose actions have left a trail (in historically narrative form) for human beings to discover, and whose intentions are the ground of the ethical response to God that constitutes the religious life.

This, of course, raises the question: if God has acted in history, how do we discover the trail and how do we interpret the narrative that tells us what has been found on it? That is the question to which we will turn next as we continue to lay the foundations for a theistic ethics rooted in the Biblical tradition.

A Biblically-based ethics will prove to be (or so I will argue) one that leads to the commitment to work actively for God's intention for justice as a means to the establishment of the minimal, necessary (but not sufficient) societal conditions for a community of persons living in relations of mutual love with one another and with God. Agapaic (mutually loving) community is the fulfillment of human persons: it is the necessary condition for their well-being and flourishing (to use two of the most widely accepted criteria for determining the goal of ethics generally, not just religious ethics). To intend community is to intend the fulfillment of all persons.

The Problem of 'Intrinsic' Value

One implication of this construal of the world's relation to God is that an ethics of response to God is, in part, the drawing of an 'ought' from an 'is', a movement that is normally suspect in moral philosophy. But within the context of my construal of the Biblical tradition, the metaphysical reality of the world is itself already an act of an intentional agent. The world (in its basic structures and historical direction) *is* the manifestation of that agent's purpose. It therefore represents not a value-neutral reality onto which *I* impose or arbitrarily draw out an 'ought' of my own making. Rather the world is already an embodiment of the value given to it by the Agent who created and sustains it. When I choose, therefore, to accept that value as my value (to value what God values), I am not committing the traditionally false move of educing an ought from a value-free 'is'.

If it *is* the case that my wife loves me, her love demonstrates or embodies a value she attributes to me (that is, that I am lovable). In responding to that value by returning her love for me, I am responding both to an 'is' and to a value simultaneously because the 'is' is already permeated or shot through with value. The 'is' is her act of valuing: the 'ought' is my response to that fact (though I am free not to respond, but in not responding I am failing to respond to a reality, namely her act of valuing me).

Similarly, if the structures of the world and the direction of its history embody the values of God, and I both accept those values as given and make them my own, then I put myself in concurrence with reality. I do not fight reality (understood as that which God intends, despite its subsequent distortion or perversion by human beings) but align myself with it. In so doing, I am accepting the world as value-laden (God being the one who gives it value) and thus not committing the naturalistic fallacy in its traditional form.

One important implication of this claim is that value is ultimately personal-agent in origin. Nothing can have value unless an agent gives or ascribes value to it. There is much talk in ethics of the 'intrinsic' value of such things as 'nature'. But it is not clear what this means. The value of nature is not self-originating. Taken in isolation from its value-bestowing source, nature cannot 'give' itself value because nature (in the ordinary sense of the word) is not a personal agent. Non-personal natural objects may be in dynamic, organic relation to other objects, but they do not form conscious intentions and then proceed to carry them out through planned actions. As such they have no power to confer value on anything, themselves included.

This is not to deny such objects value, but the value they have must originate in a being (or beings) capable of ascribing value to them. And the only beings who can do that are personal agents. One kind of value they can give is simply the value of being valued by a value-giver. I may value the sheer existence of a sunset: the sunset's value is not instrumental, or utilitarian in any narrow sense: it does not serve a purpose, but I find delight in it, and my delight is the source of its value for me. It does not give itself that value. I might not ascribe that value to it unless it had certain characteristics that strike me as value-full. I cannot ascribe value to something with no objective content of its own. My valuing is always a valuing of something with a reality that is, in some sense, extrinsic to me even when I am its creator. In the absence of a value-giver things that are not capable of giving value to themselves or others are without value, literally value*less*. They exist, but their value must be given or added to them by someone capable of doing so.

If there is a single creative source who gives, imparts, or ascribes value to all created things, any other value-giver, such as some of the created beings within 'all that is', can then accept the Creator's valuing as if it were intrinsic to the object. On this construal, it would be possible to say that nature has an intrinsic value, apart from how we human beings value it, but only because it has its ultimate value from a non-human but equally personal agent who has given it value in and through the act of creating it. We, then, have the freedom to choose whether or not to *recognize or acknowledge* its God-given value. And if we fail to recognize it, and by so doing dis-value or mis-value it (treat it as of no value, or fail to recognize its value to God), we do not take away its intrinsic value so long as God continues to value it.[5]

Interestingly enough, even the advocates of a totally transcendent God generally resort to agential and personal language when it comes to talking about God's relation to value. There is virtually no way in which a non-intentional, non-acting object can impart value. In fact, it might even be suggested that a non-intentional, non-acting object cannot even create, since creation is itself an act, perhaps the primordial act.[6] A Biblical ethics is built upon a relationship with the divine Being. It is participation in a way of life in relationship to God, a response to what Jews and Christians discern as God's actions in history. As Biblical scholar Gerhard von Rad puts it, the moral conduct of the people of God was measured by "the specific relationship in which the partner had at the time to prove himself true."[7] It is the relationship with God that is the ultimate source of moral guidance, not laws or moral theories (which only emerge subsequent to and as part of the relationship).

Notes

1 James M. Gustafson, *Ethics From a Theocentric Perspective*, Vol. 2, p. 27.

2 It is interesting to wonder why, having thrown the full weight of the 'hermeneutics of suspicion' against rationalist belief in general, they so often seem to blithely assume the validity of rationalist criticisms of belief in God.

3 This is not to say that God could not violate a natural law, but divine action does not require such violation. If God has total control over causal law, it is not clear what purpose would be served by violating it instead of simply exploiting it or deploying it for God's purposes.

4 I believe a well-reasoned, metaphysically coherent case can be made for the notion of God as personal agent and have laid out the logic of such a case in my *Together Bound: God, History, and the Religious Community*.
5 This raises the interesting question of whether God could create something and immediately disvalue it, or later come to disvalue it. There seems nothing inherently illogical about a creator coming to disvalue what he had originally valued because it goes astray, or misbehaves, or forfeits its original value in some way. Some might argue that this is what happened when God sent the flood subsequent to a decision to disvalue part of what God had created, given its willful falling away from God.
6 There are notorious conceptual difficulties in thinking coherently about a totally non-finite, non-particular, non-spatio-temporal, non-agent God 'taking thought to create' what is other than himself. But we need not, at this point, attempt to resolve the notoriety.
7 Quoted in Edward LeRoy Long, Jr., *A Survey of Christian Ethics*, (New York: Oxford University Press, 1967), p. 124.

Chapter 4

Inferring God's Agency and Intentions from History

Inferring God's Agency From History

The form of God's relationality to others, when God is understood as an agent, is historical. History, as a mode of understanding, is the stories or narratives of the acts of intentional agents. It is distinguished (though never isolated) from science, which is the mode of understanding of non-agential natural events or causes. Science tells us about what takes place in the world in the absence of intentional action. Science might better be understood as a description of the world underlying the field of action upon which agents act. It is about the world into which actions intervene. What science reveals is not a story (since it does not involve agents). Nevertheless the process by acting scientists of discovering the secrets of nature is historical and thus does constitute a story.[1]

History as we understand it comes into existence when agents begin to act intentionally on and in relation to nature and to each other. If God is an agent, then God's acts must necessarily be historical. And if they are historical, then one source of our knowledge of God will be history. It will be essentially *inferential*, that is, built upon primary and secondary experiences in which the presence of an agent acting is not necessarily immediate or self-evident, especially to those who are not present at the time of the action.[2] Inferences must be drawn from those occurrences that we take to be, or construe as, divine actions. And if this is true, then the deconstructionists who complain about an *a*historical, timeless, abstract, and ontologically transcendent being whose very ahistoricity and transcendence violate the historical embeddedness of all human agents/thinkers, have lost their target. For an acting God is, as acting, profoundly historical, and can only by known through the historical deposit of God's acts as that deposit is interpreted through inferential construals. As William Dean puts it, the religious believer's interpretation of reality "occurs in interaction with a God who is wholly historical."[3] History is the field or context for active relationality between God and other beings. The epistemology of God is grounded in historical knowledge because that is where and how God reveals Godself. And this claim is completely congruent with the Bible's construal of God.[4]

What sets this approach to ethics apart from most studies in moral philosophy, and even in theological ethics, is the centrality of God's purpose for the foundation of ethical action. Of course, many if not all theological ethics make reference to the will of God. But usually it is only as that will is discovered in the structures and dynamics of human nature. What I want to do is locate that will in the *actions* of God as construed and revealed in Scripture (the narrative of some historical peoples' experiences of what they construed as God's encounter with them over time) and in the narratives or life-stories of contemporary people who believe themselves to be the recipients or observers of divine action. I want to press to the limit the notion of God as an Agent who manifests a purpose in and through God's actions in the histories of human peoples and persons in the world. It is only in and through a correct discernment of God's intentions inferred from what one takes to be divine actions that persons can have a meaningful basis for knowing what to do morally in response to what God has done and what one believes God is intending.

For the Bible, "there was no recourse beyond history ... It is within history, within a plurality of tradition-events and interpretations, that God was to be found."[5] It is ironic that the deconstructionists, in leveling their attack on the Enlightenment's attempt to disengage reason from history, overlook this earlier Biblical tradition in which disengagement is not even contemplated. The Bible has often been dismissed by objectivist scholars for being too mired in the contingencies of history. But if God as Personal Agent acts in history, then any interpretive record of those divine acts will necessarily be 'mired' in the contingencies of history and the particularities of distinct interpretive frameworks. The tricky question is whether from that mire one can discover 'truths' (reliable beliefs, pragmatically understood) that hold up over time and prove to be reliable guides to action for all persons in all historical periods if and when they seek to conform their lives and actions to what they discern as God's will for the whole created order.

The Problematic of Biblical Interpretation

The essential religious question in this context is: is there sufficient inferential evidence, drawn from an historical record which is open in principle to all persons for interpretation, that there *is* an overarching, continuous intention on the part of a single, most powerful being, that gives unity and meaning to history? In embracing this interpretation of the evidence, the Biblical theist can claim no absolute certainty for her reading of the historical record. But presumably, she can claim no less certainty than someone who, on the basis of equally ambiguous evidence with respect to human actions, reaches the conclusion that there is a unifying thread that explains what might otherwise appear to be a random and unrelated series of occurrences. The *process* by which she interprets the data for God's action will be virtually identical with the process by which any of us interpret data about the allegedly purposeful actions of human persons whom we know inferentially through their actions.

I can only know my great-aunt Margaret (whom I met 'personally' but briefly on only two occasions) through the stories that others tell of her and from those few experiences in which I have been the recipient of her generosity. I also know that much of this 'evidence' for my discernment of her character is ambiguous. Some of the stories about her seem outlandish, a few seem 'out of character', and some are clearly made up. Nevertheless, on the whole the evidence I have from all the reports available to me, including my own limited direct experience of her actions, is that I have a pretty good 'fix' on great-aunt Margaret. Enough of the stories, coupled with my own experience, cohere in such a way that I can affirm, with a reasonable (but not absolute) degree of certainty that Margaret is a generous woman because her generosity has been a consistent feature of her most important actions as others have experienced, inferred, construed, and then narrated them.

I see no reason why something like this process of trying to figure out who great-aunt Margaret really is, and what she is up to, is not also what we do when we try to figure out who God is and what God is up to. Of course, the evidence on which the interpretation of God is to be built is both more ambiguous but also far more extensive than the evidence regarding great-aunt Margaret. There are literally millions more people who have added their interpretations to an understanding of God through what they take to be God's actions in their history. And my own experience of God's action in my personal history (assuming I believe that God has acted directly upon me) are deeper, more significant, and occasionally less ambiguous than my experience of great-aunt Margaret's actions. In the end, I can only achieve a knowledge that can be 'proved' by its ongoing, consistent, and coherent reliability in guiding my future actions in relation to what I take to be God and God's continuing intentions for my life and for the life of the world. If my beliefs about God's continuing activity ultimately fail to pan-out, if they prove continually unreliable, I would have no reason to continue to hold onto them.

History and Faith

The Problematic of Christian Belief

People steeped in the Biblical tradition, in the language of their Scripture, their liturgies, and their prayers, make reference to God's distinct, particular acts in history. These acts include (beyond the Creation) a calling of Abraham, a revelation to Moses, a sending of prophets, and for Christians an incarnation in and a resurrection of Jesus, a sending of the Holy Spirit to empower those who followed Jesus, and, for many believers, continuing specific divine interventions in their lives. These divine actions are taken to be decisive for the fulfillment, flourishing, and redemption of human beings.

At the same time, for many of these same believers the acts of God referred to by their Scripture, liturgies, and prayers are believed to be so unlike human acts, and the record of them so historically uncertain, that they are regarded as incapable of forming the basis of any reasoned belief in the God who allegedly brought them about. If one's faith, it is argued, depends on the successful validation of claims about God's historical actions in revealing Godself to Moses, or parting the waters at the Red Sea, or resurrecting Jesus, then one's faith will be unanchored because such validation is not possible.

There are two reasons for this. It is hard enough to determine the validity of claims about human actions, and cognitively impossible if the actions are those of an ontologically different reality. Some of our beliefs about human actions do, of course, have greater credibility and warrant than others. If I see you do something, I have a strong basis for believing that you did it. If I have been well schooled in philosophical skepticism, of course, I can always raise the theoretical doubt that what I think I saw may be delusory. But generally, direct experience of something is as good a foundation for believing it as any we have.

If, however, I read an account (by Parson Weems for example) about George Washington cutting down a cherry tree, I have far less basis for believing that it accurately reflects a real occurrence, let alone one that is exactly as described in the account. There is, of course, no logical, physical, or ontological reason why Washington could not have cut down a cherry tree. What he is alleged by Weems to have done is an act that is within the capability of most human beings.

What makes Weems' account of his cutting it down problematic is the reliability both of witnesses and of the transmission of the story. Weems was notorious for embroidering stories about Washington. We have good reason to believe that his account of this 'event' is something other than a 'strictly' accurate unvarnished depiction of an objective historical fact unclouded by interpretive overlay.

Now when the agent in question is not human but divine, when the witnesses are caught up in a cultural/psychological framework that is not insistent upon (or even aware of the possibility of) distinguishing between 'objective historical fact' and myth, or 'embroidered narrative', then the validity of claims about such an agent's acts becomes problematic, even, for some, incredible. Add to that the problem of claiming the reality of acts that violate what we normally take to be natural laws (for example, parting waters, raising from the dead, and so on), and we have the problematic of theistic belief based on claims that God acted in history.

The only way around this problem, as I see it, is to accept the tenuousness of belief in particular historical actions (whether divine or human) that are remote from us in time and transmitted to us only through narratives that blend myth, interpretive overlay, and objective fact. There is no question that we can only get at what 'really' happened through a series of narrative accounts that themselves are shaped by the beliefs of the narrators who are culturally/psychologically conditioned. Their beliefs are not simply a 'photograph' of the past as it really was. Our appropriation of these accounts is filtered through our own cultural/psychological frameworks. At best, therefore, we can draw uncertain inferences and create provisional construals of what happened in the past. These construals are always subject to further testing, as I have tried to set forth in my rendering of a moderate realist epistemology. We can agree wholeheartedly with Georges Florovsky when he says that "all historical interpretations are provisional and hypothetical. No definitive interpretation can ever be achieved ... Our data are never complete, and new discoveries often compel historians to revise radically their schemes and to surrender sometimes their most cherished convictions, which may have seemed firmly established."[6] Historical interpretations of divine action are no exception to this principle.

The Objectivity of History

This does not mean that the historian simply bypasses the question of the objective facticity of past events or actions. There can be no doubt that there were definite historical acts that stand in the background of the Biblical narrative. The problem is how we can determine, with what degree of certainty, what happened and who did it.

My interpretation of a purported historical act can be more or less certain depending on the reliability of my memory and the corroborating evidence. I must draw inferences from the data available, and I must trust that my inferences reflect more or less accurately what happened. Beyond that absolute certainty is impossible.

Discerning Patterns of Action

Spread out over time, my inferences from the historical data normally seek to discern a pattern of action in conformity to a consistent and coherent intention on the part of an agent or agents. In the case of Washington, I need to know whether the claim that he cut down the cherry tree is consistent with what I know of his overall character and the course of his life especially as defined by the pattern of his overarching intentions. All readings of an agent's actions presuppose a continuing, consistent, and coherent set of intentions that inform that agent's acts. Without some sense of the agent's character and defining purposes, the interpretation of an isolated, contextless, atomic act is impossible. The cherry tree incident 'fits' what else we know of Washington (from more reliable sources) whereas the claim that he spit on his dying father does not and therefore is more 'suspect' with respect to historical accuracy.

The dilemma for theists, of course, is that they want more than an uncertain construal of God's reality and purpose. They want to justify a firm conviction that God is real and that God acts in their lives. But this conviction cannot come solely by way of getting a completely reliable basis for believing in claims about the past actions of God.[7]

There is, however, the problem of whether the actions attributed to God form a coherent picture of an Agent whose intentions are ones that incline us to commit ourselves to them and their author. This is partly the problem of a selective reading of the Biblical material. Are *all* references to divine action to be taken as constituting the core of divine intention? When God commands the people of Israel to lay waste the people of the surrounding nations, is that divine intention to be taken as equally normative as the commandment to love one's neighbor as oneself? If, as seems apparent, these commands conflict, which is to be taken as more central to God's intention, and how can one justify that particular 'taking'? If both reflect God's intention, how are they to be reconciled?

Faith

I do not believe that reconciliation of these problems can be wished away or brought about by a simplistic appeal to 'faith'. Whatever faith is, it is not the ability to justify or validate a belief in an historical inference that is otherwise without evidential warrant or support. I do not verify or justify a belief in Washington's cutting down of a cherry tree simply by saying that I 'believe' he did it in the absence of further corroboration. On the other hand, faith may be synonymous with one's construal of a pattern of meaning in a series of actions that might, without that construal, reveal no pattern, continuity, or meaning. What might otherwise appear to be a random, meaningless, or even contradictory series of occurrences, might be construed as actually a clever working out of a hitherto unperceived purpose. Chess players often appear to be making random or contradictory moves on the board, only to reveal as they capture the Queen that there was, in fact, a hidden plan informing their moves, cleverly disguised from their opponent but now, at the end game, clear for all to see. Believing in this hidden but operative purpose is, until the purpose is revealed more fully at the end of the game, an act of faith.

But it is not a blind faith, nor does it in itself validate a claim that any particular move or event is, in fact, an act expressive of an agent's intention. Faith, in this context, is a reasoned inference to what is not (or not yet) obvious or clear to just any observer. Faith not does overleap the less than complete historical evidence and claim an absolute certainty about what is 'really going on'. Faith does not, in itself, reconcile conflicting inferences. Faith does not make certain what is historically uncertain. Faith cannot make historically real what is only myth. As Van Harvey said many years ago, "faith has no function in the justification of historical arguments respecting fact. When faith is used as a justification of historical claims that otherwise could not be justified by our normal warrants and backings, the machinery of rational assessment comes to a shuddering halt."[8] As Wolfhart Pannenberg insists, the essence of faith is to *trust* that one's inference is correct. "Trust primarily directs itself toward the future, and the future justifies, or disappoints."[9] Whatever faith is, its truth is dependent, in the last analysis, upon what really happened, even if cognitive access to what happened is provisional, limited, and incomplete.

But faith does permit the faithful person to infer a purpose behind a series of events/acts presently not obvious to everyone provided there is some reasonable degree of evidence to support the construal. The clever chess player *knows* he has a purpose behind his moves. He *intends* that purpose to remain hidden from his opponent. The observer, however, can *infer or believe* that he understands that purpose.

The clever player *cannot know* until the game is over whether his purpose has succeeded. The observer does not have his faith (in the discernment of that purpose) validated until and unless the end game comes about as his faith or trust would have predicted that it would.

The fact of the realization of a construed purpose needs to be distinguished from the actions that are construed to be expressive of it. For the theist what is crucial is the belief in an ongoing, overarching, unifying intention on the part of a divine agent. It is not knowledge of isolated, contextless occurrences. What the believer finds meaningful is an overarching *purpose* that unifies (and thereby gives meaning to) a series of historical actions that ultimately includes the believer herself.

If there is no overarching pattern or purpose that one can discern, the verification of the historical facticity of a putative act exemplifying it becomes extremely difficult. It cannot be shown to be impossible, but without the context of an overarching purpose there is no context in which to place its meaning. It may, at best, simply demonstrate a characteristic of its author (for example, honesty) that would have been demonstrated in other acts more directly accessible to the observer.

In the context of a Biblical faith in a God who acts in history in accord with an overarching purpose, the relationship between God's alleged acts and God's overarching intention is less than abundantly clear. Not every act attributed to God seems to be part of the fulfillment of an overarching purpose. Other alleged acts seem to be, literally, at cross-purposes to each other. The question for the Biblical theist is whether there is, in and among the various acts ascribed to God, the possibility of inferring an overarching, unifying, continuous purpose that seems to remain invariant and progressive throughout the history of what are claimed to be God's acts.

If God has a purpose for the world that purpose should be inferable from actions that take place 'in the open', as part of a 'public' or world history, as it were. It has sometimes been argued that there is a radical difference between world history and 'salvation' history. If that difference refers only to the fact that not everyone sees the same acts as acts of God or sees the significance of those acts in the same way, then the difference is to be expected and not overly troubling. If, however, the difference refers to a history that only believers can see with the aid of a cognitive faculty called faith, then the difference is unintelligible.

Pannenberg has argued that "the historical revelation is open to anyone who has eyes to see. It has a universal character. ... The revelation ... of the biblical God in his activity is no secret or mysterious happening." [10] This does not mean, of course, that human beings could see God's purpose if God had not acted, or could see it by considering nature alone, and not history as well. Not all people will see God's hand at work in the world around them now or in the past. But this does not mean that the truth of God's actions "is too high for them, so that their reason must be supplemented by other means of knowing. Rather, it means that they must use their reason in order to see correctly." [11]

The religious believer commits herself to a faith in God's purpose in part because others have made a similar commitment and have testified that their lives (so far) have been fulfilled by it. They have trusted in God's ongoing actions in fulfillment of God's purpose, and have found new life in and through that trust.

Revelation

Theology often calls upon a notion of revelation at the point when one has obtained less than certain inferential evidence. And it is true that if God is an historical agent, our knowledge of God is, ultimately, a knowledge based on revelation, but of a very particular sort. Revelation is the absolutely appropriate mode of action for disclosing what we as personal agents are (and what we are up to) to other agents. If I want you to know who I am, then I want you to know what my basic values and purposes are. The deepest possible knowledge of agents has to do with their fundamental choices, with the values they try to live by, with the decisions they make, with the intentions they adopt, and with the responsibilities they undertake. And the only way we can reveal our defining choices and values is by what we choose to do. It is only by actions of some sort (and the range is quite large) that we can reveal ourselves to others. Therefore, in the context of historical acts, revelation as the mode of knowledge is absolutely meaningful.

No revelation of who I am can occur when I am the passive victim of the actions of others, when I 'suffer' rather than 'perform' actions (except that I am not truly an agent). It is only when I 'act' that I can reveal the innermost part of me that makes choices and forms intentions in accordance with chosen values. Even a psychology that focuses solely on 'drives' or forces beyond the intentional control (or at least modification) of the person herself is inadequate to a full knowledge of who she is.

Inferring Character from Action

When it comes to inferring the character of God from the historical record coupled with personal experience, that record must not reveal radically conflicting or incompatible divine traits. It will, in the normal course of things, reveal a whole variety of *different* traits (for example, generosity, love, compassion, steadfastness, anger, justness, and so on), but these do not necessarily conflict with each other. It is only when we infer that God is both loving and spiteful that we run into problems in inferring a consistent, coherent divine self. And if the historical record bears out equally both of these incompatible traits, then the basis for our belief that we are dealing with a trustworthy and reliable being is significantly weakened.

Should this happen, our only recourse is to find a way to interpret one of the traits as a provisional or strategic mode of action that is ultimately subsumed under an enduring and universal trait for which the former is a tactical means to an end. Spite and love presumably cannot be compatible in this way, but love and anger could be. One could love another so much that when the loved one betrays that love the spontaneous response is anger. But if the record shows that on some limited occasions, the lover acted angrily, but eventually and on the vast majority of occasions subordinated that anger to or overcame it by love, one would have a way of reconciling these apparently conflicting modes of action. (Note that the reconciling of conflicting traits often occurs over the course of time, not all at once. This is the way in which historical temporality can resolve contradictions that logic, which operates atemporally, cannot. But this is what one would expect of agents who must act in time.)

What matters in the long run, assuming the relationship with the other agent is a long-run affair (and in the case of God one that runs as long as the world's history runs), is whether there is a sufficient basis for inferring an overarching, unifying, consistent, and reliable pattern of action revealing an underlying and continuous intention manifested in divine actions in history. And it is that long-run inference that Biblical theists have drawn and by which they relate themselves to the God they believe is the author of that unifying intention.

Drawing a long-run inference of this type does not, of course, replace the need for beliefs drawn upon immediate, extremely short-run experiences. The religious believer will, presumably have some experiences in the here and now from which she will conclude that she has been in the presence of God, or that God has acted directly in her life. These experiences form an essential component of her overall knowledge of God. But they have to complement and be complemented by the inferences about the enduring character and long-range historical intentions of the being with whom she believes she is in immediate and mutual relationship. Both of these dimensions of the human being's experience of God are necessary if her knowledge of God is to be both a form of justified true belief and existentially meaningful.[12]

It should be noted that unless someone has some experience that seems *prima facie* to be an experience of an overwhelming power bearing down on her, and unless she finds some resonance of that experience in the experiences of other persons, both contemporaneous to her and in the past, she would have no particular reason to even consider the possibility of the existence of a divine Personal Agent. A self-proclaimed Biblical theist who neither experiences God in any way, nor finds credible the testimony of people (both now and in the past) who do claim such experience would be hard-pressed to explain why he considers himself a Biblical theist. I am assuming, contrary to some contemporary theologies, that no case for a knowledge of God can even get off the ground unless it is based, at some point, in one's personal experience of God's saving power or grace (no matter how mediated the articulation of that experience is by a religious tradition and cultural/historical patterns of interpretation). A purely logical, rational proof of the existence of God that does not also touch one's heart and soul, will provide precious little in the way of knowledge of a personal, dynamic, living God.

Responding to the Other

The Primordial Moral Situation

Once one has drawn an inference about the unifying intention of the Other with whom one experiences a relationship, one has to make a response. If I discern that the other person's intention toward me is one of generosity, I can hardly remain indifferent to her. I may choose to retreat from her (because I cannot stand too much generosity), or I may choose to reciprocate her generosity, but I normally will not simply ignore her, especially when her actions continue to impinge upon me. I must, in short, develop an 'ethics of response' to her. The primordial *ethical* question is: what must I now do in light of what she has done? She is an Other over-against me and to the degree that ethics begins in the relationship of selves to each other in a mutual field of action, I am now in the primordial ethical situation. The motivating force behind this 'ought' (derived from the 'is' of her action) can range from sheer selfishness, to reciprocal generosity to her and to others. I might be moved either to retreat from the relationship or out of gratitude to act generously toward others in imitation of her actions toward me.

Obviously the power and influence of the other to whom I am responding will affect how much attention I have to give to her. If she turns out to be someone with whom I have had only a fleeting and impersonal encounter (for example, I sell her a ticket for the train she wants to catch) and who can be expected not to affect my life in the future, my response to her can be fleeting. On the other hand, if she is someone who can be expected to have an ongoing, decisive relationship with me, and she has a degree of power sufficient to enable her to make her intentions continue to impact upon me should she choose, then my response to her cannot be indifference. An infant has his world almost totally determined for him by the reality and power of his mother. There is virtually no decision he can make about his overt actions that does not have to take into account the intentions of his mother since they determine almost all of the significant structures and the arena for his actions. (Ultimately, of course, as their relationship matures, the good mother will give him more and more freedom from her determining power if she intends to make their relationship more mutual and loving.[13])

Given the epistemological position we have adopted, in which obstruction to our will first determines for us the reality of the 'other', an agent has no choice but to take full account of another agent's power. If the other agent dominates the field of action, the first agent either conforms to that presence or she suffers constant frustration in attempting to realize intentions contrary to those of the more powerful agents. In the short run it is to her advantage to figure out exactly what the dominating agent wants and then to adapt her intentions to it accordingly. Unless her actions are in conformity to the other agent, her actions will fail assuming the other agent continues to 'hold all the cards'. (She could, of course, try to figure out a way to undermine or nullify the power of the dominating agent, but even this counter-maneuver presupposes the need to take the power and reality of the other into account.)

There have been some theologians who believe that this notion of responding to a determining power is a relatively accurate picture of humankind's relation to God. God's omnipotent power has, they argue, predetermined the course of events by an eternal and immutable edict. Human beings have the choice of conforming to that edict (and thus of being 'saved'), or opposing it (and thus ensuring their damnation). The only 'choice' left to human beings is whether to accept their predestined fate.

While many religious people would reject this view as cold, impersonal, coercive, and demeaning (an extreme example of heteronomous coercion), especially if God is a loving person who expects genuine free choices from God's creatures, it has a measure of truth in it. Surely if God is to serve the God-function, God must have the power to establish and maintain the conditions of reality that set the boundaries for successful human action. As James Gustafson puts it, "The divine governance 'demands' some conformity to it; failure to consent to these demands is perilous both to human well-being and to 'nature'."[14] Few people complain of the fact that 'nature' has set boundaries or limits to what we can do simply by willing it. I cannot will to suspend the causal law that 'determines'[15] what will happen (provided nothing interferes) if I let my chest receive the full impact of a bullet fired from a gun 10 feet away from me. Even in my relations with powerful significant others, I cannot simply will that if I betray their love and trust in me that our relationship will remain unchanged. In this sense my 'autonomy' as a moral being is always highly conditioned.

If God, therefore, has the power to establish and maintain the conditions of reality within which I live and carry out my intentions, and if one of those conditions is that God will ultimately bring God's intentions for the world to successful completion, then those conditions set the boundaries for my successful actions. I cannot ignore them or ultimately act contrary to them if I want to succeed in doing what I intend to do. If God is working out a specific and overarching intention for the created order by God's actions in history, then I may choose to act contrary to that intention, but I cannot choose to do so with impunity or expect that my actions will encounter no obstacles or resistance. There will be consequences of a negative kind for violating, undermining, and acting against God's will. These consequences are not the result of God being vindictive or vengeful against violators of the divine will. They are the necessary result of acting against established and firm conditions of reality, including those that are created for our ultimate well-being, even though we do not recognize them as such at this moment. (We do not think of our chest being smashed by a bullet as the vindictive act of nature, nor do we think that the spouse who is reluctant to forgive us when we betray their trust is acting irrationally. They are, in fact, acting exactly as we would predict given our knowledge of what constitutes loving personal relationships and what happens when those relationships are betrayed.) And the upshot of this fact is that my response to God's actions must be based, at least in part, on my recognition that the achievement of my own intentions depends upon their conformity with God's intentions.

The specific nature of God's intentions will, of course, determine the specific nature of my response. If God's intentions are for communities of love, trust, compassion, and justice, and if those communities are the preconditions for my flourishing and well-being, then in responding to God by conforming my intentions to God's I am not working against my own well-being. Doing God's will does not become an action that is unnaturally coerced or contrary to my nature: in fact, it becomes the means to the fulfillment of my nature.

There are those who have stressed the element of command as a form of coercion in referring to God's will. Whatever God wills, God commands. And a command is usually understood as a heteronomous overriding of my autonomy. But, as Richard Mouw has pointed out, it is quite inappropriate to describe a Christian's relationship with God as simply one of receiving commands from an 'external other'. "A heteronomous account of Christian morality does not capture the intimacy of the relationship between commander and commandee as it is described in the Bible ... it is an interpersonal intimacy, a *unity of purpose* within the context of covenant."[16] This fact becomes the basis for transcending the problem of autonomy vs. heteronomy. If we desire autonomy as a means for our own flourishing, and if willing conformity to another's will turns out to be a more effective means to that same end of flourishing, then we would be silly to insist on absolute autonomy as the overriding virtue. Everything here will turn on whether there is such a thing as a human nature that is, in fact, fulfilled only in loving relationships that are to some degree dependent on (or better put, interdependent with) others.

We also have to avoid the danger of assuming that God serves the God-function *solely* or primarily by advancing my own interests or human interests generally. I may have a very distorted view of what is in my ultimate best interest, and God will presumably have a much larger view of how my interests serve the interests of God's whole creation. In a genuine relationship of love and mutuality with God, there will be dimensions of my own self-understanding and self-interest that are radically altered or transformed by that mutuality. I may need to have my present self-understanding shaken to its core before I can begin to see what is truly in my own interests. Nevertheless, we have to be careful not to turn God into a mere device for securing what I take to be my self-interest in a limited, parochial way. And we have to be equally careful not to turn ourselves into a mere device for securing divine pleasure unrelated to our own need for fulfillment. Neither alternative is appropriate for genuine mutuality in relationship.

Science and the Revelation of Human Nature

If we are to discover what, in fact, fulfills persons, we need to turn to history and the sciences of human nature. The first of the divine acts, according to the theistic reading, is the creation of the structures of reality. Subsequent acts by God refined and conditioned those structures, at least in part in order to make possible the creation of human life. One important implication of this belief is that insofar as science studies the world in the absence of the defining characteristics of agents per se (consciousness, intentions, and freedom), science is the indispensable cognitive vehicle for grasping what God was up to in the creation of the structures of reality. Ontology is a form of revelation. (This does not mean that the scientist, operating strictly within the limited domain of scientific understanding, needs to factor into her understanding of reality any reference to a divine creative act since she is concerned solely with reality in the absence of intentional actions, that is, with the cosmos *after* God's initiating, creative act brought it into being and before human actions intervene upon it.)

Therefore, if one intends to understand something of God's (as well as our) intentions and the conditions for their realization, one would have to study the totality of the relevant empirical evidence as revealed in nature. This would be true not only of the evidence taken under consideration by the physical sciences (biology, physics, chemistry, genetics, and so on), but also that under the purview of the social sciences (sociology, psychology, anthropology, economics, and so on). As James Gustafson has put it, "in the light of empirical research the moralist is likely to gain insight into the potential consequences of various courses of morally determined action."[17]

The Non-uniqueness of Christian Ethics

The Core of Human Flourishing

If the patterns and conditions of reality extend to all human beings and God intends the well-being of all, then there cannot be a uniquely Biblical ethics, that is, one that applies only to Jews and Christians. A Biblically-based ethics will have to be one that is congruent with nature generally and with the nature of human beings in particular. Unless evidence suggests that God has created human beings with quite different essential natures, one from the other, and intends them to limit their expression of these natures to different cultures, and unless God has created the empirical conditions of reality quite differently in different parts of the world at different times, one has to assume that what fulfills the human being (at the most fundamental level, not necessarily in more superficial ways) in one time and place will fulfill all human beings at different times and places. God may well intend multi-cultures without having created such a vast variability in the nature of the persons who inhabit them that one can flourish only in one type of culture and not another.

This claim does not deny that there is a real and experienced difference between some of the *modes* of fulfillment and the underlying *core* of fulfillment. If, for example, the evidence suggests that no human being can reach fulfillment or well-being in the absence of care and nurture in relation to loving others, that need for loving mutual relationship (as both giver and receiver of love) may be at the core of human fulfillment but the mode of its expression may vary greatly from culture to culture, person to person. Care may be expressed toward infants either by a single mother/father in a so-called nuclear family or it may be shown in a communal setting with more than one care-giver. There may be no evidence showing conclusively that one of these forms of care-giving is superior to the other with respect to providing the ideal conditions for the child's later fulfillment and well-being. But without some form of personal care and loving nurture, the infant will grow to adulthood radically impoverished in all those core areas that constitute the healthy, flourishing, mature individual, capable of relating wholesomely to others as an adult. In some cultures love may be expressed primarily by touch, in another by word, in still another by silent dedication to the well being of others. Cultures do shape the various ways in which people give and receive love. The point is that a theistic ethic must be grounded in the realities of human beings as such and be open to revision with respect to what the empirical evidence reveals about what enables human beings to reach the maximum levels of personal flourishing.

In this context, history becomes a kind of temporal laboratory for experimenting with different forms of loving relationship, some of which, over time, prove more and others less reliable and successful in guiding human beings toward fulfillment. (And there is no reason to suppose that God, as the Biblical narrative tells it, has never engaged in these kinds of experiments, from the period prior to the fall of Adam and Eve, through the period of the Law, into the time of Jesus and his attempt to entice others toward love through self-sacrifice. In each of these historical moments, God might be interpreted as trying out different ways of having people relate to each other. God might 'know' in some sense what will work ultimately, but the experiments might be ways of figuring out how best to get human beings to use their freedom and creativity to discern the truth about their own nature without simply imposing it on them without their consent.)

Human beings themselves contribute to the historical experiments in human flourishing. The Jesuit moral philosopher Joseph Fuchs has argued that God's creation is humanity and its world. God's will is that the human being "himself construct the 'blueprint' of genuinely human conduct, that he take into his own hands the reality of man and his world, in order to lead it to its highest human potential, and turn himself and humanity toward a lofty, truly human history and future."[18] The full implications of this observation will be worked out shortly, but the point is that for the theist there is one humanity, one underlying reality of being human even in the midst of a plurality of cultural settings and modes for the expression of the mutuality that is the heart of human flourishing. And there is one God with one overarching, unifying intention for all humankind. Therefore, there cannot be a ground-ethic, a fundamental form of response to God's intention, just for Christians, or for Jews: it must be an ethic for all persons.

According to John Macquarrie, the differences between a Christian and a non-Christian ethic "have to do with the different ways in which [various peoples and traditions] understand and engage in the moral obligations laid upon all, or with the different degrees of explicitness to which the idea of an authentic humanity has emerged in the several traditions."[19] But these differences do not obviate the fact there is a kind of "fundamental moral knowledge, given with human existence itself."[20]

This does not foreclose the possibility that human nature changes over time: the notion of an essential core to human fulfillment is compatible with emergent insights into that core and with some degree of mutability in the core itself. As Fuchs puts it, somewhat paradoxically, "mutability belongs to man's immutable essence ... [The human being] has to actualize what is sketched out for him as possibility. In the process of his self-realization he continually modifies his existence."[21]

But claims for *radically* different forms of human nature or for total incommensurability and pluralism seem exaggerated. Some moral philosophers recognize that the more we study moral codes the more we find that they do not differ in major principles. They all aim at the development of a fuller, richer, more personal human life.[22] There will always be a distinction between the human person's "unchangeable metaphysical nature" and his or her "changing historicity ... The extent to which man [sic] remains the same through historical change is a problem for metaphysical anthropology, not ethics. Precisely to the extent that man's being changes with time must the applicable ethical norm also change in every case."[23]

We cannot, as the postmodernists insist, escape the contextualization of moral response. And these contexts are surely different for different persons at different times. God may be, as Gustafson puts it, "enabling men [sic] to discern what God is enabling men to do; but the locus for the discernment is in the self as it relates beliefs about the God in whom it trusts to the situation in which it acts."[24]

But historical discernment is not incompatible with a human nature that in its fundamental dimensions, needs, and aspirations does not change radically, at least with respect to the fact that its ultimate fulfillment is found only in and through mutual love. No matter what the variation of cultures and epochs, no human fulfillment is possible through lives essentially characterized by alienation, hate, fear, indifference, exploitation, abuse, or domination of others. There are, in short, some forms of human life that simply will not, in the long run, prove ultimately satisfying or fulfilling for the persons who adopt them, no matter in what culture they live. A Biblically-based ethic is a human ethic to the extent that it reveals and articulates the appropriate response to an unchanging divine intention that sets boundaries within which human intentions can succeed. The modes and variations of response to that divine intention in particular historical situations must be built upon an understanding of what the core of human fulfillment was intended by God to be.

An individual may have some particular insight into God's intention, she may believe that she has been given the ability to discern that intention in a specific and vivid way, she may construe a particular person at a particular moment of time as the paradigm of God's intention (that is, Jesus, if she is a Christian), but the insight is into what God intends for *all* persons. In Jesus, the Christian may believe she sees an historical realization of what it is to be fully and decisively human.[25] Likewise, in the community that arises from a common response to that vision of fulfilled humanity in Jesus she may begin to experience in a preliminary, fragmentary, but real way, something (a foretaste, a first-fruit) of what will be experienced more completely by all persons when God's intention has run its course, been embraced by all, and become fully realized.

A Biblically-based ethic may faithfully reflect the ethic that will prove to be the most reliable response to God's intention for all humankind. It may discern more accurately than other religious ethics what God is up to. But whatever it discerns about human nature, whatever it learns from the experience of Jews and Christians who are trying to live out that ethic, as well as from the 'secular' study of nature, it will apply to all persons.

A Biblically-based ethic, therefore, is incompatible with a *radically* relativistic ethic. It insists that there are some (not overly vague and thin) core dimensions of human life that need to be nurtured, developed, and fulfilled if persons are to lead lives of well-being and flourishing. Each of us must live the truth of this ontology of human nature in particular, historically-contingent modes of life since we are always particular, historically-contingent people living in particular, historically-contingent communities. Nevertheless, we must live *that* ontology's ethic and not any or all ontologies as if there are no significant differences between them. If that ontology's construal of God's intention is wrong, it will ultimately fail to guide human behavior successfully, and if it is right, it points the way toward the ultimate satisfaction of human life.

An incorrect construal of ethical reality only disproves itself in action. That is the insight of pragmatism. It is only by acting over time upon what we discern of reality that we can 'know' whether we have gotten it right. The theistic ethic is based both on a construal of reality and upon the claims of Biblical theists that they have found that construal to have proven reliable and life-giving, life-enhancing, over and over again in their own lives.

In this respect the theistic ethic is teleological: it orients us toward a goal (the fulfillment of life in community). And it gives us a reason to adopt it (we want that fulfillment). It is also an ethic that, in a sense, binds God to us. Some earlier theologians raised the possibility that God's power and freedom are such that God could change God's will and intend things that are radically destructive of human interests. They have praised the virtue of people who would, in effect, be willing to be damned for the glory of God should God command it, but this possibility and its corresponding virtue are ultimately nonsensical. There is this much truth in moral autonomy: we are compelled to choose what ethic to adopt. No one can force choices on us because a forced choice is no choice. Not even God can make us adopt an ethic except by removing our free will, and fulfillment without free will is incoherent. Therefore, we find ourselves with the mental freedom to construe reality as we wish and to embrace any ethic we wish (within limits). But our construals and our embracings are not without constraints and consequences. There are ontological conditions that impinge on our reality and our choices. As long as we believe that these conditions are ultimately capable of fulfilling or frustrating us, provided we construe them correctly, we can accept their reality *and* freely embrace the correspondingly appropriate ethic of response without undermining the essence of human autonomy.

If, however, we came to believe that the conditions of reality are such that they work against our fulfillment (because God now intends to deny us fulfillment), we would be silly to adopt an ethic that leads to our own ultimate frustration. If God were to command us to do something that we find fundamentally wrong (such as to torture or abuse children) then we would be right to conclude that God's character had so changed (from what we had inferred from God's previous pattern of actions) that God no longer deserves our loving response and no longer serves the God-function for us. In this sense, a theistic ethic is based on our prior acceptance of what a morally right way of life is.[26] Human beings value some things independently of their relation to God's commands (for example, the protection of children from abuse). At the same time they believe that the right and worthy way of life that they have chosen has been built into the conditions of reality by God.

Loyalty to God, as Robert Merrihew Adams has argued, is primarily loyalty to a God who, as all-powerful, has willed a particular state of affairs and values, not to what God *might* have willed or to a radically different set of values God might will in the future. It is a loyalty to God because of the kind of character God *in fact* has revealed Godself to be through what God has *actually* done. It is not a trivial truth that God bestows on creatures things that they value.[27] Goodness and not power is fundamental in relations of human trusting. It may be better to trust God because of God's goodness than to do so because God has absolute power. "Religiously, it is better to make value rather than being, primary."[28] And if we come to believe that the conditions of reality, as created and valued by God, are not ultimately supportive of the way of life that we have come to value for ourselves, we can only remain moral by retaining our vision of the moral way of life and letting go of our attempt to conform our actions to the conditions of reality and to the God who values them. In short, if we have to choose between a God with power and no love, and human love that is actively opposed by God, we ought to choose the latter. In choosing love without God, we may have to accept the conditions of reality that 'conspire against us', but we certainly do not need to dignify that acceptance with an ethic that requires us to love the God who created the conditions that nullify love. We can and ought to choose, in that situation, an ethic of defiance and resistance (futile to be sure, if God's will prevails). It may be the only honor left to us.

Fortunately, however, the Biblical discernment is that the conditions of reality and God's intentions 'conspire to our benefit'. How they do and why they lead to an ethic of community as the core of the Christian ethic is the subject of Chapter 5.

Notes

1 Roy Bhaskar, *A Realist Theory of Science*, p. 33. A causal law that is without the actions of agents is discovered by the active intervention into it by intentional agents. "In an experiment we are a causal agent of the sequence of events, but not of the causal law which the sequence of events, because it has been produced under experimental conditions, enables us to identify." The distinction between nature and history is fully worked out in numerous studies. For an overview of the relation between science and the knowledge of agents, see my *Together Bound*, Chapter Five, 'Persons and Agents'.

2 This does not rule out present experience, even perception, of God. See William Alston, *Perceiving God: The Epistemology of Religious Experience*, (Ithaca: Cornell University Press, 1991).

3 William Dean, *History Making History*, p. 18. Presumably Dean does not mean to say

that God's reality is *exhausted* in God's historical agency.

4 I do not mean to suggest that some of the rationalistic arguments for God's existence (for example, the ontological, cosmological, and teleological) are not important. But most such arguments do not tell us much, if anything, about the *character* of God as discerned through God's actions. They may produce a rational conviction that God is the unmoved mover, first cause, ground of being, and so on, but these references to God are notoriously empty of the kind of specific content one gets about a person only by observing or inferring his/her actions as revelations of his/her personality.

5 Dean, *History Making History*, p. 38.

6 Georges Florovsky, 'The Predicament of the Christian Historian', in C.T. McIntire, ed., *God, History, and Historians*, (New York: Oxford University Press, 1977), pp. 423–424. Recently a number of Biblical scholars are questioning the fundamental facticity of Biblical accounts of the settlement of the land of Canaan by the early Israelites. Such questioning certainly undercuts any absolute certainty that the Biblical narratives are historical records as we normally understand that term today. See, for example, Israel Finkelstein and Neil Asher Silberman, *The Bible Unearthed*, (New York: Free Press, 2001).

7 The problem is not, as was pointed out previously, that God is different from human agents. If God is an agent, then God's acts are acts: they do what all acts do, they 'interfere' in the otherwise natural course of events to bring about a change intended by the agent. God's acts do not violate, interfere, transcend, or interrupt the course of events in any other way than do human acts. God's *range* and *power* of action may be greater, but as actions, God's acts are still acts, subject to the same kind of interpretation and analysis as any agent's acts.

8 Van Harvey, *The Historian and the Believer*, (New York: The Macmillan Company, 1966), p. 112.

9 Wolfhart Pannenberg, 'Revelation as History', in MacIntire, ed., *God, History, and Historians*, p. 123.

10 *Ibid.*, p. 122.

11 *Ibid.*, p. 123.

12 Alston in his *Perceiving God* shows how mystical experiences of God occur in the context of overriders and underminders based on knowledge of God gleaned from other sources.

13 Some of the important implications of this observation regarding the 'healthy' maturity of originally dependent infants, especially as they affect our understanding of our relationship with God, will be explored in Chapter 6 in which I will draw upon the insights of the psychological theory known as 'object-relations'.

14 James M. Gustafson, *Ethics From a Theocentric Perspective*, Vol. 2, p. 1.

15 Technically, laws do not 'determine' anything. Only agents have the power to determine things. Laws may describe the *means* through which agents exert power, but we must not anthropomorphize laws. In science a natural law is a description of how things work in a regular and predictable way but it begs the question to assume that laws are forces. And forces (or causes) need ultimately to be grounded in a power that utilizes them. This suggests that the ultimate power in the universe must be an agent. But this suggestion cannot be developed fully here.

16 Richard J. Mouw, 'Biblical Revelation and Medical Decisions', in Stanley Hauerwas and Alisdair MacIntyre, *Revisions*, (South Bend: University of Notre Dame, 1983), pp. 188–189.

17 James M. Gustafson, 'The Relationship of Empirical Science to Moral Thought', in Ronald P. Hamel and Kenneth R. Himes, ed., *Introduction to Christian Ethics*, (Mahwah, NJ: Paulist, 1989), p. 433.

18 Joseph Fuchs, 'Is There a Specifically Christian Morality?', in Charles Curran and Richard A. McCormick, eds., *Readings in Moral Theology, No. 2: The Distinctiveness of Christian Ethics*, (Ramsay, NJ: Paulist, 1980), pp. 10–11.

19 John Macquarrie, 'Rethinking Natural Law', in Curran and McCormick, *Readings in Moral Theology*, p. 126.

20 *Ibid.*, p. 139.

21 Josef Fuchs, SJ, 'The Absoluteness of Behavioral Moral Norms', in Hamel and Himes, *Introduction to Christian Ethics*, p. 496.

22 Macquarrie, 'Rethinking Natural Law', p. 142.

23 Bruno Schuller, SJ, 'Can Moral Theology Ignore Natural Law?', in Hamel and Himes, *Introduction to Christian Ethics*, p. 411.

24 James M. Gustafson, 'Moral Discernment in the Christian Life', in Hamel and Himes, *Introduction to Christian Ethics*, p. 594.

25 See Richard A. McCormick, 'Does Religious Faith Add to Ethical Perception', in Hamel and Himes, *Introduction to Christian Ethics*, p. 143.

26 See Robert Merrihew Adams, 'A Modified Divine Command Theory of Ethical Wrongness', in Paul Helm, ed., *Divine Commands and Morality*, (New York: Oxford University Press, 1981), p. 86.

27 *Ibid.*, p. 100.

28 C. David Grant, *God the Center of Value: Value Theory in the Theology of H. Richard Niebuhr*, (Fort Worth: Texas Christian University Press, 1984), pp. 132–133.

Chapter 5

Constructing an Ethics of Community
The Theistic Response to the Intentions of God in History

The Biblical Response to the Intentions of God in History

T.S. Eliot has said: "What life have you if you have not life together? There is no life that is not in community, And no community not lived in praise of GOD."[1] And John Macmurray, the philosopher of community for our time, has said "It is only in relation to others that we exist as persons. ... We live and move and have our being not in ourselves but in one another ... and we relate ourselves rightly to the world by entering into communion with God, and seeking to understand and fulfill his intention."[2]

These claims express deep ontological or metaphysical truths both about human as well as divine nature. They are grounded in the empirical and historical realities of the human experience of persons who struggle to live in conformity with what they construe as God's will enacted and revealed in history. They are the heart of the Biblical understanding of God's relation to both the human race and the cosmos generally. They are, in short, the ontological ground as well as telos of a Biblically-based ethics.

The recognition of the centrality of community in Biblical ethics is virtually universal among its ethicists and theologians. But the significance of that recognition in the light of the postmodernist critique of ethics has not yet received the full attention it deserves. The great irony is that some of the themes most dear to the hearts of deconstructionists and postmodernists are already present within a community-based understanding of Jewish and Christian ethics. It is these themes I wish to probe more fully in this chapter. They include the following:

1. The recognition that ethical action and reflection originate in and from a communal context, and not abstractly, or by solitary individual reflection, or as an attempt to capture a 'transcendental signified' in some ahistorical, non-contextual reality.

2. The centrality of history as the locus for the acts of community building. Real communities, by their very nature, exist, change, and develop in history.

3. The historical reality of plural, divergent forms of living out an ethical vision of the good. Again, it is ironic that only a community-based ethic can incorporate both plurality and unity in a single dynamic whole comprised of distinct, uniquely individual persons living a common life. A community, ideally, is the mutual nurture and celebration of different ways of expressing and embodying what it

means to be a flourishing human being: and only in community can these diverse ways be empowered and supported without breaking apart into radically antagonistic factions.

4. The significance of 'the other'. Community is by its very nature the recognition, endorsement, and nurture of the particularized otherness of distinct persons because it encourages the fullest possible development of the uniqueness of each 'other' individual who constitutes one of the partners in the experience of mutuality. Mutuality means individual persons celebrating the otherness of other distinct persons who are, reciprocally or mutually celebrating all the others who are celebrating them.

5. A deep appreciation of the pragmatic nature of testing the truth-claims of a theistic moral ontology. If mutuality and fulfillment are the means and goal of human relationships, then ideas must be tested for their reliability in achieving this goal. And as historical, communities must pragmatically determine what works to bring about the greatest degree of mutuality and fulfillment. As historical circumstances change, so too will the concepts that point to the future experience of mutuality.

The Experience of Mutual Community

Living in mutuality is the fulfillment that persons ultimately desire (even when they do not know it and misguidedly adopt non-communal ethics instead). And it is only within a community of mutuality that a place can be found for reconciling, without dissolving, diversity and plurality in the expression of one's values.

For a Biblically-based theistic ontology, as we have already argued, the concept of a personal divine being who acts historically is essential. God's historical actions are attempts to realize a divine intention for the world whose human inhabitants are ultimately to be fulfilled in and through the establishment of a universal and inclusive community of mutual love inclusive of all persons.[3] God's intention is not realized abstractly or in such a way that it overrides the historical reality of the world in which it is to be realized. God is a personal 'Other' who is in intimate and historical relationship with human persons (as well as with the non-human world). For the divine intention to be realized, however, requires human beings to respond freely to it. The nature, character, and form of that response is the heart of a Biblically-based ethics.

Christian Ethics as Relational Ethics

What all of this means is that Christian ethics built upon the experience of community is what Edward LeRoy Long calls a *relational* ethic. It is an ethic that is situated alongside but distinguishable from the teleological and the deontological approaches to ethics. The teleological approach assumes that there is an intrinsic good or proper end (telos) for human life by which it will be fulfilled. It is a non-moral good to which moral behavior is a means. A moral action is determined by whether or not it contributes to the achievement of that good or telos. It therefore is interested in what the actual consequences of our actions are, whether or not they retard or advance the pursuit of one's telos or ultimate non-moral good.

The other approach to Christian ethics, the deontological, denies that the morality of an action is simply a function of what is non-morally good. This approach focuses on one's moral duties no matter what their consequences with respect to the attainment of a non-moral good. In deontology, some actions by their very nature are intrinsically right or wrong. Teleology focuses upon the effective means for attaining the non-moral end of the action, deontology upon the intrinsic moral worth of the action itself.

In the context of Biblical and Christian reflection, the deontological approach centers upon moral duties construed as divine commands (for example, as found in the Ten Commandments, the Sermon on the Mount, the legal codes in God's covenant at Mt. Sinai, the moral prescriptions as set forth by St. Paul, and so on). This approach, while quite diverse in its various expressions, and more or less sensitive to changing circumstances, tends to identify moral action with behavior that accords with moral prescriptions, which can range from strict legal codes to moral injunctions (for example, in Paul's letters regarding sexual behavior). These prescriptions are always linked directly to what is construed to be God's unchanging will for persons in all situations. The teleological approach centers upon the end for which God has created the world, and in particular, human beings. If that end is construed as union with or love for God and other persons, then ethics is constituted by the discovery and implementation of the various means by which this end can be achieved in fact.

The relational ethic moves beyond the teleological and the deontological by focusing upon the primordial reality of God whose overarching intention and ongoing historical creative acts both establish the non-moral good for human beings and prescribe (with various degrees of flexibility and always providing for free human response) the means for attaining it. In a now famous summary of the three types of moral theory, the American Protestant moral philosopher H. Richard Niebuhr notes that the theory of teleology, or purposiveness, "seeks to answer the question: 'What is my goal, ideal, or telos?' Deontology tries to answer the moral query by asking, first of all: 'What is the law and what is the first law of my life?' " His own alternative to these two theories, what he calls an ethic of responsibility, "proceeds in every moment of decision and choice to inquire: 'What is going on?' ... [T]he differences among the three approaches may be indicated by the terms, the *good*, the *right*, and the *fitting*; for teleology is concerned always with the highest good to which it subordinates the right; consistent deontology is concerned with the right, no matter what may happen to our goods; but for the ethics of responsibility the *fitting* action, the one that fits into a total interaction as response and as anticipation of further response, is alone conducive to the good and alone is right."[4]

It needs to be clearly understood that the relational ethic of response to God *includes*, as subordinate parts of itself, teleological and deontological elements. There *is* a highest *good* for the cosmos and for human beings. There *is* also a divine *will* that expresses itself in various prescriptions for appropriate behavior if persons wish to conform themselves to the highest good for them. A prescription in this sense is a guide to action and has about it a strong consequentialist dimension: if you want to achieve this end, this is the action you need to take. (Think of a medical prescription: it is not one's *duty* to take it *unless* one wants to achieve the non-moral good of being healthy. But if one's telos is health, the prescription may be virtually mandatory, that is, nothing else will work as well to achieve health, and failure to take it will ensure a decline in health. The only stipulation is that one must freely intend health before the prescription becomes operative and effective.) Now if God intends health for us (understood in its broadest possible sense as well-being or flourishing, the full realization of all the potential that God has given to us to become fully human), then we have a non-moral telos toward which we may aim, which is underwritten by the structures of reality as they were created by God, and we have a set of prescriptions by which we can learn how to increasingly approximate that telos.

It is crucial, however, that this ethics of response to our telos and to God's actions in establishing and empowering its possibility takes place within the overall context of community. What counts as having the force of deontological duty is contextually determined. What counts as teleological is also contextually framed insofar as the very telos of human life is living fully in the context of loving relationships with other persons and with God. The nature of our telos and the purpose of divine action is rooted in God's intention to create mutual love as the intrinsic character of human flourishing. Within this intention deontology and teleology, properly contextualized, take their natural place.

If we isolate, as a paradigm of relationship, the mutual love of two persons-in-relation, we might see more clearly the contextual nature and place of prescription and goal. Two lovers discover experientially that maintaining a mutual, loving relationship is enhancing, empowering, and fulfilling for each of them but only when each puts the interests of the partner ahead of her own. (But since the 'other' is also putting the partner's interests ahead of her own, each of the partners is flourishing even though each intends the other's flourishing as her primary concern. This is the paradox of genuine mutuality, resolved ultimately in the practice of mutual heterocentricity.[5])

Now in such a mutual relationship, the telos is the fulfillment of the human. Being fully human is not completely open-ended, since empirically (due to the structures of reality and human nature as such) some experiences are more central and fulfilling than others (for example, those of love and trust). Therefore, some actions prove in practice in the long run to be effective prescriptions for achieving the telos. In a long-term relationship the partners may come to know each other so well that they normally appropriate and utilize rule-of-thumb prescriptions for maintaining and deepening the relationship. They might adopt a practical 'policy' (it would never become abstract or formal) of always saying 'I love you' before going to bed at night (even when they may not feel particularly loving on any given night). This and similar practices become tried and true prescriptions for sustaining the vitality of the relationship. They might almost reach the level of duties if the partners come to believe that such practices are almost always reliable and trust-worthy insofar as they have proven themselves in and through their contribution to the maintenance of the relationship. Regarding them as duties may turn out to be a reliable way of ensuring that they are done, even when one's immediate inclination might be to act in a contrary manner. But their trustworthiness is, in turn, based on their effectiveness in helping the persons who rely on them to achieve their telos or goal of fulfillment-through-loving-mutual-relationship.

If we move from the isolated example of a loving couple to the context of an intentionally inclusive community, the entire structure of telos, will, and action presupposes beings in relation to each other against the background of an ontological reality created and sustained by one of those beings. Each of the elements in this cosmic order is implicated in all the others. The telos is someone's telos (ours), created and sustained by someone (God), and the actions taken in pursuit of this goal are *for* the attainment of the telos. They are always *in* the world as it was created to enable its attainment, and in *response to* actions taken by God that are construed as supporting or enhancing its attainment. The co-implication (literally, the articulation or fitting together) of all the parts is underscored, of course, given the claim that the telos (the end in itself) *is* the full experience of relationality in the form of an inclusive and mutual community of love. If the telos (human good) is only achievable by and in mutual, loving relationships, then by its very nature the telos is relational. If 'true' community is achievable only in harmony with the underlying structures of the world, then it is profoundly related to the world. And if God intends the telos, God is intimately related both to the world and to human beings. Since there are no intimate relations between persons except through inter*action*, God must act where persons are, where they live out and experience their fulfillment, namely in the 'warp and woof' of human history.

Christian Ethics as Response to What God is Up To in the World

The Christian Moral Philosophy of H. Richard Niebuhr

Putting things this way places the Christian ethics I want to develop in harmony with H. Richard Niebuhr's construal in a decidedly theistic framework. God is a singularly decisive reality with whom persons have to deal. (God is a reality they must take into both theoretical and practical consideration because God is *there* impinging upon their field of action. As such, God's reality cannot be successfully ignored or bypassed *if* persons want their actions with regard to their ultimate telos to succeed.) At the same time, a theistic framework is not an exclusively Christian one. If God's relation to reality is basic and universal (God underwrites the underlying structures of reality as a whole), then God's work and presence in and through those structures cannot be understood to occur solely in Jesus or in the Christian community alone. (God may be experienced by Christians as present in their community in some particularly significant ways, but not exclusively present there.) And if ethics is our response to what God is up to (to how God is a decisive part of what 'is going on') as we seek to attain the fulfillment God intends for us, some of our ethical understanding will be universal: it will apply to all persons in so far as they are constituted as persons like us who can be fulfilled ultimately only in and through certain types of relationship with others (that is, mutually loving ones).

The Christian may have some historically particular insights into and experiences of those relationships that emerge out of some particular actions of God (and may lack other insights due, for the same reason, to her historical particularity, insights more readily available to persons in other religious traditions). Nevertheless, within a theistic framework the Christian must utilize the insights available to her to illuminate the kinds of relationships *all* persons will find fulfilling and that constitute their telos.

Human fulfillment cannot consist (and still be consistent with a single, unified, coherent overarching divine intention) of modes of satisfaction that are radically hostile to or divergent from each other. There is a limit to moral incommensurability. One group of persons cannot find ultimate fulfillment by living lives of deep suspicion, hostility, mistrust, fear, and hate while others find true satisfaction in trust, openness, love, and compassion. Such radical diversity is ultimately incoherent and those who argue that we, as a race, must now acknowledge such a broad range of diversity simply do not have the empirical evidence to back up such claims. (This forces the question of what the evidence *does* support and we will return to it shortly.)

Niebuhr's Christian moral philosophy echoes many of the points we made earlier. Persons are agents existing in a field of action. Each agent must both initiate actions and respond to the actions of others. All of our actions, he argues, have "this character of being responses, answers, to actions upon us. ... [I]n all our actions [we] answer to action upon us in accordance with our interpretation of such action."[6]

This means that ethical reflection already begins from within a communal, situated context. Too often rationalist secular or purely philosophical ethical theory, within the Enlightenment tradition, attempts to abstract the self from its empirical communal setting in order to eliminate anything that might contingently constrain or qualify the purity of a transcendental rational moral response. Kant's categorical imperative was developed in large part in order to *free the self from* its embeddedness in contingent reality, especially that which constituted its 'desires' and inclinations. This embeddedness needed to be surgically removed by conceptual abstraction so that the self could determine its autonomous moral responses without the distorting influence of its empirical ties to its world. Only by such removal could it permit a clean and pure reason to determine what it ought to do, free from any emotional or empirical bondage with which the non-rational part of the self was held by the world. Kant argued that the only truly autonomous moral response was one that overrode the heteronomous inclinations or desires that necessarily (in his view) qualify the self's moral freedom.

While there are some virtues in Kant's position (for example, it helps us avoid action that is *solely* based on selfish desire), it goes too far in stripping the self of its communal bonds. Niebuhr's understanding of the situated self as agent "begins with the question, not about the self as it is in itself [that is, the self as abstract rational thinker], but as it is in its response-relations to what is given with it and to it,"[7] namely 'what is going on' in its situated context. (The primacy of situatedness has been the hallmark of much of contemporary communitarian thinking and we will draw some connections between it and a Christian ethic in a later section.) Niebuhr argues that our first question as moral agents is 'what is being done to me?', not what is my end or what is my duty or what prescriptions must I follow.

A mother called to her child's bed in the middle of the night by a series of sobs, does not first consult her own telos or a list of moral prescriptions. Rather she begins by determining empirically (not, of course, as a theoretical abstraction, but concretely), what is going on. This may involve some reflection, discrimination, and discernment, in order to figure out whether the sobbing is due to a wet bed, an object onto which the child has rolled, a fever, and so on, in the particular situation. She wants to know, practically, what is going on and what her participation can accomplish. In short, the mother must *interpret or construe* what is going on.

The third element in responsible action (in addition to being an interpreted response), according to Niebuhr, is accountability or, literally, *respons*ibility. A responsible action is done "in anticipation of answers to our answers . . . [I]t seeks to meet, as it were, to fit into, the previous statement to which it is an answer, but is made in anticipation of a reply. . . . No action taken as an atomic unit is responsible. Responsibility lies in the agent who stays with his action, who accepts the consequences in the form of reactions and looks forward in present deed to the continued interaction."[8]

This description of the situated, interactive, responding and responsible action bears a striking resemblance to the notion of truth as that claim that is made as part of an ongoing conversation (note the same image in Niebuhr's language) by a community of discoursers (in the ethnocentric sense set forth by Richard Rorty). The difference between Rorty's and Niebuhr's views, however, is that for the latter God is one of the conversants. As such, God's action works to dissolve the barriers to trans-communal communication that Rorty seems to think are not transgressible. If God's action were to be taken seriously one is struck again by how much of a difference the reality of God as Agent could make to the deconstructionist, postmodern conviction that we are trapped within our parochial, ethnocentric communities of discourse. According to the deconstructionist the 'radical' differences between one community and another and the lack of any reality powerful enough to unify them without destroying their distinct communal identities preclude universal community. Without a personal, acting God no such community is possible and deconstructive postmodernism therefore has no place for such a God.

But the three essential elements in an alternative theistic construal of ethics must be co-present and co-implicated: God as personal, acting agent; the self as responding agent; and community as the context (and goal) of ultimately fulfilling mutual action and love between responsible agents.

Narrative and Reality

Does this view of the self as responsible and responding agent conform to the Biblical picture of reality and the narrative of God's dealings with its human inhabitants? Narrative is a central notion here. It connotes a story, and a story entails agents in relation to each other in and through history. The Bible is the construal of God's actions in human history that involve human response and God's counter-response. In this sense God's work meets Niebuhr's criteria for responsible action: God is an agent, God's actions are both initiatory and responsive to human actions, and God remains responsible (that is, faithful) to God's intention by always structuring God's action so as to 'stay with his action' and to look forward to how God's future action can effectively continue the realization of God's intention.

This means that the Biblical picture of reality is just that. It is not simply a myth whose primary revelation is of the mind-set of the myth-makers and not of the central agent in the myth. This does not mean that the Bible is, therefore, always an accurate and literal picture of reality. It is and remains a construal. Nevertheless, those who accept this construal, subject to its revision, commit to the belief that it is fundamentally right in essential respects: that it has gotten the reliable (true) sense of what God is up to and where God is taking those who conform to God's intention. This is clearly not Biblical literalism, but neither is it a view that would relegate the Bible entirely and exhaustively to myth, poetry, or simply fanciful (and evocative) imagination. The litmus test of Biblical interpretation will be its reliability in discerning what human beings are, what fulfills them, and what they must do to help bring about that fulfillment, what powers bear down on them in the process, and what the intentions of those powers are.

Its discernment will certainly need to be informed, supplemented, even revised by the best insights of those disciplines that study reality in its natural setting: natural science and in particular the social and psychological sciences that try to understand human beings in their fullness as persons in relation to others. In many respects the Biblical picture of human beings is crude, oversimplified, and subject to cultural distortions due to the ignorance and superstition of its writers, at least in some respects. But its underlying picture of who human beings are, what fulfills them, and what role God plays in that fulfillment must remain essentially reliable (true) if the Bible is still to inform contemporary Christian ethics.

What then, is the Biblical construal of reality, and what, in particular, does it think God is up to? What has God done and what is God intending to do? Biblical scholar Paul Hanson believes there are four essential *ontological or metaphysical* theses[9] implicit in the Biblical narrative, with which my own construal of God and God's action is in fundamental agreement and which undergird the portrait of community that I am about to draw.

Four Biblical Metaphysical Theses

1.   "Since the world's beginning, God has been active in fidelity to a creative, redemptive purpose, and will remain active until this world has completed its divinely ordained intention."

2. "God's purpose has included fellowship with the human family, fellowship arising out of confession of God's sovereignty and expressing itself in gratitude and praise. Such confession has in turn motivated the desire within the responding community to pattern its life on what it grasps to be the nature of the divine Sovereign."

3. "The sacred writings of many peoples reflect this pattern of fellowship and response. Among them, the writings of the Bible assume a unique role for Jews and Christians." They have arisen as confessional responses of a people experiencing God's fellowship. When "interpreted historically, critically and with theological sensitivity" these writings "constitute a trustworthy witness to the order God

intends as the basis for human society ... Their trustworthiness resides ... in the transcendent dynamic discernible as the unbroken strand running throughout Scripture."

"A community of faith is able to confess that no human formulations or institutional structures are eternally valid and at the same time maintain a healthy communal stability if it lives from the belief that its life is created ever anew as an aspect of God's ongoing creative, redemptive activity, of which it is a modest part. The true community of faith is thus a pilgrim people, seeing its forms and structures as provisional within a world being transformed from brokenness to wholeness, and trusting that ultimately its own transformation is being guided by a God whose promises are trustworthy and whose purposes are dedicated to the redemption of all creation."[10]

4. "Within God's purpose for creation, a specific vocation as human partner and historical agent is accorded the individual and the community responding in faith to God's creative, redemptive activity."[11]

The Biblical Construal of Reality as Community Bound

The movement of the Hebrew people from bondage to freedom "gave birth to a notion of community dedicated to the ordering of *all* life, for the good of *all* life, under the guidance and empowerment of a righteous, compassionate God."[12] God's intention is universal, incorporating all persons. And the community that God intends is "based on the pattern of *divine initiative and human response*."[13] This conforms with Niebuhr's notion of action as response and with our claim that such response presupposes some degree of human freedom.

At the same time, this Biblical notion of community presents itself as a "dependable vision of the One who is active in all history to guide the human family to a common life of justice, compassion, and shared prosperity on a mended and peaceful earth."[14] This claim underscores a number of things to which we have already alluded. First, genuine community is dynamic and life-enhancing. It is not static or ahistorical. It fulfills, empowers, or helps people to flourish. Second, it is dependable. In our terms it is, as a vision or construal, reliable. It proves itself in action and experience. Third, it involves the activity of a single One who guides (not imposes or coerces) people to a common life. God was revealed to the Hebrew people "as a personal agent [sic] committed to the battle against injustice and oppression in the world."[15] Fourth, that to which it is a guide is not yet fulfilled. The world must be 'mended'. It is part of the task of human persons to share in the mending process and they can do so only by conforming their actions to God's. Fifth, it includes the history of more than the Biblical people (it will guide the 'human family' to a 'common life') and is inclusive of a diversity of forms of expression. As Hanson goes on to say, the Biblical notion of community is "richly diverse and multifaceted in its unfolding". It includes various forms of living in community. It does not deny "the multiplicity, diversity, nor imperfections of the actual communities"[16] that have arisen in response to God's call. God's acts of mercy and righteousness are not "directed inward in the manner of the 'introspective consciousness of the West', but ... outward in dedication to the construction of a healthy community ... in which a compassionate openness to those falling outside of its orbit of protection would be preserved."[17]

When community is neglected as the focus of human and divine effort, moral philosophy becomes focused on the reflective unsituated individual in isolation from encumbering ties and, in the process, loses the fullness of the self-in-relation. When that happens, ethical theory becomes incomplete, truncated, and incapable of reflecting the fullness of what it means to be human. Finally, community finds its "final unity and focus" in the work of "one true God"[18] who is "true to one universal purpose."[19] Community is both universal, inclusive of all persons, and decisively (though not exclusively) the work of a single divine Agent.

In the Biblical construal, the first historical act of God intended to bring authentic and fulfilling community into being[20] was the liberation of the Hebrew people from slavery in Egypt and their creation as a people called into existence by God. Worship constitutes the central response of the Hebrew people ("the human side of the living covenantal relationship"[21]) to the God of their deliverance. Response to God also "meant acting toward other humans even as Yahweh had first acted toward them."[22] As Brueggemann says, Israel understands itself "as a community of persons bound in membership to each other, so that each person-as-member is to be treated well enough to be sustained as a full member of the community. [In particular this entails] a mandate to order public policy, public practice, and public institutions for the common good and in resistance to the kind of greedy initiative that damages the community."[23] This is a concrete example of what it means to 'conform' one's actions to God's purpose: to act as God has first acted toward oneself: to do as God does, to adopt God's intention as one's own. This is not the grudging acceptance of an imposed heteronomous moral law, but the willing grasp of a vision that will lead one to greater fulfillment and flourishing.

When he reaches Jesus and the early Christians, Hanson argues that they want to enlarge the boundary of community to all peoples. "The Kingdom of God knew no such boundaries [as those between people on the inside and those on the outside of the community of faith], but issued an urgent invitation to all to enter into fellowship with God through repentance and faith."[24] As the Jews could have reminded the Christians, however, there is a long history of God attempting to gather the nations into one community. It did not begin with Christianity.

Pauline Community

In Hanson's reading, St. Paul continued the communal inclusion motif of Jesus's teaching and example. "In the eschatological concept of the 'new creation' – that is, the order of reality with which God brings to fulfillment the divine plan for creation by breaking down all human distinctions that had led to the exclusion of certain groups and individuals – we find the heart of Paul's notion of community."[25]

Paul's community encouraged a diversity of gifts. "[T]he unity that he envisioned was dynamic enough to integrate the many different gifts of individual members into the whole. Thus the body was not threatened by the individuality of its members, nor was the individuality of the members threatened by the corporateness of the body."[26]

Each local Christian community saw itself as "the visible manifestation of a universal and eternal commonwealth in which men [sic] could become citizens."[27] At its heart is the practice of *agape*, or other-directed love. The acts that characterize love are "acts of identification ... the solidarity of the members with one another, [that] goes beyond mere sociality, for each is inextricably involved in the life of the other."[28] Its focal point was "*a set of relationships* ... God communicated himself to them primarily ... *through one another.*"[29]

The community is to be a foretaste, a foreshadowing, a living image, a first fruit of the inclusive community toward which God is calling all people. It is only within this community that a specifically Christian ethic becomes both conceivable and doable. "Jesus's ethic is not directed to isolated individuals, but to the circle of disciples, the new family of God, the people of God which is to be gathered. It has an eminently social dimension. Whether or not this ethic can be fulfilled is something that can only be determined by groups of people which [sic] consciously place themselves under the gospel of the reign of God and wish to be real communities of brothers and sisters – communities which form a living arena for faith, in which everyone draws strength from each other."[30]

Living together with and for one another is crucial to what it means to be in Christian community. These Christians were to live "in harmony with one another" (Rom. 12:16), "outdo one another in showing honor" (Rom. 12:10), "welcome one another" (Rom. 15:7), "greet one another with a holy kiss" (Rom. 16:16), "have the same care for one another" (I Cor. 12:25), "be servants of one another" (Gal. 5:13), "bear one another's burdens" (Gal. 6:2), "comfort one another" (I Thess. 5:11), "build one another up" (I Thess. 5:11), "be at peace with one another" (I Thess. 5:13), "love one another from the heart" (I Pet. 1:22), and "have fellowship with one another" (I John 1:7).[31]

Only in community can one find one's telos, one's non-moral good toward which moral action is directed. But community requires that moral character and moral virtues take on meaning and can be realized only in relation to other persons (including God), not simply by obedience to an autonomous moral law whose morality is determined by and for the autonomous individual in abstract non-relation to others. Moral duty becomes essentially a question of loyalty to a community that sees itself as righteous (by God's grace) and under attack by those who are threatened by it.[32] *Agape* is 'confused' when it is identified with Kantianism and utilitarianism. Agape has to do "with the friendship between the divine and those who are freely responsive."[33]

As does Hanson, Gerhard Lohfink sees the elimination of artificial human distinctions and barriers as the essence of the early *koinonia*. He calls such intentional communities "contrast-societies".[34] In them there is no discrimination against women, the poor, Greeks, or slaves, all of whom, as groups, were subject to social discrimination in the surrounding society. These *koinonia* lived a common life that set them apart from life lived in the larger society. But it is important to note that while their internal life of fellowship was in part an end in itself (insofar as it was a foretaste of the fulfilled life God intends for all persons in the kingdom), it was also in part a means to an end. The *koinonia* experienced the fullness of life (though not without some ambiguity) but its experience was not just for itself but also for the world. It was a church not without guilt but one "in which infinite hope emerges from forgiven guilt", a church with divisions but one which "finds reconciliation despite all gulfs", a church not without conflicts, but one "in which conflicts are settled in ways different from the rest of society."[35]

Its life as community, as contrast-society, was to be a sign or paradigm for others so that they, too, might see prefigured the beginning of the realization of their telos, of their fulfillment. In order to maintain its vitality and validity as a sign, it was crucial that the churches did not become the world but instead think of themselves as part of a genuinely *universal* history, encompassing the 'real' story of the world.[36] In fact, Wayne Meeks argues that:

> if anything may be said to be unique in Christianity's contribution to Western ethical sensibilities, it is this dramatic history of everything and all peoples, centering on the erratic response of God's elect people to God's speaking and acting, and culminating in the calling to account of every creature for what they [sic] have done in God's world.[37]

Reconciling Difference and Universality

This fact opens up the possibility of reconciling difference with universality, a problem endemic to modern suspicions of a universal morality. Within a Christian moral theology it makes sense to assert that difference *from* the other may be a gift *for* the 'other'. The self-understanding of the Christian community lives in the tension between the here/now (partially) and the not/yet (fully). But its experience of mutual love as the down payment on God's promise of fulfillment, while distinguishing it from many other communities (and non-communities) of the world, is also *for* those other communities just as much as it is in and for itself. As Stephen Post observes, in this time and place, "agape should never be considered a principle acceptable to all rational persons whatsoever. ... It is a peculiar people who carry on the life of agape",[38] even when they do so, ultimately, for all the others. And this being for others is consistent, ultimately, only with the actions of a God who has not yet accomplished the divine plan. It makes sense only for a God who works in and through particular, distinct historical moments, not one of which is complete in itself but all of which, taken together, constitute the temporal realization (not without experimentation) of a divine intention for a universally inclusive community of *all* persons. Only a God who acts in history could bring it about that some historical moments are situated for and directed toward other, more inclusive, more complete moments. The Church *does* live a different life, but its life is true for others and must be seen, at least in part, as motivated by a desire to include others within it if it is to be faithful to God's universal and inclusive intention.

Only in and through the acts of God can what modern moral philosophy takes for granted (the incommensurability of self-interest and a concern for others) be brought into harmony. As John Reeder, Jr., puts it:

> the relation to the divine being provides ... a reconciliation of what are often opposed in ordinary experience, namely, self-fulfillment and concern for others. ... What we prefer is *both* to have self-fulfillment and to be so devoid of self-seeking that our desire can be

wholly directed to the good of others ... in which the good of the self is provided by
another and the self seeks the good of others.[39]

Macmurray and Bonhoeffer

This is precisely what John Macmurray calls for in his *Persons in Relation*, namely
a "universal community of persons in which each cares for all the others and no
one for himself", a community in which the members constitute a fellowship and
are oriented toward each other "heterocentrically" (that is, the 'other' is the center
of value). "Each ... acts, and therefore thinks and feels for the other, and not for
himself ... [but] ... each remains a distinct individual; the other remains really
other. Each realizes himself in and through the other."[40] The Christian theist insists
that this 'mode of existence' is achievable only in a community brought into
existence and sustained by the ongoing activity and grace of God.

> In the kingdom of God, the individual does not experience 'countervailing appetites or
> desires of self-interest' – there is no experience of constraint – and there is no necessity
> for a system of moral pressure or legal enforcement. The transformation of human nature
> [that God effects] enables the concepts of duty and obligation ... to wither away.[41]

Macmurray is bold enough to claim that God has created human beings such that
when they intend what is contrary to God's intention they necessarily intend what
will prove in the long run to be "self-frustrating." Persons cannot successfully be
in opposition to God "since they cannot be in opposition to him without being in
opposition to themselves. They themselves are, after all, God's act, and his
intention is embodied in their nature. To act in defiance of the will of God is to
intend the impossible."[42] When we act contrary to God's intention for us (for our
fulfillment and flourishing) we in effect negate our own nature. Thus our wish for
fulfillment is perfectly attuned to God's intention for us, provided we appropriate
that intention as our own (which, in a way, it really is). And when intentions blend
or converge, any sense of an 'imposed' morality, or a duty 'laid on' one against
one's own best-interests, becomes incoherent. Heteronomy and autonomy fade
from opposition to each other into harmony with each other.

This reference to the withering away of duty and obligation echoes one of the
important themes in Dietrich Bonhoeffer's *Ethics*. If the human being is in full
communion with God, Bonhoeffer argues, there is no need for ethics as we know it.
"Man at his origin knows only one thing: God. ... He knows all things only in God,
and God in all things. The knowledge of good and evil shows that he is no longer at
one with this origin."[43] Through the embodiment of divine love, Jesus has
recovered the original pre-moral unity with God. This recovered unity "is now the
... 'point of decision of the specifically ethical experience'."[44]

Bonhoeffer elides too easily some of the more difficult questions of ethics, but
his underlying point is that if one is in a mutual relationship with God, one no
longer approaches ethics from the primacy of (and domination by) principles, rules,
duties, and obligations. "Not fettered by principles, but bound by love for God, he
[the Christian moral agent] has been set free from the problems and conflicts of
ethical decision. ... He belongs simply and solely to God and to the will of God."[45]

Human ethics then becomes conformation with Jesus: to conform to the full human being that God intends us to be. "To be conformed with the Incarnate is to have the right to be the man [sic] one really is."[46]

To be fully human, however, is to be 'for others', which is, of course, the hallmark of the true mutual community. This is universal for all persons. But it is always universal only if it seeks the good of others. This is not Kantian ethics in which the primary moral concern is whether one's own maxim, as an expression of one's moral autonomy, can become a principle of general legislation. Rather it is "whether my action is at this moment helping my neighbour become a man before God."[47] God was not, for Christians, incarnated as a moral theory, a law, a duty but as a full and concrete human person. This means that the form of Christ takes form "in the real man, that is to say, in quite different guises. Christ does not dispense with human reality for the sake of an idea which demands realization at the expense of the real."[48] So there are diverse 'guises' for the real [Bonhoeffer's nod in the direction of a deep appreciation of the uniqueness and particularity of each human 'other'], but ultimately only one humanity. And the diversity can be reconciled only when it is 'for' others and not for itself (since the others will be for it, mutually and reciprocally). The primary and essential locale for being for others is a community of mutual love out of which grows what constitutes a theistically-based morality.

The Generation of Moral Narrative

Meeks insists that the most "prolific consequence" of belief in an acting God who brings about both the Kingdom of God and its outposts in the early *koinonia* is the "generation of moral narrative."[49] At the heart of this moral narrative are what Meeks calls "preliminary theses" on Christian morality.[50] Thesis 1 is that "making morals and making community are one, dialectical process." In a strong echo of the deconstructionist theme, Meeks says that neither rational reflection alone nor the forms of rationalism "ha[ve] succeeded in finding a place to stand outside the particularities of a human community and its tradition, nor a first premise purified of interest."

Thesis 4 speaks directly to the pragmatic, provisional nature of truth. In the New Testament, according to Meeks, there was no such thing as "new testament ethics": rather one finds a record of experimentation, of trial and error in response to God's creative acts. One who responds to God's call is a "guinea pig of the Kingdom."[51] Thesis 5 echoes the importance of diversity in the process of trial and error. "The Christian community ought always to strive and pray for unity – but to admit a considerable measure of diversity." In this light, the most that can be required is "moral confidence" (Thesis 6), not moral certainty. And this confidence emerges from the very experience of healthy communities: of those that are truly what Lohfink calls contrast-societies. And this happens only when they are focused upon their task of serving the world by being themselves communities of mutual love. "Christian communities are healthy not when they are worrying about their health, but when they are trying to do what they are here for."

And, finally, thesis 7 recognizes that "God tends to surprise." All thought of an ahistorical transcendent divine being who plays no role in history is completely absent (suggesting that Christianity's contemporary cultured despisers are woefully ignorant of what they despise). Because of God's own entry into history, history becomes the locus for understanding an ethics founded upon God's will. As Bonhoeffer puts it

> the concept of historical inheritance, which is linked with the consciousness of temporality and opposed to all mythologization, is possible only where thought is consciously or unconsciously governed by the entry of God into history at a definite place and a definite point of time ... Here history becomes a serious matter without being canonized ... It is precisely in its temporality that it is history with God's consent. Consequently when we ask about the historical inheritance we are not asking the timeless question about those values of the past of which the validity is eternal. Man himself is set in history and it is for that reason that he now asks himself about the present and about the way in which the present is taken up by God in Christ.[52]

One of the ways in which God may well 'take up the present', Meeks suggests, is that Christians and Jews together,

> perhaps will discover that the flourishing ... that God wills for all earth's creatures is only possible if Christians and Jews can find ways to affirm the narratives and rhythms of yet other peoples and traditions, once again revising and rehearing, but not abandoning, their own. A faithful hermeneutic of the Pauline kind requires confidence in the God who, determined to have mercy on all and to bring into being the things that are not, will astonish those who are loyal to the story of God's past actions, but will not abandon them. In this way the process of inventing Christian – and human – morality will continue.[53]

Perhaps the last word on how the process of 'inventing' Christian and human morality can continue can be given to Paul Hanson. If every significant moral human act is a response to God's actions, it is necessary to find those forms of life that truly are 'fitting' to the occasion of God's work of bringing universal community into being. God's work is primary: it is the ontological reality on which our moral work is built. And "this thoroughly relational aspect of the biblical and Judeo-Christian ontology explains both the enduring quality of Jewish and Christian faith and the error implicit in construing the Bible as a manual of timeless answers to specific personal, political, or social problems."[54] (This suggests, incidentally, the weakness in the position of contemporary fundamentalism: it is profoundly ahistorical and, as a result, misunderstands the centrality of history in the development of God's intention and our response to it.)

Notes

1 T. S. Eliot, 'Choruses from "The Rock",' in *The Complete Poems and Plays, 1909–1950*, (New York: Harcourt, Brace, 1952), p. 101.
2 John Macmurray, *Persons in Relation*, (New York: Harper and Brothers, 1961), pp. 211, 217.
3 'Inclusive' means both human and non-human realities. James Gustafson has warned us not to limit God's concern just to human beings. There is a larger cosmic interest that God has and there is, therefore, a cosmic community that must be included in God's

overarching intention. That there is something more than just human interests does not, of course, entail that human interests are at odds with or diverge in any significant way from this larger cosmic concern provided that they are properly aligned or in conformity with God's inclusive intention for all creation.

4 H. Richard Niebuhr, *The Responsible Self*, (New York: Harper and Row, 1963), pp. 60–61.

5 For a further exploration of this odd term, see pp. 91ff.

6 Niebuhr, *The Responsible Self*, pp. 56–57. There is a voluminous literature on the notion of the self as agent. One of the foundational works in this area is John Macmurray's *The Self as Agent* on which I have drawn extensively. I have developed the notion of agency as a basic category for understanding both human and divine beings in my community and, more recently, in *Together Bound: God, History, and the Religious Community*.

7 Niebuhr, *The Responsible Self*, p. 60. The words in brackets are mine.

8 *Ibid.*, p. 64.

9 The following points are all from Paul D. Hanson, *The People Called: The Growth of Community in the Bible*, (San Francisco: Harper and Row, 1986), pp. 524–525.

10 *Ibid.*, p. 493.

11 *Ibid.*, p. 525.

12 Hanson, *The People Called*, p. 2. Hanson's claim has been echoed more recently by Walter Brueggemann who claims that the Biblical narrative underscores the conviction that "human persons are not isolated individuals, but are members of a community of those authorized by the life-giving breath of Yahweh, and so have humanity only in that membership." *Theology of the Old Testament*, (Minneapolis: Fortress Press, 1997), p. 453.

13 Hanson, *The People Called*, p. 3.

14 *Ibid.*, p. 5.

15 *Ibid.*, pp. 76–77.

16 *Ibid.*, p. 7.

17 *Ibid.*, p. 80.

18 *Ibid.*, p. 5.

19 *Ibid.*, pp. 8–9.

20 It seems clear that the Biblical portrayal of God's work in the creation of the people of Israel both assumes the reality of many different kinds of communities (Egypt under the Pharaoh was certainly a community, or society, of sorts) and the supremacy of one particular kind of community (the kind that God intends and that is foreshadowed in part by Israel, and later by the Christian *koinonia*). Not all communities stand on a moral par: some are clearly more conducive to human flourishing and well-being than others.

21 Hanson, *The People Called*, p. 25.

22 *Ibid.*, p. 44.

23 Brueggemann, *Theology of the Old Testament*, pp. 421–423.

24 Hanson, *The People Called*, pp. 424–425.

25 *Ibid.*, p. 442.

26 *Ibid.*, p. 449.

27 Robert Banks, *Paul's Idea of Community*, (Grand Rapids: Wm. B. Eerdmans, 1980), p. 49.

28 *Ibid.*, p. 59.

29 *Ibid.*, p. 117.

30 Gerhard Lohfink, *Jesus and Community: The Social Dimension of Christian Faith*, (New York: Paulist Press, 1984, p. 62.

31 See the full list in *ibid.*, pp. 99–100.

32 *Ibid.*, p. 179.

33 Stephen Post, *A Theory of Agape*, (Lewisburg: Bucknell University Press, 1990), p. 116.

34 Lohfink, *Jesus and Community*, p. 122.
35 *Ibid.*, p. 147.
36 Wayne Meeks, *The Origins of Christian Morality*, (New Haven: Yale University Press, 1993), p. 191.
37 *Ibid.*, p. 210.
38 Stephen Post, *A Theory of Agape*, p. 80.
39 John P. Reeder, Jr., 'Assenting to Agape', *Journal of Religion*, 60, 1, p. 27.
40 John Macmurray, *Persons in Relation*, pp. 159, 158. For a fuller explication of how a community of heterocentric mutuality can be considered 'realistic', see my article 'The Logic of Mutual Heterocentrism: The Self as Gift' in *Philosophy and Theology*, 6, 4, Summer 1992, pp. 353–368. See also my *The Ethics of Community*, (Oxford: Blackwell, 2001), Chapter Four, 'Building a Philosophy of Community.'
41 Reeder, 'Assenting to Agape', p. 27.
42 John Macmurray, *The Clue to History*, (London: SCM Press, 1938), p. 95.
43 Dietrich Bonhoeffer, *Ethics*, (New York: Macmillan, 1965), p. 17.
44 *Ibid.*, p. 26.
45 *Ibid.*, p. 68.
46 *Ibid.*, p. 81.
47 *Ibid.*, p. 85.
48 *Ibid.*
49 Meeks, *The Origins of Christian Morality*, p. 173.
50 *Ibid.*, pp. 213–219.
51 Hanson, *The People Called*, p. 512. The image is from Krister Stendahl.
52 Bonhoeffer, *Ethics*, pp. 88–89.
53 Meeks, *The Origins of Christian Morality*, p. 219.
54 Hanson, *The People Called*, p. 488.

Chapter 6

Theistic Ethics, Moral Philosophy, and Psychology

The Foundations of a Conversation

Opening Theistic Ethics to Conversation with Moral Philosophy

If a theistic moral ontology is to be relevant to the material and social world of God's creation, then what it has to say about human beings must cohere with what the sciences of human nature have to say. This is particularly true regarding what some forms of modern psychology have to say about the nature of human persons. Biblical theism wants to talk about renewed, transformed persons, persons who are capable of living new lives in and through the power of God's grace. But the renewed life is, in important ways, continuous in certain essential ways with the lives that all persons lead. Grace, as Thomas Aquinas claims, does not abrogate nature but completes it. And as long as the theistic ethicist is concerned about the effects on persons of orienting their lives one way rather than another, she needs to know how that concern is supported by the realities of human nature that God continues to sustain even in an 'unredeemed' state. At the very least, the theist needs to know how the moral responses she recommends are likely to work out in the 'real' world of human life and activity. As James Gustafson puts it, "in the light of empirical research the moralist is likely to gain insight into the potential consequences of various courses of morally determined action."[1] Without that empirically grounded insight, moral recommendations are self-defeating and out of kilter with the nature of the world the theist believes God has created for our well-being and flourishing.

Flourishing and Psychological Analysis

One of the issues that faces moral philosophers is how to reconcile human well being with the psychological dimensions of an individual's belief in God. True belief always has a psychological dimension, but its truth cannot be determined solely by its psychological effects. Ever since the critique of religious belief by Freud, it has been taken for granted by many, if not all, psychologists that religious belief is a form of psychological impairment that can be cured only by what Freud called 'education to reality' (to the world as it is without supernatural grounding or intervention). But as in numerous other areas of contemporary thought, the increasingly accepted fact of interpersonal relationships as a necessity for flourishing has come to undermine some of the more outlandish claims for individual autonomy and a freedom from unnatural dependence on others, of which Freud's is one outstanding example. One of the areas in which the stress on personal relationships, and a questioning of the value of unrestricted moral autonomy and self-sufficiency, has been most evident is in the psychological school of object-relations. Its work can be seen to have implications for an understanding of the individual's personal relationship with a personal God that does not undercut individual integrity.

Freud

Sigmund Freud's psychological theories dealt a serious blow to the religious understanding of God as a personal 'Other' with whom one could have positive, fulfilling relations. For Freud, God is a mental, psychological construct: an 'exaltation' of a child's experience of his father. This view of God is rooted, for Freud, in humankind's experience of its helplessness in the face of natural forces from which people want protection as well as consolation. "Man's seriously menaced self-esteem craves for consolation, [therefore] life and the universe must be rid of their terrors, and ... man's curiosity ... demands an answer."[2] One way to achieve all this is to project upon (transfer to) the universe a picture of powerful personal beings in control of things. This has the distinct advantage of allowing us to negotiate with (bribe) them, person to person "and so rob them of part of their power by thus influencing them."[3]

This 'peopling' of nature with 'gods' has an 'infantile prototype': our relationship with our parents. The forces of nature are given father-like attributes and made into gods following an 'infantile prototype'[4] so the human person can "recover the intimacy and intensity of the child's relation to the father."[5]

But the image of God as Father, in order to do its psychological work of comfort, protection, and consolation, need not be objectively true. It is a psychological 'illusion', derived from the wishes of the believer. Despite Freud's belief that religious ideas are "incompatible with everything we have laboriously discovered about the reality of the world," their objective falsity turns out to be irrelevant. It is their psychological power that matters, whether the realities to which they ostensibly refer are real or not.

Scientific belief, however, is no illusion because it permits its hypotheses to be objectively tested regardless of the wishes of the scientist. While science may not give us all that we wish (education to reality may be harsh and discouraging), it would be an illusion "to suppose that we could get anywhere else what it cannot give us." It follows that an individual who remains wedded to the image of God, instead of to the picture of reality slowly but surely developed by science, is increasingly acting in an immature and ultimately psychologically impaired way.[6]

Central to psychological development, in Freud's view, and essential to overcoming the illusions of religious belief, is the idea of transference. This notion of transference has become the controlling idea of much contemporary psychoanalysis. "Impulses, feelings, and defenses pertaining to a person in the past have been shifted onto a person in the present."[7] Transference is a regression to infantile thoughts and feelings (which, of course, are the source of a belief in God, according to Freud). All those whom the grown child gets to know later become "substitute figures for these first objects ... All of his later choices of friendship and love follow upon the basis of the memory-traces left behind by these prototypes."[8] Transference results from impulses that are blocked or frustrated. It signals a failure to connect with or to allow one's beliefs to be tested by reality. And insofar as 'God' is a creation of transference, successful flourishing in the world requires the overcoming of the God-belief.

A second dimension of transference in Freud's thought is the dominance of instinct. "The basic motivation for human behavior is biological drive. Psychopathology results from the person's repressing these instincts and the fantasies and wishes they generate, rendering them unconscious, and then engaging in defensive maneuvers – denying feelings, projecting them onto others, keeping an overly tight rein on them – to keep them unconscious."[9]

And as long as contemporary moral philosophy (and especially postmodern deconstructionism) is committed to a Freudian understanding of religious belief, it cannot take seriously the idea of God as a real, acting, person with whom one can have a mature, healthy relationship as a prerequisite for fulfillment. Consequently, it cannot take seriously an ethics of response to God's actions in the world.

Object-Relations Theory

The contemporary psychological theory of object relations attempts to correct much of the Freudian picture and in the process gives us, by extension (or so I would argue), a way of integrating a Biblical view of God into a psychological understanding of human health and well-being that coheres well with the telos of theistically informed moral activity. At the heart of the object-relations theory is the conviction that "a relationship with an object and not the gratification of an impulse" is the ultimate aim of human beings.[10] W.R.D. Fairbairn, one of the earliest of the object-relations theorists, rejected Freud's drive or impulse theory. Pleasure, or the satisfaction of frustrated drives, is not, he argued, the goal of impulse, but rather a means to its real end – relations with 'another'. "Human experience and behavior derive fundamentally from the search for and maintenance of contacts with others."[11] (These 'others' or 'objects', it should be clearly understood, are real personal beings, not ideas or fantasies.)

Correspondingly, psychopathology is understood not as the repression of instincts "but as reflective of disturbances and interferences in relations with others." The psychological task, therefore, is a process "through which the capacity for making direct and full contact with real other human beings is restored," and suggests to Fairbairn that "the crucial aspect of healthy maturity is a capacity for a rich and intimate mutuality with another."[12]

This suggests strong correspondence to a relational model of ethics that maintains that

- only in and through personal relationships can full personhood (flourishing) be achieved, and
- theoretical knowledge of another person is pragmatic in the sense that it seeks to find a way to restore the primacy of the actual experience of mutuality through

the instrumentality of thought that will finally be proven true in the practice of relating fully to others.

Philosopher John Macmurray's emphasis on fellowship in community echoes much of Fairbairn's.[13] He was also deeply influential on Fairbairn's pupil and fellow psychoanalyst, Harry Guntrip. Macmurray's epistemology parallels the psychological process of object relations theory. When the intention of action is frustrated, one must engage in a temporary withdrawal from the fullness of active relationship in order to reflect on what has gone wrong. By withdrawing for the moment from full involvement in the relationship, the self can use its reflective faculties to figure out what is not going on as intended. Once it has reached, in theory, some new idea of what the reality of the field of action is like and formulates a plan of action that it thinks can resolve the problem by a more effective engagement with that reality, it can re-engage practically with the Other and 'try out' its theory, act upon it and thereby test it by its reliability in practice. "The reflective moment in a practical activity is itself concerned with the means to the realization of a practical end,"[14] and if that practical end is the re-establishment of the fullness of personal relationship that has in some way been broken, then theory is necessary to the restoration of lived wholeness.

Similarly, object-relations theory assumes the primacy and telos of full mutuality and regards the psychotherapeutic task as a means to its achievement or restoration. "If relations with others were nonproblematic, if satisfying contacts could be established and maintained, psychology would consist simply of the study of the individual's relations with other people."[15] (And, we might argue, to the extent that the theological task is a means to the achievement or restoration of a previously broken relationship of mutuality with God, it is similar to the psychoanalytic task. Both are reflective activities concerned with the re-establishment of broken relationships and both have their ultimate meaning only when they contribute practically to that task. Both object-relations theory and theology assume the reality of the objects with whom one is in relation. In this sense both break decisively with the Freudian picture of the origin and truth of our religious beliefs even though not all object-relations theorists are theists or even show an interest in religious life and thought.[16])

Like Freud, Fairbairn and other object-relations theorists trace (as does Macmurray) disruption in relationships back to childhood. If the child's relation to its mother[17] is a bad one (due to deprivation of appropriate affection and caring), the child compensates for the deprivation by establishing "internal objects inside himself, which act as substitutes and solutions for unsatisfying relationships with real external objects ... The greater the degree of interference and deprivation in relations with its 'natural' objects, real people, the greater the need for the ego to establish relations with natural objects ... [which become] psychopathological structures."[18]

And the primary form of deprivation is that of absence, of an unavailable, unresponsive parent. (This suggests that if a person's view of God is of a distant, abstract, remote, and unavailable being, that person is reflecting theologically a very infantile and unhealthy relationship with God.) When the child, who cannot in reality do without his parents, experiences relations with them as unbearably painful, he takes their bad characteristics and attributes them to himself. It is he who is bad, not they. And he thinks that if he were somehow different, they would love him.[19]

If the badness is 'inside' himself, he can hope eventually to overcome it since it is easier to control what one 'owns' than what is external to, or 'other' than, himself. As long as the objects are internal, the child can believe he has control over them. D.W. Winnicott suggests that the healthy person emerges when he moves from a state of "illusory omnipotence" to a state of "objective perception" in which he accepts the "limits of his powers and becomes aware of the independent existence of others" who presumably are not controllable in the same way the self is.[20] (Again one might see the immediate analogy with a relationship to God: if God is truly a powerful Other, accepting one's own limits in the face of that power would be a step toward "objective perception". Ironically, such perception is objective just to the extent that it takes cognizance of the objective reality of God – and that would be truly, Freud notwithstanding, education to reality! If this theistic claim is true, then Freud clearly had a truncated and impoverished view of reality.)

The crucial psychological question for the theist is not whether God exists or whether God is a projection of infantile wishes, but what *kind* of God exists and what *kind* of relationship we can have with God. If God intends human fulfillment, God must intend psychologically healthy persons. If our relationship with a loving God has been broken, if we now internalize God as a 'bad' object, then the reality of God has not been changed but the nature of our relationship with God clearly has. We see God from within the distorted image of the internalized object 'God'.

This is the truth behind the psychological observation that our emotional, feeling relations with others shape our understanding of God, and vice-versa. What concept of God we hold cannot be divorced from the full panoply of feelings that accompany our relationship with God and other persons. H. Richard Niebuhr has observed that "emotional relations to otherness, to objective being, are prior in meaningfulness to intellectual relations ... love of God or enmity to God, hate of God, is prior to all articulation of our idea of who God is."[21] Only by restoring a healthy relationship with the external object, God, who is truly worthy of our love, can we return to authentic psychological health.

It is sometimes said that the therapist must ask of the patient who says she hates or does not believe in God, 'which God' do you hate or not believe in? If God is internalized as distant, remote, unavailable, indifferent, or unloving, then one might have good reason for hating or not believing in that God. The restoration of a positive and healthy relationship with the living God might well require becoming an atheist with respect to destructive and life-denying Gods.

James Jones creatively develops the links between self-images and God relationships in his recent study of transference and the dynamics of religion. As a practicing therapist, as well as scholar of religion, Jones is in a unique position to see how patients' self-images correlate with their images of the divine. For example, he often treats people who have grown up with the image of a harsh, judgmental God. Through therapy in the object-relations mode they have shifted their God image to that of a loving Person who cares for and forgives them. Jones suggests that an infant or child who is in deep psychological pain and "is left alone to make sense of that as best she can without much comfort from others (and the lack of comforting may be the worst part of the pain)" can initially make sense of the experience by blaming herself because she is 'bad'. Every child goes through some experience like this "and a judgmental God will resonate with her experience."[22] Such a God, through transference, can reinforce the patient's feeling that she can never be good enough (who can be good enough for the judgment of an absolutely good God?).

Through therapy, the patient may be able to come to a stronger sense of self that grows beyond "paralyzing fear or guilt". When this happens, "a chronically angry God has no psychological function to perform for the more autonomous or cohesive self. Thus, as the patient's psychological development resumes and the nature of the self's selfobject relationships change, this change is likely to be reflected in the person's relationship to his God. More specifically, a move from a fragmented and diminished sense of self toward a more autonomous and cohesive self might be mirrored in a shift from a vengeful to a nurturing deity."[23] (The autonomy to which Jones refers is not the individualistic isolation, or self-sufficiency so highly valued by much modern thought. Rather it points to the fact that until a self is itself, and is able to enjoy and exercise freely that which is unique to it, it cannot be a genuine partner in mutuality. It still needs relationships, but it must be a full, healthy, integrated self in order to be a truly worthwhile partner in relation. Being and becoming a full self is a dialectical process of separating from, while still belonging to others.)

Jones' conclusion bears careful attention: "people need an awareness that the ultimate nature of reality supports and legitimates their fundamental sense of themselves and undergirds their basic stance toward the world ... The coming of a new sense of self in each case [of therapy] demanded a new image of God to ground it."[24] The whole thrust of my argument so far is that there is a reality whom we call God and that the character of that reality, as revealed in God's ongoing actions in the world, is of a loving, caring, available, supportive, and ultimately relational Person. Without the reality of that God, the possibility of becoming ourselves loving, caring, available, supportive, and ultimately relational persons is severely diminished, perhaps ontologically impossible.

But if God is objectively real, then a relationship with God can be part of the healthy, mature self's orientation toward the world. And if God is active, in a decisive, powerful, and not-to-be-ignored way in the world, then maturity and healthy relationships must take account of God and what God is up to. The God-relationship can then become the ground for one's ethical action. Ethics, from within a theistic construal, proceeds from and reflects a vision of a healthy God-relationship, and seeks to extend it universally. Object-relations theory, while few if any of its proponents advocate a God-relationship (Guntrip is an exception), at least lays down the conditions that a healthy God-relationship would have to meet and establishes the necessity of interpersonal relations for fully effective functioning in the world. Extended inclusively and universally, this suggests the indispensability of mutual community for complete fulfillment and health, and provides the context for successful moral action.

To restore a healthy relationship with the persons from whom one has been estranged requires a movement toward "mature dependence" which, for Fairbairn, is a process of moving from infantile dependence to a "a capacity for adult mutuality."[25] This form of mutuality does not flee from dependence but lives in and through it with a healthy sense of one's own contribution to the other's well-being. Heteronomy is perfectly compatible with autonomy as long as both are grounded in mutuality.

Like Macmurray, who influenced him, Harry Guntrip believes that a religious view of the self as a person-in-relation to other persons, including the person of God, is essential to the full development of the self. In this sense, religion and therapy are not opposed. "Religion has always stood for the saving power of the good object relationship."[26] Religion (as practice, not theory) "relates us to a personal heart of reality, that we refer to by the indefinable term 'God'."[27]

Ultimately, for Guntrip, the person *can* be free from anxiety and conflict. The healthy person will be free to form significant personal relationships "in which there is a genuine meeting of kindred spirits ... and to exercise an active and spontaneous personality free from inhibiting fears." This can be accomplished through agape love which the therapist must provide for his patient because the latter did not get it from his parents in an adequate way.[28]

Agape **Love and Mutuality**

Agape, of course, is the Christian term for mutual love. But mutuality is a form of mature interdependence. In mature relationships people are truly inter-dependent. But for authentic personal relationships to be truly mature, according to object-relations theory, the child must learn separation from its infantile dependence on its mother. The child needs to feel that her own love is "welcomed and valued."[29]

Children must differentiate themselves from their parents in order to enter into more mature and healthy forms of relationship with them. Healthy parents are those who understand and encourage the separation and differentiation in order to enjoy their children at another, and higher level, later on. There may well be a parallel movement in our relationship with God. Only after we have struggled against God, and worked through our separation and differentiation from God as unique, free beings, can we re-enter relationship with God as the healthy and mature persons God intends us to be.

A healthy theology, therefore, might well want to encourage a healthy differentiation between human beings and God in order to bring them beyond the unhealthy kind of infantile dependence that Freud exploits in his rejection of religion. At the very least, separation and differentiation underwrite the theological importance of human freedom: if we are not free in relation to God, we cannot have a healthy relationship with God because we cannot enter it intentionally and maturely. Walter Brueggemann, who draws upon object-relations theory in his development of theology of the Old Testament, has argued that Israel's understanding of its relation to Yahweh requires conflict and self-assertion on the part of both partners. "Complaint and petition whereby the speaker can be fully honest before Yahweh and expect Yahweh to accept the self so expressed requires a strong sense of self on the part of the petitioner."[30] Without the distance between God and the believer, 'false selves' who cannot be honest with God will necessarily emerge. The authentic human self needs a certain degree of autonomy and power over God if the relationship is to be truly mutual and fulfilling.

James Jones has also observed in his most recent work on the relation between psychology and theology:

> the connections in which we are embedded may include a connection to a larger, sacred reality without doing violence to human selfhood, because selfhood and interconnection are not antithetical but potentially mutually strengthening. Likewise, dependency on a higher power may not contradict individuation, as the need for interdependence stays with us all our lives. The deepening of interpersonal relationships may lead us to the experience of the sacred.[31]

There must be real persons in real relations with the self for it to be truly healthy. The myth of fulfillment through self-sufficiency and autonomy is ultimately untrue to reality if this object-relations analysis is well-founded. A *kind* of healthy autonomy is necessary for mutual interdependence. The apparent paradox of autonomy/dependence is resolved only in the practice of genuine community. If the primary intention of each member is that the other flourish, then each will intend that the other exercise gifts, capacities, and abilities that enhance that person's sense of authenticity, uniqueness, and identity as a distinct, valuable other. The study of persons in their full personhood in the world undergirds what might otherwise be taken as the fanciful flights of the theological imagination as it invites us to experience the full fruits of agape in relation to a loving God.

This is precisely one of the most important dynamics of the mutual *community*, to provide each individual within it the support of all the members so that she can feel free enough from the need to defend her own defenseless ego so as to be able to love others in return on the basis of a healthy and strengthened ego. (Fairbairn does not develop the notion of community nearly as extensively as one might have hoped, but the seeds of communal relationality are clearly there in his theory. I will develop them much more fully in my analysis of the work of John Macmurray.) Object-relations theory ultimately makes sense and is fully applicable in a community in which mutual efforts are made to restore broken selves to wholeness and to provide all the members with ongoing experiences of comfort, consolation, care, compassion, and availability. When communities of mutuality really work, they will also foster more accurate images of the God who undergirds them by God's own work on their behalf: a truly objective God who mirrors, not the images of deprivation and unavailability so characteristic of Freud's deprived patients, but the images of healthy selves in open, flourishing relationship.

Incommensurable Moralities and Moral Ontology

Despite the claims of object-relations theory that there is something essential about the human need for relationality, the existence of different, often incommensurable, moralities is the basis for much of the postmodernist critique of traditional theistic ethics. It is now a truism among moral philosophers that there are rival views of human flourishing that are so different from each other that they cannot be reconciled by a common 'measure' or compared by a common standard (hence they are 'incommensurable').

If there were a common measure, then, logically, one view could, in principle, prove to be superior to all the others. This fact, in turn, threatens both the autonomy human beings claim for themselves in holding whatever views they wish, free from external coercion, and the tolerance they have learned to expect from and to show to other similarly autonomous people holding views different from their own. Modern secular people are

> hostile to any idea or beliefs which derive their authority or sanction from outside the self [that is, any traditional religious view in which God is an 'Other'], and consequently unable to understand or deal with [these] alternative and contrary world views except in terms of pejorative encodings, for example, blind faith, fundamentalism, and a form of zombiism (those who continue to live in a world that is godless as if it were not!).[32]

Christian ethicists Gene Outka and John P. Reeder, Jr. have identified two important fears that drive the secular hostility to the idea of a "common morality" that at a deep level would be the same for all persons. The first is the fear of "the tyranny of particular communities."[33] This fear is *of* a radical relativism in which some communities gain hegemony simply because they have the power to do so and not because they have ontological truth on their side.

The second fear is 'epistemic hubris'. It is the fear of invoking a 'God's eye' vantage point, or an absolute knowledge that can be used to suppress moral and cultural differences, forgetting that all human construals are finite and limited.

As Outka and Reeder have noted, allied with the secular suspicion of religious belief is the fear that there is a true ontology reflected in theistic belief. If such an ontology can survive the epistemological onslaughts of relativism that we discussed in Chapter 1, then it would presumably trump the secular conviction that there is no single true ontology. Epistemological skepticism and relativism therefore become inextricably linked with moral pluralism and the radical autonomy of the individual self. As long as the question of an ontology of moral behavior can be kept off the agenda, a pluralism of incommensurate views can be taken for granted. Whether it is as pervasive as it seems, and whether there might, in fact, be deeper underlying commonalities in human nature and action, can be safely ignored.

Charles Taylor

Philosopher Charles Taylor has noted the importance of this 'unholy alliance' of epistemological and ontological relativism. "There is a great deal of motivated suppression of moral ontology among our contemporaries, in part because of the great weight of modern epistemology ... and behind this of the spiritual outlook associated with this epistemology."[34] This outlook tolerates all views except the religious.

The unquestioned assumption in this secular outlook is that a religious moral ontology *is in fact* incompatible with (let alone not strongly supportive of) *all* versions of moral pluralism. Only when the underlying assumptions of this version of secularism are brought to light, according to Markham, can we get at the deeper questions ignored by pluralism.[35] Only when we take what Taylor calls "our deepest moral instincts" seriously, can we begin to gain "access to the world in which ontological claims are discernible and can be rationally argued about and sifted."[36] It is not, of course, that secular moral philosophers are without a moral ontology or framework: it is simply that they suppress it in order to gain the moral and epistemological 'payoff' for ignoring it. The studied neglect of ontology permits them to avoid messy and interminable metaphysical debates that might lead to conclusions with universalist implications for how all of us ought to act that would qualify our unrestricted autonomous freedom.

One consequence of moral philosophy's avoidance of ontological questions is its lack of concern with a notion of the good "as the object of our love or allegiance".[37] Taylor's critique of this neglect leads him to consider the ontological implications of our moral assent to what we take as our deepest moral instincts, namely those that respect the "life, integrity, and well-being, even flourishing, of others."[38] Our moral instincts thoroughly implicate ontological claims. They "seem to involve claims, implicit or explicit, about the nature and status of human being. ... [A] moral reaction is an assent to, an affirmation of, a given ontology of the human."[39] Given the rise of deconstruction and postmodernism, of course, any ontology on which these claims are grounded will fall, Taylor concedes, under epistemological suspicion.[40]

But Taylor wants to argue that our feelings about some objects can, in fact, be revelations and indices of their objective reality. In this respect, Taylor is not far from Macmurray's insight that emotional reactions can be perceptive revelations of the reality of that to which they are responses. Emotions are, in fact, one of our central forms of relational contact with what is 'other' than us.

Feelings and Values

Taylor seems to be agreeing with Macmurray's claim that feelings are rational when they correctly orient us to reality when he argues that our moral reactions are "implicit acknowledgments of claims concerning their objects. The various ontological accounts try to articulate these claims."[41] This entails that "there is such a thing as moral objectivity." Or as Macmurray puts it, "objective emotion ... is an immediate appreciation of the value and significance of real things. Emotional reason is our capacity to apprehend objective values."[42] Ultimately, for Macmurray, love "is the ultimate source of our capacity to behave in terms of the object [and not simply in terms of our own desires]. It is the core of rationality."[43]

Many modern psychologists make the same point. Joseph de Rivera has said that "true value can only be revealed by true emotion."[44] And Ronald de Sousa has argued that when we desire an object "we experience value as inherent" in it.[45] In this sense, our emotional perception of value in the Other can help us transcend selfish desires. If love is a true emotional reaction to the other, then love will urge the lover to "give to, or care for or affirm, an object that is perceived as good in its own right ... [it will instruct] the person to 'surrender' his or her will and *give* to the beloved."[46]

In psychology, if one starts with the self as disengaged and non-relational, one can get no purchase on the role of emotions as revelatory of the value of the other (except in a purely subjective way), and reciprocally, of oneself. Drawing explicitly on Macmurray's work, de Rivera argues that if persons exist fully only in personal relations, then the emotion that will reveal the true worth of each of the partners is love, not fear. Fear is essentially an emotion shaped by a deep concern only for one's own self and driven by the belief that the other is a threat. If fear is the dominant emotion, the person will either have no regard for others or sacrifice his needs to others. In either case he cannot develop true individuality. "Real individuality can only develop out of the caring that occurs when love dominates over fear."[47]

But in a mutual relationship, emotions are "*between* the self and the other ... the behavior [of one] can only be completed by a response from the other."[48] This psychological analysis perfectly complements a theistic moral ontology's claim that only in relationship with God (and through God with other human persons) can one flourish. But such flourishing must include the fully developed emotional components of a person's mature life. Ironically, these components are not simply add-ons to an essentially intellectual grasp of the Other; they are both primary and essential to a full revelation of the value of the Other.

In a complementary argument, Thomas Wren has suggested that underlying all our moral actions are "constitutive desires" or feelings that "constitute the moral agent's 'identity.'"[49] Taylor agrees: "The notion of an identity defined by some mere *de facto*, not strongly valued preference is incoherent."[50] But the emotional desires of the self need not be solely self-interested. They can include a basic concern for the well-being of others, just as a theistic moral ontology would insist they do.

Now if all this is the case, Taylor is correct in asserting that "one or another ontology is in fact the only adequate basis for our moral responses."[51] One way into an ontology, he argues, is through the "inescapable frameworks" by which we "make sense of our lives spiritually."[52] A framework helps people define the moral demands by which they judge their lives and measure their fullness or emptiness.[53] While it is true that frameworks have problematic aspects, especially those that include a place for a divine agent and intention, they are inescapable. "Doing without frameworks is utterly impossible for us ... [M]y identity is defined by the commitments and identifications which provide the frame or horizon within which I can try to determine from case to case what is good, or valuable, or what ought to be done, or what I endorse or oppose."[54] Radical pluralists believe there are many frameworks, most of them incommensurable with the others, and not one of which is common to all people or superior to all others.

All human beings, according to Taylor, want to know "what kind of life is worth living, e.g., what would be a rich, meaningful life, as against an empty one."[55] We want to connect our life to some greater story or reality, to become rightly placed in relation to the good.[56] It is precisely in answer to these fundamental questions that Biblical theology rehearses a narrative of God's acts in history and the human responses to them, because it contends that this divine/human dialogical action points to a deeper ontology in which human fulfillment and the divine will come together in the formation of human community as precursor to the Kingdom of God.

Theism, I would argue, provides one example of what Taylor calls a "best account" (BA) that "make[s] the best sense of our lives ... [by] ... offering the best, most realistic orientation about the good but also allowing us best to understand and make sense of the actions and feelings of ourselves and others."[57] Part of this BA is that we cannot help having recourse to "strongly valued goods for the purposes of life," nor can we avoid the question of reality ("what you have to deal with, what won't go away just because it doesn't fit with your prejudices"). Taylor's definition of the real is, of course, consistent with our earlier construal of a pragmatic moderately realist understanding of the relation between the knower.

Hypergoods

According to one's framework, some goods (hypergoods) are 'incomparably more important than others' and provide the critical point from which all other goods are to be ranked or compared. These are the goods that *move* us to moral action. But because different people hold different hypergoods, there will be moral tension in any society. This will be true not only with respect to the hypergoods themselves, but also with respect to their correlative views about human nature.

A hypergood of self-sufficiency or autonomy, for example, is allied with a view of the self as radically independent of others and as able to achieve fulfillment in their absence. A hypergood of mutuality, on the other hand, is allied with a view of the self as radically interpersonal and as able to achieve fulfillment only in mutual loving relations with them.

According to Taylor an ethical outlook organized around a hypergood gives rise to moral conflict within that outlook. The highest good subordinates other goods to it and can on occasion challenge or reject these other goods. "That is why recognizing a hypergood is a source of tension and of often grievous dilemmas in moral life."[58] This means that a moral ontology committed to a hypergood (for example, the fulfillment of God's will for mutual love) has to recognize the reality of plural, and sometimes competing hypergoods. It can reduce the level of tension between itself and them either by a hierarchical ranking in which the other hypergoods in effect lose their 'hyper' status and become complementary second-level goods under the hypergood. (For example, when freedom becomes not a freedom to do whatever one wants, but a freedom 'for others' under the hypergood of responding to God's intention for human well-being in community.) Sometimes the hypergood must oppose other hypergoods directly (for example, when the Biblical value of the dignity of all human life leads to unqualified opposition to slavery or capital punishment).

When we put the good into a form of discourse that gives it meaning it becomes a "constitutive good ... the love of which empowers us to do and be good."[59] And stories about the constitutive good, woven into narrative form, supplemented by liturgies, rituals, and prayers, can be powerful forces in motivating us to act morally. The question is whether underneath these narratives and practices there is an ontological reality that gives them metaphysical support. It is the theistic moral philosopher's claim that there is and that it is centered upon God's will and action in history. It is also her claim that within this reality there is a place for the reconciliation of much of the plurality of goods in the world, provided that they are properly ranked in relation to each other. Those that cannot be so hierarchicalized, must be opposed.

A theistic moral ontology meets all the relevant conditions laid down by Taylor for coherent moral thinking: it offers a moral ontology, an escapable framework, a hypergood, a best account, a narrative, and a way of dealing with the pluralism of values within the world. Within a theistic ontology based on the primacy of the divine will for human (and cosmic) well-being and flourishing, there are limits to what kind of moral action will prove ultimately satisfying or fulfilling. If, as secular moral philosopher John Kekes argues, moral pluralists believe that "good lives require the realization of *radically different* [emphasis added] types of values, both moral and non-moral, and that many of these values are conflicting and cannot be realized together,"[60] then theistic ethics cannot be radically pluralist. The theistic metaphysic assumes that God has created persons with enough similarity in what constitutes the core of their flourishing that they can (and must) comprise a mutual community if they wish flourishing to take place. Community presupposes some standard of basic commensurability. Radically different types of values (for example, the denial of the value of the life of children vs. its unqualified affirmation) simply could not co-exist in a mutual 'heterocentric' community based on agape love. The question is whether radical ontological pluralism with a concomitant moral incommensurability is the only kind of pluralism that we can recognize.

Commonalities and Differences

Christian ethicist Michael J. Perry has claimed that the Christian presupposition "that human beings are all alike in some significant respects is not inconsistent with the pluralist view that human beings are also different from one another in many respects, that human beings have many different needs and wants, even different biological needs." Nevertheless, he argues, there are some needs that are common to all persons and that what satisfies a common human need is good for any person. There are some things that all of us must possess if we are to live good lives. And while pluralism must be respected, a true conception of human good "can acknowledge sameness as well as difference, commonality as well as variety."[61]

The really difficult task is identifying precisely wherein the commonality lies and what differences in human moral life it permits. Taylor has said that "there may be different kinds of human realization which are really incommensurable ... I think this is a real possibility, but I doubt if it is true."[62]

Certainly a theistic moral ontology is not committed in every respect to the alternative to pluralism that Kekes calls 'monism', the view that there is one and only one reasonable system of values, the same for all human beings, always, and everywhere.[63] Even individual persons can have different values at different times in their lives without undermining an essential continuity and consistency in their moral outlook and personal integrity. (For example, a parent can value her child's dependence upon her in his early years and value that same child's increasing independence as he grows older. This example is more than random, in that community is often developed by the gradual alteration in values as they correspond to the various stages of moral growth among its members. God, for example, may value the subservience of persons up to a certain point in their growth toward moral maturity and after that point, value much more their freedom to create spheres of (relative) autonomy and differentiation *vis-à-vis* God.)

However, there is a standard of measurement grounded in a theistic ontology that lifts it beyond complete incommensurability. That standard is what conforms to the will of God. And if the will of God is for human flourishing, and if that will is determinative in setting the conditions of reality, then no system of values that contradicts human flourishing can be recognized as valid or true. So the question comes down to: 'what counts as human flourishing?' This is the question of whether there are, in fact, 'universally human' forms of flourishing and well-being. These forms, if they exist, would constitute what Kekes calls 'primary' values. But there could be 'enormous differences' in the *ways in which* these primary values are enacted and experienced by human beings constituted similarly with respect to their 'essence' but expressing that essence differently at different historical times and places. These differences constitute the 'secondary values' of persons that would vary with individuals, societies, traditions, and historical periods. Even a monist, Kekes concedes, could accept this distinction between primary and secondary values. However, the monist would still insist on there being an overriding value (for example, God's will for human flourishing) which always takes precedence over any other values with which it might be in conflict (that is, the tension between hypergoods).

Strict pluralists reject the idea of there being such an overriding value. They would hold out for there being *only* unique, variable, and individual conceptions of the good life, which are not ultimately commensurable with each other or with some external standard of measure.[64] In this sense, theistic moral ontology is monist with respect to the overriding value of God's will that all human beings have the need for mutual love as the essence of human well-being and flourishing.

This does not mean that it has to deny either that there are various ways to satisfy such a need or that our particular beliefs about our needs are socially constructed.[65] What is denied is that all views of human flourishing are equal in weight or truth.

Even Hilary Putnam, a non-theist, has emphasized that "belief in a pluralistic ideal is not the same thing as belief that every ideal of human flourishing is as good as every other. We reject [presumably for good reason, some] ideals of human flourishing as wrong, as infantile, as sick, as one-sided."[66] The only alternative to rejecting or accepting various proposals for human flourishing is to accept, without reservation, a totally relativistic ownership of whatever ideals one happens to find attractive for no reason beyond one's immediate subjective desires. And this acceptance could lead to the "tyranny of particular communities" that Outka and Reeder have noted.

To avoid moral relativism does not, of course, commit us to an absolutist position with respect to our epistemic certainty regarding the 'eternal' truth of our moral ontology or judgments. We cannot rule out the possibility that present reliable beliefs might prove to be inadequate in the future in a variety of ways.[67] But this is just what we would expect given a (neo)pragmatist, historical understanding of the contextual nature of belief. If there is a telos to human history, guided and informed by a divine intention for human flourishing, then there is, in principle, a ground for the ultimate determination of the truth of what counts as human flourishing. Some accounts will simply prove to be unworkable and unsustainable. The same empirical basis that now leads secular philosophers to extol the ultimacy of incommensurable, purely subjective versions of flourishing may also prove to be the foundation for discovering a common morality built on a common vision of what is truly good for human flourishing generally.

Outka and Reeder have said that:

> if the case against the efficacy of universal appeals is indeed empirically based, it remains tentative and subject to revision. And it commits us to acknowledge in advance that the question of important cross-cultural similarities in human beings is a matter we can determine through empirical-theoretical investigation.[68]

This claim justifies our examination of some of the secular literature, such as that of object-relations theory, that has investigated the life of human beings in social and personal relation.

The theistic moral-ontological claim is that ultimately only those lives that are led in responsible love toward others in the context of mutual community, that is, lives informed by agape, can be truly flourishing. It is, in Perry's words, a vision of a "final and radical reconciliation, a set of beliefs about how one is or can be bound or connected to the world – the 'other' and to 'nature' – and, above all, to Ultimate Reality in a profoundly intimate and ultimately meaningful way." And a moral vision is one about how to live a 'truly human' life compatible with this religious vision, how to live a life "oriented by and to the way in which life is trusted and believed to be ultimately meaningful."[69]

The religious vision of the Biblical theist is that we flourish when we live a moral life in open, trust-based relationships of care, compassion, and responsibility for the others with whom God intends us to dwell.

Charles Taylor's own construal of the best account is close to the theistic one that we have been arguing for. He wants the theistic moral sources that give life to the spirit to again empower modern people.[70] Modern unbelief, he argues, is based upon valuing the autonomous, self-sufficient, and disengaged individual.[71] Such a self glories in his unrestricted individual freedom. "Pure untrammeled freedom ... has become the underlying ideal ... of all modern goods."[72] The end result of this ideal is, however, spiritual and psychological emptiness. "Nothing would count as a fulfillment in a world in which literally nothing was important but self-fulfillment."[73]

Taylor himself suggests that the potential of a theistic perspective is greater than that of naturalism[74] though he does not spell out how that potential can be realized. He does not deny that spiritual ideals have on occasion been "poisoned chalices" that have laid "the most crushing burdens on humankind."[75] Nevertheless, when compared to a secular alternative that "involves stifling the response in us to some of the deepest and most powerful spiritual aspirations that humans have conceived,"[76] the theistic best account gains plausibility. When it is combined with the element of hope that is present in the Judaeo-Christian version of theism, "and in its central promise of a divine affirmation of the human, more total than humans can ever attain unaided,"[77] it can lead to an empowering conviction that

God is real and works historically for our well-being. And that conviction is, as we have argued, the basis of the moral life as, in Niebuhr's notion, our response to what God is up to in the world.

While Taylor does not argue directly for a theistic position, he does, as Michael L. Morgan points out, show how God *could* play a central role in our moral lives and how a moral ontology can reflect that role.[78] The moral life, Morgan argues, is "a human response to a divine impact ... Meaning arises out of the human response to an encounter with God."[79]

Nevertheless, Morgan asks, how can one affirm the teachings of one religious tradition as "available and appropriate to all human existence but somehow peculiar to each community, with its texts, its formative events and its special understanding of God's acts in history"?[80] That problem is the nub of a Biblical moral ontology that is grounded in a belief that God has acted, does act, and will continue to act, in history. I am trying to address just that problem through a construal of theistic ethics as a response to the changing actions of God, the freedom of human persons and community to respond historically to those divine actions, and the overarching divine intention to nurture human flourishing in and through the historical development and experimentation in creating human community. Only a divine agent who acts in history can provide the theistic grounding for a life-affirming ontology. A divine agent can affirm human diversity and moral pluralism providing both are part of the maturing process and the experience of human flourishing.

Notes

1 James Gustafson, 'The Relationship of Empirical Science to Moral Thought', in Ronald P. Hamel and Kenneth R. Himes, eds., *Introduction to Christian Ethics*, p. 433.
2 Sigmund Freud, *The Future of an Illusion*, (Garden City: Doubleday, 1964), p. 22.
3 *Ibid.*
4 *Ibid.*
5 *Ibid.*
6 James Jones, *Contemporary Psychoanalysis and Religion: Transference and Transcendence*, (New Haven: Yale University Press, 1991). Jones notes, drawing on the work of Meissner, that Freud's own attitude toward religion was the working out of 'unresolved infantile conflicts' that led him to wish never to submit to the demands of religion. Freud assumed atheism required no explanation but religious belief did. He failed to notice, in Jones' words, "that just as there can be a psychoanalysis of belief, so there can be a psychoanalysis of unbelief. Just as there are neurotic reasons for believing in God, so there are neurotic reasons for refusing belief." (p. 37)
7 The quotation is from R. Greenson, *The Technique and Practice of Psychoanalysis*, Vol. 1 (New York: International Universities Press, 1967), as found in Jones, *Contemporary Psychoanalysis and Religion*, p. 11.
8 Quoted in Jones, *Contemporary Psychoanalysis and Religion*, p. 10. From 'Some Reflections on Schoolboy Psychology'.
9 *Ibid.*
10 *Ibid*, p. 13. The quotation is from one of the earliest object-relations theorists, W.R.D. Fairbairn (1943).
11 Jay R. Greenberg and Stephen A. Mitchell, *Object Relations in Psychoanalytic Theory*,

(Cambridge: Harvard University Press, 1983), p. 156.

12 *Ibid.*, pp. 156–157.

13 John Macmurray, *The Self as Agent*, (London: Faber and Faber, 1957), p. 15.

14 *Ibid.*, p. 182.

15 Greenberg and Mitchell, *Object Relations in Psychoanalytic Theory*, p. 158.

16 For an illuminating comparison (and ultimate complementarity) between the object-relations theory and the systems theory of the self, see Linda Olds, *Metaphors of Interrelatedness: Toward a Systems Theory of Psychology*, (Albany: State University of New York Press, 1992). Olds argues that systems theory (built around the notion of integrated but increasingly inclusive levels of organization in the self) is committed to a view of the self as a thoroughly interrelational being. Olds even builds into her systems view "an ethics of being, of the outflow of caring and love, and ethics of response-ability" (p. 100). Implicit in this ethic is an ontology that is similar to the Biblical one: namely, that if "one moves outward in love, the universe responds in kind ... this is the essence of the fabric, the ultimate reality of which we are a part" (p. 100). The weakness in Olds' argument is her somewhat indiscriminate openness to metaphors of inclusiveness that sometimes seem to abandon the centrality of the person (and a personal God) for such vague abstractions as "the dance of cosmic energy", "totality", "wholeness" or "the All", and to speak of God as "It, That, That which is" in order to free God from "partial attributes" (p. 122). God becomes, in effect, something so abstract that God can be captured only by impersonal or transpersonal metaphors (which are at odds with the Christian ontology's claim that God *is a Person*), such as "interconnection" or simply as "a name for my personal relationship with the universe" (p. 133).

17 The mother is normally the paradigm of the significant 'other' with whom the child has continuing relationships. However, nothing significant hangs solely on the gender of the supportive and responsive parent.

18 Greenberg and Mitchell, *Object Relations in Psychoanalytic Theory*, p. 159.

19 *Ibid.*, pp. 170–171.

20 *Ibid.*, p. 195.

21 Quoted in John McDargh, *Psychoanalytic Object Relations Theory and the Study of Religion*, (Lanham, MD: University Press of America, 1983), p. 61.

22 Jones, *Contemporary Psychoanalysis and Religion*, p. 82.

23 *Ibid.*, p. 83.

24 *Ibid.*, pp. 83, 85.

25 Greenberg and Mitchell, *Object Relations in Psychoanalytic Theory*, p. 160.

26 Guntrip, quoted in McDargh, *Psychoanalytic Object Relations Theory and the Study of Religion*, p. 207.

27 *Ibid.*, p. 212.

28 Harry Guntrip, quoted in Greenberg and Mitchell, *Object Relations in Psychoanalytic Theory*, p. 219.

29 Greenberg and Mitchell, *Object Relations in Psychoanalytic Theory*, p. 161.

30 Walter Brueggemann, *Theology of the Old Testament*, (Minneapolis: Fortress Press, 1997), p. 475, note 52.

31 James W. Jones, *Religion and Psychology in Transition: Psychoanalysis, Feminism, and Theology* (New Haven: Yale University Press, 1996), p. 68. Jones' work on the relation between psychology, especially its object-relations school, and theology, especially its relational model school, is the best I know bringing these two areas of insight together without reductionism and with genuine sympathy for what each brings to the table of understanding the human person in relation to herself, other persons, and the sacred.

32 Ian S. Markham, *Plurality and Christian Ethics*, (Cambridge: Cambridge University

Press, 1994), quoting Gavin D'Costa's criticism of 'intolerant secularism' in the writings of Salman Rushdie, p. 77.

33 Gene Outka and John P. Reeder, Jr., 'Introduction', in Outka and Reeder, Jr., eds., *Prospects for a Common Morality*, (Princeton: Princeton University Press, 1993), pp. 24–25.

34 Charles Taylor, *Sources of the Self: The Making of the Modern Identity*, p. 10.

35 Markham, *Plurality and Christian Ethics*, p. 77.

36 Taylor, *Sources of the Self*, p. 8.

37 *Ibid.*, p. 3.

38 *Ibid.*, p. 4.

39 *Ibid.*, p. 5.

40 *Ibid.*, p. 5.

41 *Ibid.*, p. 7.

42 John Macmurray, *Reason and Emotion*, p. 31.

43 *Ibid.*, p. 32.

44 Joseph de Rivera, 'Choice of Emotion and Ideal Development', in L. Cirillo, B. Kaplan, S. Wapner, eds., *Emotion and Ideal Human Development*, (Hillsdale, NJ: Erlbaum, n.d.), p. 8.

45 Ronald de Sousa, *The Rationality of Emotion*, (Cambridge: MIT Press, 1987) has made a similar point. Emotions, he argues, have "indispensable biological foundations" (p. 332), have their "deepest roots in the experiences of sociality", and are a kind of perception that can help us to apprehend axiological or value reality, so much so that we have an "emotional responsibility" to *feel things as they really are* (p. 315). Emotions can be useful or not useful in helping us find our way around in the world. Emotional integrity "apprehend[s] and celebrate[s] the fullness of what it is to be human. The ideal of emotional rationality is *adequate emotional response*" (pp. 332–333).

46 de Rivera, 'Choice of Emotion and Ideal Development', p. 14.

47 *Ibid.*, p. 25.

48 *Ibid.*, p. 24.

49 Thomas Wren, *Caring About Morality*, (Cambridge: MIT Press, 1991), p. 161.

50 Taylor, *Sources of the Self*, p. 30.

51 *Ibid.*, p. 10.

52 *Ibid.*, p. 18.

53 *Ibid.*, pp. 16–17.

54 *Ibid.*, p. 27.

55 *Ibid.*, p. 42.

56 *Ibid.*, pp. 43–44.

57 *Ibid.*, p. 57.

58 *Ibid.*, p. 65.

59 *Ibid.*, p. 93. I am not suggesting that Taylor would draw any or all of the religious implications that I am drawing from his work, even though it is clear that he is a committed theist.

60 John Kekes, *The Morality of Pluralism*, p. 11.

61 Michael J. Perry, *Love and Power*, (New York: Oxford University Press, 1991), pp. 30–31.

62 Taylor, *Sources of the Self*, p. 61.

63 Kekes, *The Morality of Pluralism*, p. 8.

64 *Ibid.*, pp. 18–23.

65 Perry, *Love and Power*, footnote 5, p. 157.

66 *Ibid.*, footnote 6, p. 157.

67 Alasdair MacIntyre, *Whose Justice? Which Rationality?*, p. 361, quoted in *ibid.*, p. 61.

68 Outka and Reeder, 'Introduction', p. 24.
69 Perry, *Love and Power*, p. 77.
70 Taylor, *Sources of the Self*, p. 520.
71 *Ibid.*, p. 106.
72 *Ibid.*, p. 489.
73 *Ibid.*, p. 507. The further implications of this view for political philosophy, or our understanding of the self in society (as distinct from community) will be explored in the final chapter.
74 *Ibid.*, p. 518.
75 *Ibid.*, p. 519.
76 *Ibid.*, p. 520.
77 *Ibid.*, p. 521.
78 See Michael L. Morgan, 'Religion, History, and Moral Discourse', in James Tully, ed., *Philosophy in an Age of Pluralism: The Philosophy of Charles Taylor in Question*, (Cambridge: Cambridge University Press, 1994), p. 51.
79 *Ibid.*, p. 63.
80 *Ibid.*, p. 66.

Chapter 7

Flourishing, Altruism, Trust, and Love

On Flourishing

If God has created and sustains all human beings, and intends for all of them a fulfillment that is constituted by mutual love, then, in one sense, all persons will ultimately flourish in ways that are not radically in conflict with each other. But not only are there different historical and existential forms of this ultimate fulfillment, there are also forms of flourishing that may be unique to those persons who have already begun to appropriate the divine gifts of the foretaste of fulfillment in and through their reception of God's grace in specific religious communities. Nevertheless, a secular understanding of flourishing informed by the sciences of human nature (even ones that do not see the signs of the kingdom in their present form), cannot be radically at odds with a Biblically-based theistic vision of fulfillment if it is to successfully reflect the realities of human flourishing. There must be some continuity between the present, empirically-based picture of what fulfills human beings and what will ultimately fulfill them when they have entered, by God's grace, fully into the community of mutuality God intends for all.

As we saw in the previous chapter, a theistic-moral ontology needs to be in conversation with historical as well as philosophical views on human flourishing. One of the most important of recent non-religious attempts to develop a view of 'non-relative' virtues that are at every point immersed in the concrete circumstances of history and culture is that of Martha Nussbaum.[1] Drawing heavily on the philosophy of Aristotle, Nussbaum wants to retrieve something of his commitment to "a single objective account of the human good, or human flourishing." Such an account appeals in part to "features of humanness that lie beneath all local traditions and are there to be seen whether or not they are in fact recognized in local traditions."[2]

Nussbaum's Reading of The Aristotelian Account

Among these features, according to Nussbaum's reading of Aristotle, is friendship, which includes "mutual benefit and well-wishing, mutual enjoyment, mutual awareness, a shared conception of the good, and some form of 'living together.'"[3] This stress on mutuality is central to Nussbaum's reading of Aristotle. People in a relation of *philia* (not agape, interestingly enough) "know each other, feel emotion for one another, wish and act well towards one another, and know that these relationships of thought, emotion, and action obtain between them."[4] This is a love of the other for the other's own sake. These are also features of a Biblical understanding of community and suggest that its moral ontology has much in common with this non-theistic construal of the non-relative virtues that constitute human fullness.

As Nussbaum also points out, however, there may be many concrete specifications of friendship depending upon particular local practices and conditions.[5] But the 'context-sensitive' nature of virtue does not imply that it is no more than *relative to* a local context, "any more than the fact that a good navigational judgement [sic] is sensitive to particular weather conditions shows that it is correct only in a local or relational sense. It is right absolutely, objectively, anywhere in the human world. ... The value of contextual responsiveness and the value of getting it right are seen by the Aristotelian as mutually supportive."[6] We do not need to give up what she elsewhere calls "the ethical value of surprise, contextuality, and particularity," as we pursue the objective commonalities of human nature. "However varied our specific conceptions of friendship and love are, there is a great point in seeing them as overlapping expressions of the same family of shared human needs and desires."[7]

Part of this 'family' of overlapping expressions is human flourishing. David Wong, also writing from a non-religious perspective, and arguing in support of a pluralism of conceptions of flourishing, has nevertheless claimed that a necessary condition for all forms of human flourishing is 'effective agency' in achieving our ends.[8] Certainly a theistic ethic would accept Wong's notion of effective agency (without which there can be no authentic self in genuine relation to others), as well as his claim that one of its necessary conditions is that certain sorts of relationships with others must obtain.[9]

A Thick Notion of Flourishing

It is important to note the qualifier 'certain sorts' of relationships. A meaningful theistic ethic cannot rely solely upon a 'thin' conception of the good. Such a conception is too vague to carry any moral weight. To say simply that people need other people, or that persons are 'constituted' by their relations with others, allows far too much room for not only a complementary pluralism of views about relationships, but contradictory, incommensurable, or conflicting views as well. That is why the theistic moral ontology must always stress the particularity and superiority of *certain kinds* of relationships it sees as constituting human fulfillment and flourishing, that is, ones of mutuality, trust, love, compassion, other-centeredness, and so on.

To get at the appropriate sorts of relationships necessary for effective agency and, ultimately, flourishing, Wong argues that we cannot be effective agents without a sense of our own identity. Having an identity involves knowing what one stands for and believes in. One's identity "covers the characteristic set of ways that a person has for interpreting and behaving in the world, her views as to what is important, and her actual ends and desires."[10] This ties in very nicely with Charles Taylor's notion that " 'identity is defined by our fundamental evaluations,' ones that form the 'indispensable horizon or foundation out of which we reflect and evaluate as persons.' "[11] Among the primary desires and goals of human life and identity, Wong argues, are those for "relationships of affection and intimacy,"[12] precisely the specific kinds of relationships that are at the heart of the Biblical understanding of mutuality and love (though Wong does not specifically make this connection).

Part of our effective agency is, of course, shaped by how others treat us, especially at the earliest stages of our life. If the object-relations theorists are right, then our ability to seek out fulfilling relationships with others is determined to a large degree by how fulfilling our relationships with our parents were.

Trust

If we are to have a healthy identity, trust must play a major role. We want to be able to trust that the power others have over us is intended for our well-being. Trust is an essential part of any fulfilling mutual relationship that contributes to human flourishing. Getting help from others and being able to use it effectively "presupposes a substantial degree of trust."[13] We have to trust that others will give us true information about ourselves and, if it is negative, that it is intended for our well-being by those who care for us.

Many secular moral philosophers have begun to claim the virtue of trust for (and, in the process, to add 'thickness' to) their descriptions of what counts as human well-being. At least some others must be committed to my nurture and they must expect some reciprocity for those commitments if our relationship is to be fulfilling.

Challenging the deconstructionist claim that there is no such thing as 'human nature,' Wong, a pluralist, goes so far as to claim that there are "deep satisfactions obtained from nurturing, and deep tendencies to reciprocate ... So duties of care and of reciprocation through gratitude and obedience find some hospitable soil in our natures."[14] Such a claim clearly suggests that within or underneath the wealth of pluralistic and contextual views, there is no escaping the necessity of something fundamental and common that constitutes the core of 'human nature', just as a theistic moral ontology claims.

The secular moral philosopher Laurence Thomas goes even further in support of a thick notion of that nature when he argues that the amount of care human nurturing requires makes it reasonable to assume that "natural selection would favor human beings having a motivational structure capable of varying degrees of altruism, with the altruism of parental love being the most basic and generally the richest expression of altruism among human beings."[15]

And Robert Adams notes that, logically, what we consider to be our good must have been received initially from others. "An appropriate concern for one's own good has roots in one's relations with other people ... insofar as one's own good is a common project that one shares with others."[16] Our sense of our own good was initially acquired "from people who not only had the concept of our good before we did, but also cared about our good before we could even conceive it."[17] It seems to be a fact about human nature that we find much of our good in the act of advancing the good of other persons. Thus in caring about our own good we are likely to be more effective agents in caring about others.[18]

For this reason, Thomas has argued that "there has to be more altruism in our bones ... than contemporary moral philosophers have allowed."[19] This suggests at the very least that the view of the human self as inherently disposed toward self-interest is, at best, only a partial view and, at worst, fundamentally off-track.

Thomas is also correct, I believe, when he claims that "individuals who do not have their altruistic motivations manifestly realized in their lives flourish less than those who do."[20] Like the object-relations theorists, Thomas finds the most important modeling of altruism, or what he calls 'transparent' love, in the original parent-child relationship. Such love "is unconditional love ... because there is no belief about that individual's behavior, performances, or what have you, that constitutes a conceptual bar to so loving that person. There is nothing a person can do, nothing a person can become, that would cause one, on conceptual grounds, to cease loving him."[21]

Such love, of course, on theistic grounds, is what one experiences from God, assuming one's relationship with one's parents early on has been such as to open up the possibility of receiving and construing God's love in this way. (Persons can be so deprived of love as children that they cannot constitutionally receive God's love unless God decides, almost in a miraculous way, to break through the inevitable resistance the love-starved often exhibit. But that is, of course, the mystery of what Christians, for example, call 'redeeming love' and 'conversion'.) One crucial effect of the altruistic love by parents is that it provides the child with such transparent love that the child is motivated to conform to her parents' wishes and to choose their values as her own.[22] This motivation is not an imposed or coerced morality. It is not a threat to moral autonomy since the child retains freedom of choice in the selection of her values and, in addition, the parents desire to support and enhance that freedom. But it is clearly a *response* to what has *already been given by others* and thus fits nicely into the kind of ethics of response that I have been claiming is at the heart of a theistic ethics.

Heterocentric Love

One aspect of the kind of altruism that Thomas develops is that when it takes mature form in our relations with lovers and friends, it is not simply a reciprocal response to their love for us. It is a love that is, to use Macmurray's term, *heterocentric*. "Companion friends," Thomas says, "are committed to each other's flourishing, not to responding to each other's altruism."[23]

All of this underscores the importance of trust in the establishment of deep personal relationships. Annette Baier, a non-theist, has argued that attention to the importance of trust is almost completely lacking in modern moral philosophy.[24] This is largely because moral philosophy is focused on the needs of the self for protection from others and leads, more often than not, to an individualistic and utilitarian calculus. For Baier, however, trust is a human need that cannot be neglected without damage to human flourishing. Without trust there can be no basis for a loving relationship. As Thomas remarks "to trust another is to voluntarily make oneself vulnerable with respect to some good, having been led to believe by the other's actions toward one that no loss or harm will come to one as a result."[25] (This, of course, is absolutely consistent with the Biblical theist's reasons for trust in God: by God's actions, God has given one the confidence that one can be voluntarily, non-defensively, openly vulnerable to God with respect to the good, that is, fulfillment or well-being, that God intends for one.) When trust is real, a relationship between trusting persons is such that there can be a mutual fulfillment of each. Genuine trust enables us to rely upon others for the very fulfillment we desire for ourselves, thus removing, or at least greatly diminishing, the need to rely upon ourselves or to put our own self-interest ahead of the interest of others. Both the desire to realize one's talents and the desire to be treated equitably "are compatible with taking considerable delight in the flourishing of others."[26]

In fact, Thomas argues that being loved by others frees us to be able to love ourselves, not, as is usually claimed, that we have to love ourselves first (on what grounds?) before we can love others. It is through being loved especially by one's parents, that one can come to have self-love.[27] Baier agrees that "unless some form of [trust] were innate, and unless that form could pave the way for new forms, it would appear a miracle that trust ever occurs."[28] This self-love is not egoistic, however, nor is love of the other a willingness to do whatever the other desires. True other-love (heterocentric love, in Macmurray's terms) involves regarding some things as ontologically good and other things as bad. "Thus, at the very minimum, to love a person is necessarily to subscribe to a conception of the good for that person"[29] even when the other might not share that conception. And this, of course, is just what a theistic moral ontology claims: that God's will and power are such that, ontologically, some things will in fact prove to be good for human beings and other things less good, or even downright evil. As Thomas concludes, it is because we love that we are moral. "It is in virtue of love that doing what is right has ontological priority in our lives … And if love is part of the Good, then the Right, namely morality, is anchored in the Good."[30]

In religious terms, if love (both freely given and freely received) is the essence of flourishing, then we have a basis for morality that coheres with much in secular moral philosophy's understanding of human nature. The moral task becomes that of figuring out what actions will enhance love and then doing them, and what actions work against love and avoiding or opposing them. But above all and underneath all is a conception of the non-moral Good, anchored (for a theist) in God's will and those divine actions that implement the divine will, and (for a non-theist) in the realities of human nature as such. And for the theist the divine will is found, at least in part, in the realities of human nature which is that will's creation and sustainer.

The Need for Community

If the end result of focusing on human flourishing, according to Wong, is that bonds of trust and care do in fact promote effective agency,[31] then those bonds require the appropriate form of community. We simply cannot be fully effective agents, with a healthy mature identity, unless we commit ourselves to trusting and loving others in the context of community life. "Getting the best out of ourselves means getting the right company."[32]

One of the tensions in modern moral philosophies is that between "getting the right company," finding the right community in which one can flourish, and at the same time acknowledging, even celebrating, the genuine otherness of the 'other' with whom one is in communion. Propelled to a large degree by what it takes to be the flattening out of differences required by a universalistic ethic, postmodern moral philosophy wants to stress the radical uniqueness, the individuality, the 'difference' between one being and another.[33] And communities, even liberal ones, have a tendency, because the very nature of communities is to have some kind of commonality, to have a point of communion for all within them, and to stress similarity, not difference. Such stress on similarity is taken to be a threat to the sacredness of moral autonomy, the right of each individual to develop her own unique moral stance, and to exercise her unique gifts and talents.

Respecting the Otherness of the Other

The autonomy of each individual self is always qualified by the presence of the 'Other', of that which is different and to which one must make a response. Sometimes the presence of the Other is an inescapable, perhaps even lamentable, intrusion upon the more fundamental singularity of the individual self. As Zygmunt Bauman puts it, from within a rationalist or pre-deconstructionist mentality, "as a moral person, I am alone [solitude marks the beginning of the moral act], though as a social person I am always with others; just as I am free though entrapped in the dense web of prescriptions and prohibitions."[34] The tension and paradox of an essentially solitary self in communion with other, equally solitary selves, is an intrinsic part of this Enlightenment construal of morality. The community that emerges from solitary selves "entrapped in the dense web" is one that is understood as "the achievement of lonely moral persons reaching beyond their solitude in the act of self-sacrifice." But, given its starting point, this ethic can only heroically and paradoxically affirm that at "the heart of sociality is the loneliness of the moral person."[35]

Certainly a Biblical theistic ethic would uphold the significance of sociality. But it would do so in a far different spirit than that outlined by Bauman's depiction of the solitary moral self who reaches community only on the basis of heroic, and even tragic, attempts to break free of its essential prison of loneliness. For Biblical ethics, each self is grounded and has its being in a primordial relationship with its creator and primary, abiding, and completely trustworthy lover, God. Even when that relationship is partially broken it is never destroyed. Our very being remains grounded in God's love even when we refuse it.[36]

If Bauman is right that postmodern ethics breaks with modern moral philosophy precisely by readmitting the Other "into the hard core of the moral self" and recasts the Other "as the crucial character in the process through which the moral self comes into its own,"[37] then it is just catching up to insights that have preceded it by thousands of years in the experiences that constitute the religious core of both Judaism and Christianity. But where it differs from the theistic construal is in terms of the primordial reality of the self-Other relation. If the Other is already knit tightly into the hard core of the moral self, it nonetheless remains true for postmodern ethics that "being for the Other" has no ontological foundation, no cause, no ultimate reality on which it rests.

Postmodern morality is what Bauman calls "an act of creation *ex nihilo*, if there ever was one."[38] This leaves postmodern philosophy with the right result (responsibility for the Other's flourishing) and the wrong (or no) reason why. It has no place for the act of a divine personal being whose will and power have established the conditions of reality such that human beings are primordially, ontologically bound together with God and with each other and, through that bond, able to flourish. The result is that postmodern ethics has to proclaim sociality or solidarity with others 'irrationally'. It becomes a 'surd', an unexplainable given or ungrounded free choice for which one can give no justification. Consequently, it has to rest content with a plurality of communities (the ethnocentric turn proclaimed by Richard Rorty), and must forgo any attempt to establish ontological links (except of the thinnest kind) between these communities. The theistic vision, conversely, has at hand, in God's creative and sustaining power, the ontological link that binds all humans together with each other and with God in ways which deepen diversity and individuality without sacrificing mutuality and love.

The fear that this bond between all persons, because of God's unifying will, must flatten out differences is quite unfounded. Everything depends on *how* God expects flourishing to take place. If to flourish is to become just like everyone else in all respects, then clearly we had all better be radical pluralists and give up attempts to conform to the divine intention. But if in God's mind flourishing *entails* the celebration of individual and cultural diversity, the exuberance that comes with being in the presence of and helping to nurture the differences that vitalize community, then flourishing is not predicated on a drab and flattened sameness.

Karl Rahner has claimed, in the context of a Christian ethic, that "the human person of flesh and blood ... possesses intrinsic significance and is an end and not a means" This unique person is "more than the point of intersection of general truths and maxims, more than the particular instance of a multipliable essence."[39] There is an *individuum ineffabile* that cannot be overridden by general moral principles. Person and community are, in short, "correlative; as persons we are intended for community with God and other persons, and real community exists only where our nature as persons is protected."[40] There is no ultimate paradox between communion and uniqueness. In the words of secular moral philosopher Paul Wright, "personal relationships provide the individual with one way, perhaps the most effective way, of maintaining a sense of individuality."[41]

Relationality and Freedom

One of the apparent paradoxes of the exercise of human freedom (which is certainly one crucial element in any human flourishing) is that it can occur meaningfully only in relation to others. If there is no Other in relation to whom I can act freely, then my freedom has no limits, no constraints, no boundaries, no context within which to define itself. A limitless freedom is ultimately vacuous. A being completely without any Other(s) in its field of action is a being who would have nothing by which or by whom to orient its will. There would be no goals, purposes, intentions, or aspirations *in relation to which* one would set one's actions. A limitless self, having no other in relation to whom it can understand what makes it this self rather than that self, ultimately is no self at all. Therefore, without community, personal freedom and fulfillment are meaningless concepts:

community is the necessary condition of freedom and fulfillment.[42] This fact, it should be noted, would apply to God as well: if God is to have a self, a personality, God must be in relation to what is not God. This is the point that process theology and my own previous work has tried to substantiate. Even God's freedom to act presupposes some Other(s) in relation to whom that action takes place.

Nel Noddings, in her feminist ethic of care, has nicely captured the relationship between freedom and relationality.

> We know ... that we are irrevocably linked to intimate others. This linkage, this fundamental relatedness, is at the very heart of our being. Thus I am totally free to reject the impulse to care, but ... as I chop away at the chains that bind me to loved others, asserting my freedom, I move into a wilderness of strangers and loneliness, leaving behind all who cared for me and even, perhaps, my own self. ... When I have detached myself or because circumstances have wrenched me free, I seek first and most naturally to reestablish my relatedness. My very individuality is defined in a set of relations. This is my basic reality.[43]

Robert Adams has pointed out that the very substance of personal relationships is the "meeting of will with will, which almost always involves conflict at some level." This conflict is part of the process of differentiation by which one self becomes itself in and through the presence of other selves. Adams argues that it is only through conflict that we know the others as others. We need opposition, for example, between our wills and our parents' if we are to successfully differentiate ourselves from them. [See the earlier discussion of object-relations theory on pages 99–104]. "The fact that the world is in some ways contrary, and in some ways unresponsive, to our wills is what keeps us from regarding it all as an extension of ourselves. . . . Interpersonally, the independence of will from will ... is essential to the reality of relationship."[44] (See the earlier section on epistemology in which reality was defined as that which is 'in opposition', pp. 36–38.)

While Adams perhaps overplays the element of outright conflict, he is right on target in observing that psychologically the self needs its differentiation and distinction from the other in order to flourish as the self that it is or can be. And this means that personal wholeness, flourishing, well-being, and fulfillment require difference within a community that is predicated on mutual love. Love does not mean doing away with the self (see the section on reconciling self-regard and agape, pp. 125–129). It does mean recognizing the necessity of differentiation between lovers provided that differentiation is in the service of the personal growth of each so that their mutual love can be enriched. But this is a far cry from the notion that only by breaking all bonds and striving for self-sufficiency can one achieve genuine wholeness. Mutuality, by its very nature, reconciles both the drive toward becoming a unique self and the drive toward communion with others.

Consider a couple very much in love over a long period of time. Clearly they are bound together by a mutual concern for each other's flourishing and well-being. Each cares for the other as other, and who that other is uniquely. This means that each wants to nurture, enhance, support, and affirm those unique capabilities or gifts that distinguish the other as other. But not only will their ways of showing affection change over time, their ways will not be the same as the ways other couples show affection. In short, there is a multitude of different ways in which people express the underlying components of flourishing (given the multitude of gifts that fulfill them), but in each and every case the differences are grounded in the underlying commonality of affection, trust, love, mutuality, and nurture.

The Need for Communities of Discourse

James Gustafson has pointed out that a theocentric ethics requires 'communities of discourse' [this phrase has strong links with postmodern language such as that of Rorty] because no one person ever can have the full knowledge or abilities necessary for acquiring her well-being. The very discernment of what counts as well-being for this particular person requires a common context of support. No one has complete knowledge of all the factors relevant to predicting the outcome of a proposed course of action. The discernment of the relevant data and analyses, according to Gustafson, "ought to be a social as well as an individual process."[45]

This is the bottom line theistic ontological affirmation: we cannot be ourselves, we cannot be for others, we cannot flourish or be fulfilled except in and through relationships of mutual love undergirded and empowered by God's love and action. The commonality and the differences fit together like hand in glove because they both flow out of a common human nature created and sustained by a common intention continually enacted by a common and unifying divine power. There are many different hands and many different gloves, but all must work together, hand in hand, glove in glove, set to a common task of building up a community in which all can flourish uniquely but also together in mutuality.

Reconciling Self-interest and Love

There is much recent work trying to go 'beyond self-interest' among non-theistic-moral philosophers, especially those who have been informed by the empirical findings of modern psychology.

'Altruism,' the term most often used by such work (see Laurence Thomas' work referred to earlier), is perhaps not the best word to capture what a theistic moral ontology understands by the notion of agape, or heterocentric, other-oriented love or mutuality. Often altruism simply means an ability to consider the interests of other people. As such it is too anemic to cover what Christians, for example, mean by agape. Unless altruism is given more precise definition and refinement, it can be predicated simply on a *quid-pro-quo* basis that is essentially ego-centric rather than hetero-centric. Christian love, however, understands genuine agape to be fully centered on the needs of the other with little overt concern for what benefits one will reap in return.

There is a great deal of debate among Christian scholars about the degree to which self-interest can be made compatible with agape or altruism. One reading of the Christian tradition's notion of agape is that it is entirely devoid of *any* self-interest. As Anders Nygren understood agape, it was *completely* unselfish, focused only on the good of others, not because they had any intrinsic worth but because of God's original selfless act in loving worthless human beings. For Nygren if agape is to any degree mixed with *eros* (the pursuit of a good desired by and for the self), it ceases to be agape and reduplicates human sin and depravity. "*Eros* is always man's attempt to 'establish his own righteousness', to make himself fit for the vision of God; and it must therefore be ruthlessly extirpated to make room for the entry of agape."[46]

But in this ruthless form, agape runs the risk of devaluing the one who loves agapaically. If the self does not matter and has no worth, then one could well wonder why its love should matter to any one at all: who wants to be loved by a worthless self? What value would such love have? Gene Outka has argued that "altruism cannot be endorsed unqualifiedly, *if* endorsement signifies that the self does not matter."[47] And the theistic moral ontology makes clear why this is so: if it is grounded in the human response to God's acts and intentions, then clearly it must value what God values. And in loving human persons, God has affirmed them (in their essential being, if not in all that they do or have become under the power of sin).

If God loves us, we cannot be faithful to God's love if we refuse to love ourselves. "Love for God," Outka claims, "includes fidelity to God in loving whom God loves." This leads to the affirmation that God's love is universal, extending to all persons. Such love requires that we neither "exclude our neighbors nor ourselves as subjects of attention and care."[48] If God loves us, who are we to say that God has loved inappropriately? And if God's love gives us value, why would we want to deny that value (and run the risk of impugning God's wisdom in loving us) by denying ourselves some sense of self-worth and self-affirmation?

Of course, for Christians love for oneself is grounded in God's prior love for us. We are not the primordial givers of value to ourselves. If God does, in fact, value us, and in the process gives us the freedom and power to value what God values, then we are given the ontological support and motivation for valuing ourselves. To hate ourselves for the sake of others devalues the very thing God values.

Outka is aware of the importance of mutuality in the context of inclusive community for a full working out of agape. Altruists, he argues, "abandon any focus on a purely private self-other situation. To think of an isolated self meeting an isolated neighbor is too abstract. Our meetings always occur within an array of social relations."[49] The kind of universal love he sees as definitive of Christian agape has to take self-regard into account if, among other things, the self is to be an effective bearer of agape toward others.

If I do not pay sufficient attention to my ability to be a good father (if I do not attend to those things such as my health, my finances, my time with my children), then I cannot be a good father and being a good father is part of what it means for me to act in a true agapaic way toward my children. We need to be free enough both from ourselves and from others to ask what considerations of self-regard can make us effective agents of love.[50] A Christian ethic, therefore, is not required to choose between self-love and heterocentric love. They can be reconciled through God's love for all persons and by the empirical realities of life as it is actually lived in a mutually loving community.

Mutuality, rather than an altruism that has no place for self-regard, also provides a larger context within which the needs of all members of the community can be met without excessive or unrestricted heterocentric and egocentric love. In loving others agapaically, one does not demand a quid-pro-quo response, but "one nonetheless desires and hopes for a response, and takes actual attainment as both a genuine possibility and as the fruition it seeks. We should say then that mutuality is the internal, ideal fruition of agape."[51] The desire for our own fulfillment is simply part of the human package that God has created and given value.[52]

Paul Wright, writing from a secular perspective, has observed that while a relationship may be said to be maintained by selfish motivation, "the selfishness involved is the satisfaction of having one's individuality affirmed."[53] But the secret to mutual community is that, again as Wright notes without reference to Christian community:

> While one partner is reaping this selfish reward, the other partner is reaping exactly the same reward. ... If we found a relationship rewarding because our partner affirmed such self-attributes as loyalty or altruism, we would not be inclined to say the partner is in that relationship only for what can be gotten out of it. It would be just as accurate to say the person is in that relationship only for what can be put into it. ... [T]he participants ... seem to regard mutual rewardingness as basic to personal relationships, and not a reflection of either their own or their partner's selfishness.[54]

Concern for one's own well-being or fulfillment, therefore, should neither be singled out for excessive blame (as a sign of depravity) nor for excessive attention (as in the contemporary focus on individual self-fulfillment). If we fail to acknowledge our own need of and desire for fulfillment (flourishing and well-being), then we are unlikely to be open to receiving those forms of nurture and support that others offer us for our fulfillment. I must be at least aware of my need for fulfillment if I want to be able to inform others of what they can do to fulfill me, given that that is one of their basic motivations in a true mutual community. An individual who is so self-abnegating as to become willfully ignorant of her own needs, will wind up completely frustrated. She will lack 'effective agency' for getting what she needs for the particular form of fulfillment that is hers (for example, as a painter, writer, or teacher), and, lacking those gifts, she will not have sufficient power and self-affirmation to be a generous, intelligent, mature giver of her gifts to others.

If the one whose need for fulfillment becomes self-obscured or hidden fails to communicate with others who stand ready to provide for that need, both giver and receiver of gifts will suffer extraordinary relational frustration. At the very least, the giver will be driven to treat the unrevealing recipient more and more as an 'object', as one unable or unwilling to provide him with the knowledge necessary to make his giving effective. It would also be the case that someone who has come to believe that she, through a combination of God's grace and her own discernment of reality, now understands the nature of fulfillment and its ontological grounding, must want to share that belief with others.

This is the point at which a theistic ethic must rest on the claim that its construal of reality is right, that it reflects the way things are, or, more specifically, what God is really up to in the world. To share that construal with others means, in part, that the individual believes that it is right *for her*, as well as for others. She must be convinced that *her fulfillment matters*. If it did not matter to her, if she thought herself of no value whatsoever, then she would not value her own fulfillment. And if she could not value it, why would she want to make others aware of the possibilities for their fulfillment?

One's active concern for the well-being of others "implies a clear conception of what is best for them, which must, in consistency, be also in essential what is best for ourselves."[55] One who loves the neighbor as oneself "must be willing to offer him that view in which one finds one's own fulfillment."[56] The point is that fulfillment, in fact, comes about most effectively (given God's intention and the structures of reality that God has created) when we seek the fulfillment of others while they, in mutual love, seek ours, provided that all parties are sufficiently self-aware, mature, and able both to receive and to give intelligently, openly, and freely. And when mutuality truly flourishes, as one hopes it will in a community committed to a theistic moral ontology, then we can rely on (trust in) the love of others for our fulfillment without making our fulfillment the first or overriding intention behind our own actions. "Where benevolence is mutual, one can rely entirely on the neighbor's love."[57]

One of the great ironies of this view of mutual fulfillment is that if it should ever be achieved, if we truly lived in communities of agape and heterocentric affection, most of the issues that now bedevil ethical theory would virtually disappear. In this respect, the thrust of anti-theory is affirmed. As Bonhoeffer and others have argued, ethics only emerges when there is a *disruption* in relationality. John Hardwig has argued that most moral philosophies presuppose an impersonal field of relationships as the ground of ethics in which relationality is factored out. Most moral philosophers:

> have unconsciously assumed a context in which we mean little or nothing to each other and have then asked themselves what principles could be invoked to keep us from trampling each other in the pursuit of our separate and often conflicting interests. ... What we now study and teach under the rubric of ethics is almost entirely the ethics of impersonal relationships.[58]

Certainly a deconstructionist and postmodern ethics presumes this kind of radical discontinuity and division between persons as each struggles for his or her own vision of the good. And the ethics of most so-called realistic political philosophies is an ethics of fear of others and defensiveness for the self. The stress on moral autonomy reflects this fear for the self and of others who are perceived to be its enemies. When we cannot defeat our enemies, our so-called 'realistic' social ethics at least tells us how we can neutralize them or co-opt them into schemes of cooperative behavior that work out best for all of us. But generally there is a sense that others are necessary evils, not fundamentally essential to the core of our being. I need a political or social ethics for my relations with these others because I need to define the boundaries by which we can each negotiate our respective private 'spaces' in the social arena, not because they are essential to the very core of my being.

But as Hardwig points out, when I am fully invested in a loving and fulfilling relationship with other persons, I do not need an ethics of personal relationship. "We do not search for what we already have. ... Ethics is unnecessary where genuine care is present in a personal relationship, since we do not need an ethics to protect us from those who understand us and care about our interests."[59] Of course, in a contingent, ambiguous, flawed world, personal relationships, even those between religious persons, will always fall short of full mutuality. And so an ethics of some sort will be needed. But it might be closer to what Hardwig calls an ethics of 'aspiration' than of protection. We need a vision of the end toward which God is calling us if we are to negotiate successfully the shoals and dangers along the way. Relationships, embedded in the contingencies of individuals, time, and history, change constantly. Unless we have some sense of what direction to retune and refine them toward, we will have no sense of what to aspire to for our and others' flourishing.

The Biblical view of fulfillment through mutual love is not shared, at least with respect to its theistic and ontological foundations, by most secular moral philosophers. Nevertheless, there are, as I have tried to suggest, important secular analogues to a theistic agapaic ethic. Many secular scholars are committed to the view that persons do, in fact, want to be fulfilled and to flourish. And that fact requires some balance between self-regard and other-regard.

The insight among many non-theistic-moral philosophers that some form of community participation helps to mitigate the worst effects of selfishness opens up moral philosophy to the insights of a theistic moral ontology. What that ontology insists upon, however, is a notion of community that, unlike an army or other secular forms of sociality, is composed of members each of whom is motivated toward all the others agapaically, that is, in a genuine mutually heterocentric (as opposed to egocentric) way. This notion of community can build upon (but not be reduced to) the underlying minimal notion of sociality that grounds many secular moral philosophies. A fuller development of this idea is taken up in Chapter 9.

Notes

1 See especially Martha Nussbaum, 'Non-Relative Virtues: An Aristotelian Approach', in Peter French, Theodore E. Uehling, Howard Wettstein, eds., *Midwest Studies in Philosophy: Volume XIII Ethical Theory: Character and Virtue*, (Notre Dame, IN: University of Notre Dame Press, 1988).
2 *Ibid.*, p. 33.
3 *Ibid.*, p. 44.
4 Martha Nussbaum, *The Fragility of Goodness*, (Cambridge: Cambridge University Press, 1986), pp. 355–357.
5 *Ibid.*, p. 44.
6 *Ibid.*, p. 45.
7 *Ibid.*, p. 49.
8 David B. Wong, 'On Flourishing and Finding One's Identity', in Peter A. French, Theodore E. Uehling, Jr., and Howard K. Wettstein, eds., *Midwest Studies in Philosophy Volume XIII Ethical Theory*, p. 327.
9 *Ibid.*, p. 327.
10 *Ibid.*, p. 328.
11 Taylor's quote is from 'What is Human Agency?' in Theodore Mischel, ed., *The Self: Psychological and Philosophical Issues*, (Oxford: 1977), Wong, 'On Flourishing and Finding One's Identity', p. 328.
12 Wong, 'On Flourishing and Finding One's Identity', p. 329.
13 *Ibid.*, p. 333.
14 *Ibid.*, p. 334.

15 Laurence Thomas, 'Moral Motivation: Kantians Vs. Humeans', in French, *et al.*, *Midwest Studies in Philosophy*, p. 380.

16 Robert M. Adams, 'Common Projects and Moral Virtue', in French, *et al.*, *Midwest Studies in Philosophy*, p. 305.

17 *Ibid.*, p. 305.

18 *Ibid.*, p. 305.

19 Laurence Thomas, *Living Morally*, (Philadelphia: Temple University Press, 1989), p. viii.

20 *Ibid.*, p. 29.

21 *Ibid.*, p. 60.

22 *Ibid.*, p. 88.

23 *Ibid.*, p. 138, note 3.

24 Annette Baier, 'Trust and Antitrust', p. 347. In Joram Graf Haber, ed. *Doing and Being: Selected Readings in Moral Philosophy*, (New York: Macmillan, 1993). Originally published in *Ethics* 96, 2 (January 1986).

25 Thomas, *Living Morally*, p. 181.

26 *Ibid.*, pp. 193–194.

27 *Ibid.*, p. 194.

28 Baier, 'Trust and Antitrust', p. 356. Baier is, however, deeply suspicious of a trust that rises to a 'creator-God' because such a theological trust is, in her opinion, an "infantile residue of . . . this innate readiness of infants to initially impute goodwill to the powerful persons on whom they depend." Baier has an extraordinarily truncated and ill-informed view of God, but she is right to link infant trust to trust in God since, as object-relations theory has observed, how we are treated by and respond to our parents dramatically affects our view of God. What she completely avoids considering, of course, is whether God exists and acts toward us in ways that ought reasonably to generate our trust in God as the one who demonstrates trust*worthiness* over and over again in and through God's historical acts on behalf of human flourishing. And if we experience God's love primarily in a mutually supportive and loving community then the Christian moral ontology has a significant point of correspondence with more secular views of trust and identity.

29 Thomas, *Living Morally*, p. 194.

30 *Ibid.*, p. 232.

31 Wong, 'On Flourishing and Finding One's Identity', p. 335.

32 *Ibid.*, p. 336.

33 This may be partly understood in Freudian terms: to get rid of the 'bad' father who fails to recognize the uniqueness of each of his children, it is necessary to kill him in order to liberate each child to do its own unique 'thing'.

34 Zygmunt Bauman, *Postmodern Ethics*, p. 60.

35 *Ibid.*, p. 61.

36 Despite what I think are some fundamentally wrong turns in Paul Tillich's overall ontology, he is right on the mark at this point. We find the courage to go on being because our very being is still grounded in the power of being that comes from God. Those Protestants (and even Luther and Calvin are not unambiguous on this point, despite what some of their more radical followers would claim) who stress the utter worthlessness and depravity of human nature obscure the reality of God's continuing love toward even those persons who freely continue to reject that love.

37 Bauman, *Postmodern Ethics*, p. 84.

38 *Ibid.*, p. 33.

39 Karl Rahner, quoted by Gustafson, *Ethics From a Theocentric Perspective*, p. 71, note 109.

40 James Gustafson, *Ethics From a Theocentric Perspective*, pp. 71, 76–77.
41 Paul H. Wright, 'The Essence of Personal Relationships and Their Value for the Individual', in George Graham and Hugh Lafollette, eds., *Person to Person*, (Philadelphia: Temple University Press, 1989), p. 25.
42 See Eric Loewy, *Suffering and the Beneficient Community*, (Albany: State University of New York Press, 1991), p. xvi.
43 Nel Noddings, *Caring: A Feminine Approach to Ethics and Moral Education*, (Berkeley: University of California Press, 1984), p. 51.
44 Robert Merrihew Adams, 'Religious Ethics in a Pluralistic Society', in Gene Outka and John P. Reeder, Jr., eds., *Prospects for a Common Morality*, (Princeton: Princeton University Press, 1993), p. 106.
45 Gustafson, *Ethics From a Theocentric Perspective*, Vol. 2, p. 316.
46 'Agape', in John Macquarrie, ed., *Dictionary of Christian Ethics*, (Philadelphia: Westminster Press, 1967), p. 199.
47 Gene Outka, 'Universal Love and Impartiality', in Edmund N. Santurri and William Werpehowski, eds., *The Love Commandments*, (Washington: Georgetown University Press, 1992), p. 30.
48 *Ibid.*, pp. 2–3.
49 *Ibid.*, p. 81.
50 *Ibid.*, p. 82.
51 *Ibid.*, p. 89. For a fuller development of the notion of mutuality, see Frank G. Kirkpatrick, 'The Logic of Mutual Heterocentrism: the Self as Gift', *Philosophy and Theology*, 6, 4 (Summer, 1992).
52 See John Whittaker, ' "Agape" and Self-Love', in Santurri and Werpehowski, *The Love Commandments*, p. 228.
53 Paul H. Wright, 'The Essence of Personal Relationships and Their Value for the Individual', in George Graham and Hugh Lafollette, eds., *Person to Person*, p. 28.
54 *Ibid.*
55 Basil Mitchell, quoted in Santurri and Werpehowski, *The Love Commandments*, p. 30.
56 John Whittaker, *ibid.*, p. 232.
57 John P. Reeder, Jr., 'Analogues to Justice', *ibid.*, p. 286.
58 John Hardwig, 'In Search of an Ethics of Personal Relationships', in Graham and Lafollette, eds., *Person to Person*, p. 63.
59 *Ibid.*, pp. 64, 78.

Chapter 8

Moral Rules and Contexts

The Ethics of Feminism, Natural Law, Marxism, and Virtue

Feminist Ethics

Feminist ethics brings out a number of the themes we have examined linking secular and religious ethics in the theistic traditions of the West. Relationality is at the core of that linkage. Both feminist ethics and Biblical ethics are suspicious of the notion of the radically autonomous, self-sufficient moral individual. And both want to highlight the importance of the experience of mutuality.[1]

For many feminists the liberal privileging of the autonomous self is not the right starting point for reflection on our relationships with others. As Rita Manning puts it:

> a feminist ethic should not take competent, independent, adult humans as its paradigm, nor should it presuppose that humans are abstract individuals. It must recognize that humans are connected by social relationships, that their self-identities are colored by these relationships, and that their welfare requires that at least some of these relationships be intimate and sustaining.[2]

And Nel Noddings, who has elevated the act of caring to the highest moral level, has argued that a feminine[3] ethic (which is for men as well as women) is "rooted in receptivity, relatedness, and responsiveness. ... [R]elation will be taken as ontologically basic and the caring relation as ethically basic."[4]

As in a theistic moral ontology of mutuality, Noddings (who is decidedly non-theistic)[5] is careful to distinguish relationality from relations of contractual obligation that characterizes more traditional individualistic theories from Plato to Rawls.[6] We perceive caring as constitutive of the good and make at least a tacit ontological claim about it as being "better than, superior to, other forms of relatedness."[7] It is something all human beings strive for and long for.[8] As she develops her ethic of care Noddings touches on many of the key elements in a theistic ethic that we outlined: the pragmatic, contextual nature of moral decision-making, relationality, the respect for the other, and the restoration of healthy selves aiming for mutuality in relationship.

Caring is a very close analogue to agape and altruism because it takes the needs of the other seriously, often putting them ahead of the needs of the care-giver. (Noddings is not unaware of the problem of losing oneself in the other but believes it is a risk that the caregiver must take. Caring does increase one's vulnerability, but as I strengthen the one for whom I care, she will in turn be strong for me, and in this sense I do not fully 'relinquish myself' in the caring relationship.[9])

She argues that "caring is both self-serving and other-serving ... it has no problem in advocating a deep and steady caring for self."[10] But how this care for self is ontologically grounded in the care that others extend to the care-giver Noddings does not make entirely clear. She would have to argue that unless the care-giver cares for herself she cannot be an *effective* agent of care. She would also have to argue that if her care is 'successful' the one cared-for will then be empowered to care for her.

One crucial aspect of caring is that it takes seriously the particularities and uniqueness of the others toward whom it is directed. The care-giver must take into account the actual needs of the one being cared-for. This means that the care-giver must "try to apprehend the reality of the other ... I realize that there is invariably this displacement of interest from my own reality to the reality of the other."[11] This notion of displacement ("my motive energy flows toward the other ... I put it at the service of the other"[12]) echoes what Macmurray is getting at in his articulation of the heterocentricity of mutual relations, focusing upon the other's need before my own. And clearly, caring-for is essentially a responsive set of actions: I cannot adequately care for someone until and unless I am able to respond to *her* needs, not as I blindly think they are, but as she makes them known to me. This is the basis of my need to know *objectively* who and what the other is in herself and what she needs.

Nevertheless, even the care-giver in her appropriate context-sensitive response to the needs of others, has to be on guard against her own tendency to define *for* the other what her needs are. She must balance her responsibility to maintain her critical faculties of discernment that may not always conform to what the one being cared for demands and her responsibility to hear what the other is truly saying. We have to 'move away from the other' temporarily if we are to assess effectively what she has given us to respond to. The care-giver must not *disrespect* the rights of the cared-for and arrogate the right to define for him what he needs without his participation. But the reality of the other and our objective thinking about it must remain "tied to a relational stake at the heart of caring."[13]

Each person in the caring relation has inalienable rights that are not abrogated simply because one is being cared-for. Without these rights, Joan Tronto argues, the care-giver might be tempted to view the situation too narrowly and in the process "to stifle diversity and otherness."[14] The dependence of the cared-for is intended to be temporary, not permanent. As we have seen in our treatment of object-relations theory, any healthy mutual relationship requires the integrity, health, and wholeness of each partner. One-sided dependence, rather than healthy interdependence, cannot make for mutually enhancing relationships. It is possible, however, as some of Carol Gilligan's studies show, to understand dependence not as helplessness or powerlessness, but as signifying that "interdependence of attachment empowers both the self and the other, not one at the other's expense."[15]

Rita Manning has argued that there are seven desiderata that ought to constitute an "adequate and thus a feminist ethic".[16] Each of these corresponds, I believe, to an ethic of mutual love that reflects God's intention for the human creation (though Manning does not, like Noddings, incorporate any theistic claims into her ethic). These seven criteria are:

1. 'A picture of the self that grants the connected nature of humans.' Obviously a theistic moral ontology would argue that this connectedness is part of God's

design for the world, including what God intends for the fulfillment of human nature, broadly conceived.

2. 'A model of reasoning that is contextual, with rules of thumb grounded in experience.' A theistic ethic, understanding that persons live in specific contexts (and not just nowhere or everywhere, timelessly or spacelessly), is also highly contextual. It, too, can accept rules of thumb whose origin and 'test' are ultimately pragmatic.

3. No sharp division between theory and practice. Again, assuming the epistemology I have already developed, a theistic ethic understands practice as primary, with theory playing the important but functional role of enabling practice to be more effective in achieving the intention of mutuality.

4. An understanding of beliefs grounded in experience, and guidance about practical life. What was said above under criterion 2 would be re-affirmed here. Experience is too broad a term in Manning's ethic. Not all experiences count if some are destructive of human integrity, wholeness, health, and well-being. But on a neo-pragmatic understanding of the relation between theory and experience, this criterion is consistent with a theistic ethic.

5. No dichotomies between reason and emotion, mind/body, culture/nature. We have already argued for the importance of what Macmurray calls the rationality of emotion, the role of feeling and objectivity in ethics, and for the treatment of the human person as an integrated, non-dualistic being.

6. A concern with problematics not only of the private but of the public sphere as well. This criterion echoes (without the theistic grounding) the religious claim that God is concerned with the whole world and with our relationship to it. A purely private ethic is a contradiction in terms and severely truncates the whole moral self. We have our being in relationality and that means in public actions and relationship as well as in more intimate ones. At the very least, the nurturing of some more intimate forms of relationship can only take place effectively with the support of the more public conditions in which it occurs.[17]

7. An explicit discussion of the moral conceptions expressed by the ethic. This is Manning's nod to the importance of moral ontology. As long as theory is for the sake of practice, then we are in no danger of reifying theory or isolating it from the actual lives it is intended to serve. But because theories can differ in their hypergoods, we need to be clear about what values, what lives, and what goods are at stake in each operative theory.

A theistic moral ontology has a clear sense of these goods and they clearly have much in common with a feminist ethic. But a theist would want to raise a question about a non-theistic moral theory: what resources within that theory lead its adherent to believe she can successfully achieve her intention? If you have no room for a divine power, are you committed to the view that human beings have it within their power simply to choose to overcome the disabilities that stand in the way of caring and love? If they have it within their power, why haven't they chosen to exercise that power? Is lack of knowledge the source of the impairment in our relationships? Is the control of society by ill-intentioned persons responsible? Is the wrong form of society the culprit? Or is there something deeper, more intractable, more resistant to change without some kind of extraordinary power bearing down on us, that keeps us from achieving what we want? A theist would argue that the reality of sin must be factored into any full understanding of persons in social relations now, and would also point to the renewal of life through God's grace as playing a crucial role in those experiences that stand at the heart of the religious life.

The Fear of Heteronomy

The traditional fear of a heteronomous moral force breaking in upon the self from outside is particularly acute among women who have generally experienced heteronomous power as that which emanates from men seeking to perpetuate male control *over* subordinate, dominated women. Given the reality of political, economic, and sexual domination that women experience, it is no surprise that many feminists reject the notion of a divine being (traditionally characterized in male power symbols) setting the terms for their moral life. And when the institutions that emerge as ostensible representatives of God's power (for example, the hierarchy of Church and synagogue) exercise precisely the same male-privileging, dominating, and oppressive power as the God they claim to represent, women can be rightfully suspicious of any religious ethic that simply repeats and reflects that power structuring.

However, a new case becomes possible if God is radically reconceived as a Person who is in relationships with others that are characterized as mutual, dialogical, responsive, loving, empowering, supportive, non-alienating, and affirming. The God-issue ought to be one of *who* God is; what is God's manifest *character*; and what is God's actual *intention* for human beings? If God, being loving, intends human well-being and flourishing, then what makes women (as well as men) *actually* flourish is what God intends and what God helps to provide (when we cannot bring about full flourishing on our own). The exercise of male dominating power (which dehumanizes, exploits, and demeans) would be the polar opposite of the way in which a truly loving, empowering God would exercise power. If this is an accurate reading of a theistic moral ontology, there is nothing in it, with respect to what counts as fulfillment or flourishing, that is at odds with a feminist ethic.

Christian feminist theologian Susan Frank Parsons has brought together many of the threads binding a Christian moral ontology with a feminist ethic and, in doing so, complements the formulation of the theistic ethic attempted in this book. Accepting that the end for which human life has been made is "mutuality-in-relation,"[18] she has argued for what she calls an "appropriate universalism" for a postmodern ethic. In abandoning all forms of universalism, deconstructionist and postmodern feminists are left without any framework through which to make sense of the lives of women and of their own moral insights.[19] Parsons encourages us to recognize both the finitude which sets limits on human possibilities and the interdependence in which human life is embedded as providing for the multiple and changing possibilities of loving relationships.[20] Within this double recognition of limitation and interdependence, we can develop a framework for an appropriate universalism, "sustained by the compassionate presence of God, and continually offering opportunities for this love to be interwoven into relationships with our fellow human beings and the natural world." In the context of this framework, Parsons urges women to relate to the created world and to other persons so as to transform human life into (using Martin Luther King, Jr.'s immortal phrase) the "beloved community."[21] As a theist, Parsons also notes the significance of an appropriate universalism for grounding theological claims about the whole created matrix within which true human flourishing can be nourished and inspired.[22] She believes that openness to thinking about God is a hopeful sign among contemporary feminist moral philosophers.

Finally, a further word should be said about Carol Gilligan's work. Influenced by object-relations theory, Gilligan understands the moral problem as one of relationality, or, like Noddings, of caring. She contrasts an ethic of care which is undergirded by a "psychological logic of relationships" with an ethic of rights and rules that utilizes the "formal logic of fairness."[23] While Gilligan tends to overemphasize differences between men's and women's approaches to ethics,[24] she clearly opts for an ethic of relationships of intimacy and care rather than an ethic of moral judgments justified by rational, abstract, and transcendent moral criteria utilized by morally autonomous agents.[25] As long as autonomy remains a moral ideal, the individual will be viewed as essentially separate from others. The formal ethic is built on the primacy of hierarchical or contractual relationships. The ethic of care is built on a view of "the self and the other as interdependent and of relationships as networks created and sustained by attention and response."[26]

Gilligan takes issue with psychological theories of development that seek to define maturity as the ability to withdraw from attachments, especially those present primarily in childhood. Because she believes girls have a greater reluctance to withdraw from attachment, they may be perceiving, at a primordial level, that reality supports finding an 'inclusive' relational solution to moral problems, that is, one that keeps the connections with others with whom one may be in conflict open, rather than closing them off by premature moral judgments from the Olympian heights of morally disengaged autonomous rational thinking. This inclusivity is, of course, perfectly in tune with an ethic that sees community as the locus for the solution of moral problems that arise when relationships are disrupted, eroded, or undermined by a false and idolatrous search for radical disengaged autonomy and absolute self-sufficiency.

The only question a theistic ethic might raise about the secular feminist approach to ethics through caring, is that in an unredeemed world, simply appealing to caring may well fall far short of responding to the injustices that sinful structures inevitably produce. Without a realistic assessment of the broken condition of human beings, a condition that tends to make it impossible to rise by our own volition to become compassionate care-givers genuinely concerned about the well-being of those we care for, we may have no way to bring about the right conditions for effective care-giving. In a state of brokenness, our tendency toward idolatrously defining our private and selfish desires as God's goods for everyone needs the correction of structures of 'impersonal' justice.

Marilyn Friedman makes a good point when she argues that we have to be careful not to polarize justice and care. Concepts of justice and care are mutually compatible. Treating people justly does not mean that we cannot care for them. And even in more intimate personal relationships, individuals retain the right to be treated fairly. Fairness she argues, "can be reflected in ongoing interpersonal mutuality."[27] Friedman criticizes Gilligan for failing to recognize the potential for violence and harm in human relationships (though Friedman does not tie the reality of these to any notion of sin). Friedman argues that a justice perspective can never be entirely dissolved in the depths and intimacies of personal relationship. 'The justice perspective' arises "from a more complex, and more realistic, estimate of the nature of human interrelationship"[28] in the larger, more impersonal social arena.

An adequate theistic moral ontology must find a place between nothing-but-justice and nothing-but-mutuality, if it is to speak credibly to the real world in which we live. It must not concede the ground entirely to the so-called hard realists, who (usually on individualistic assumptions) argue for a rigorous structure of justice as the means for protecting the well-defended, fearful self looking out for its own interests in each and every relationship it has. Nor must it allow itself to be seduced into a sentimental, utopian vision of living only in fully mutual human relationships without a scintilla of exploitation and the subtle exercise of dominating power over the partner. Fortunately, a moral ontology grounded in the reality of God and in the reality of human beings responding to God can help it avoid both dangers (at least in theory).

Natural Law

The concept of natural law has always played a crucial role in much theistic moral thinking. It is present not only in the moral theologies of Roman Catholicism, but also plays a significant role in much Protestant thought. It also points to an important link between secular moral thought and religious moral philosophy, one built on the notion that there is such a thing as human nature embedded in a natural created order. As a recent Vatican declaration put it: "In the depths of his conscience, man detects a law which he does not impose on himself, but which holds him to obedience. ... For man has in his heart a law written by God. To obey it is the very dignity of man; according to it he will be judged."[29]

This natural law contains and is constituted by "immutable principles based upon every person's constitutive elements and essential relations – elements and relations which transcend historical contingency. These fundamental principles, which can be grasped by reason, are contained in the divine law – eternal, objective and universal – whereby God orders, directs, and governs the entire universe and all the ways of the human community, by a plan conceived in wisdom and love. Man has been made by God to participate in this law, with the result that, under the gentle disposition of divine providence, he can come to perceive ever increasingly the unchanging truth." Some of the precepts of the natural law have "an absolute and immutable value."[30]

Both this natural law theory and the moral ontology I have been developing affirm the ontological reality of God as the provider of the structures of reality. Both hold that God has a plan for human development (its well-being or flourishing), and that this plan is more or less fixed because it remains God's initiative (which presumably does not change in its essentials) and is sustained by God's power. Both believe that human beings have the freedom to discover through reason what God's intention is, and both hold that human beings can choose to conform to it. In addition, both believe that in adhering to God's intention, we actually contribute to our own fulfillment and well-being. In short, God does not intend for us anything that violates our fundamental nature as persons called into community with God and with each other. The natural law is not heteronomously 'imposed' on us as an alien nature but instead reflects our inner nature as God created it. We were made to 'participate' in it.

Despite their similarities in these respects, however, there is a crucial difference between a moral ontology of a human response to God's actions in the world and some of the more traditional interpretations of the natural law position as enunciated by church authorities. And that difference centers on the flexibility and variation in the application of natural law. I would claim that stressing the immutable dimension of natural law (as the Vatican declaration does) obscures the historical contingencies that have contributed to our reading of it. At the same time, immutability tends to straightjacket our ability to apply natural law principles to the unique, particular, historically different ways in which people live out their natures as human beings intended for community and mutual love.

A New (Old) Reading of Natural Law Theory: Aquinas

Interestingly, however, there are many contemporary natural law theorists who are making the argument that the interpretation of natural law reflected in the Vatican Declaration is not entirely consistent with a deeper, more open, and more nuanced reading of it which, many would argue, can be traced back to St. Thomas Aquinas himself, who is usually taken as the archetypal defender of the traditional natural law position. This more nuanced version of natural law will fit much more smoothly into the theistic ethic I am developing and therefore deserves some extended consideration.

Aquinas, after affirming that all things participate in the eternal divine reason, says that this participation is properly called a law inasmuch as a law pertains to reason.[31] But this gives little specification of what specific laws accord with reason. Aquinas therefore adds a vehicle of specification that he calls the practical reason, the first principle of which is founded on the nature of good *"as that which all things seek after."* The first precept of [natural] law, is "that *good is to be done and promoted, and evil is to be avoided."*[32] Everything that the practical reason discerns as good for the human person belongs to the precepts of the natural law as things to be done or avoided in pursuit of the human good.

But this still seems vague and abstract. Aquinas therefore goes on to claim that everything we have a 'natural inclination' toward is "naturally apprehended by reason as being good." A further specification of the natural law identifies (as a basic inclination the human being has in common with other living beings) the seeking of "the preservation of its own being, according to its nature; and by reason of this inclination, whatever is a means of preserving human life, and of warding off its obstacles, belongs to the natural law."

At a second level of still further specification, Aquinas says that man [sic], in common with other animals, has an inclination through natural law to those things *"which nature has taught to all animals*, such as sexual intercourse, the education of offspring, and so forth."

Thirdly, (now specifying that which is common only to human animals) there is an inclination in the person to that which is proper to the nature of his rationality: "a natural inclination to know the truth about God, and to live in society; and in this respect, whatever pertains to this inclination belongs to the natural law: for example, to shun ignorance, to avoid offending those among whom one has to live, and other such things regarding the above inclination."[33]

It is clear to Aquinas that every person has a natural inclination to act according to reason. And all such acts are virtuous, since virtue is grounded in the eternal reason. But Aquinas observes that there are many things that are done virtuously, "to which nature does not primarily incline, but which, through the inquiry of reason, have been found by men to be conducive to well-living."[34]

Aquinas also concedes that the practical reason "is concerned with contingent matters, which is the domain of human actions; and, consequently, although there is necessity in the common principles [which is the domain of the speculative reason], the more we descend towards the particular, the more frequently we encounter defects." At the theoretical level, moral principles are the same for all rational persons. But at the practical level, Aquinas concedes, "truth or practical rectitude is not the same for all as to what is particular, but only as to common principles; and where there is the same rectitude in relation to particulars, it is not equally known to all. ... As to the proper conclusions of the practical reason, neither is the truth or rectitude the same for all."

Aquinas suggests a situation in which the practical reason can reach different conclusions depending on the circumstances. From the principles of natural law one can conclude that property should be returned to its rightful owner. But in a particular situation, the return would be 'injurious, and therefore unreasonable'. This would be the case if the property would be used to fight against one's country. The overriding of a general moral principle becomes more frequent as one descends towards greater contextual particularity and adds more conditions, "because the greater the number of conditions added, the greater the number of ways in which the principle may fail."[35]

Still further, Aquinas admits that additions to the natural law can be added to in certain respects "for the benefit of human life." Two examples he gives of such 'additions' are the distinction of possessions and slavery, which were not brought in by nature, but devised by human reason for the benefit of human life, even though *"the possession of all things in common and universal freedom"* are of the natural law. And second, a precept may be changed "in some particular cases of rare occurrence, through some special causes hindering the observance of such precepts."[36]

Now it is not at all clear, given Aquinas' increasingly qualified and nuanced understanding of the practical applications of natural law to more and more contingent and particular cases, what if anything remains of the notion that virtually every aspect of human life is ordered by a specific, immutable, absolute moral law. In fact, if Aquinas, invoked as the defender of an absolutist reading of natural law, is taken in the full context of his work, his application of moral law is always towards the particular, the unique, the variable, and the historically contingent (just as anti-theory and a pragmatic notion of moral response to the ongoing work of God in the world have also held).

Aquinas himself says very little about the precise precepts of natural law. Despite this lack of detail, Aquinas scholar Daniel Mark Nelson has argued that Aquinas grounds the practical reason ultimately in the virtuous character of the moral agent. Every agent intends the good, but agents may incorrectly apprehend or construe the good. What will determine their apprehension is the virtuous or vicious nature of their dispositions.[37]

Now a virtue is a habitual or customary trait of character. It is like a second nature. It is an "excellence which enable[s] a human being 'to attain the furthest potentialities of his nature.'"[38] It also presupposes something of an ontological account of human nature, or at least as Jean Porter puts it "a notion of what counts as growth and health for that sort of creature."[39] This means, for Aquinas, that what is in a person's true self-interest is what the person 'ought' to do. As Porter argues, on Aquinas' terms it would not be moral or rational to act "contrary to the well-being of the individual. ... That is why, for Aquinas, moral claims have motivational force even though they are grounded in truths about human nature."[40] And this presupposes a basic view of what constitutes the fullness of human self-interest. Departure from this view, in the actions of the individual, would ultimately express itself "pathologically, if that ideal is indeed grounded in the realities of what it is to be human."[41]

This reading of Aquinas stands in tension with the more tendentious reading of virtue ethicists such as Alasdair MacIntyre and Stanley Hauerwas who tend on occasion to condemn appeals to a universally true notion of human nature.[42] The antidote (that MacIntyre and Hauerwas argue for) to the alienating freedom of the liberal vision of life must be grounded in the objective reality of human fulfillment as lived out in practicing freedom for others. And that, in turn, rests on something like a natural law theory of the self in which failure to obey natural law will entail a loss of true freedom and a stunting of one's full development as a free agent.[43] The problem with MacIntyre's apparent rejection of an objective good for human persons leaves him, according to Porter, with little more than another "liberal/romantic vision which suffers from all the inadequacies of liberal programs that MacIntyre himself identifies."[44] Porter argues, on the contrary, that for Aquinas the goal toward which the successful life must be directed must be the right one, not just any one at all.

On the basis of this reading of Aquinas' treatment of the natural law, Nelson concludes that the basic virtue by which the goal of moral life can be reached is prudence. By focusing on this virtue, one can avoid understanding natural law as providing inflexible moral rules that overdetermine a moral action in any given situation.

Aquinas defines prudence as "right reason about things to be done, not merely in general, but also in the particular, where action takes place."[45] The secondary principles of moral action are acquired by discovery through experience. Nelson suggests, therefore, that we think of these secondary principles as "prudential rules of thumb, moral generalizations based on the experience of a community or of prudent individuals, which are universal in the loose sense that they apply most of the time. ... [T]hey are experientially rather than naturally known."[46] If carried to its logical conclusion, Nelson's distinction between Aquinas' primary and secondary moral principles means that some general moral judgments cover a large number of instances that fall under them, but there is only one first principle of the natural law, namely to do good and avoid evil. Not all moral judgments can be validated by "locating them at some point in the hierarchy of natural law."[47] Each distinct moral judgment is a 'prudential specification' of the general first principle of the natural law that good is to be done and evil avoided. Aquinas clearly admits that there can be legitimate disagreement about the details of natural law. He also contends that "the common principles of the natural law cannot be applied to all men in the same way because of the great variety of human affairs; and hence arises the diversity of positive laws among various people."[48] This sounds almost exactly like a postmodern ethicist arguing from the fact of moral pluralism and contextualism across a wide array of disparate moral communities.

Even the natural inclinations toward which we are directed by our human nature do not, in themselves, provide much specificity with respect to particular moral acts. At best they provide the "very wide boundaries within which prudential reason operates."[49] And the rough guide for prudential reason seems to be what will be conducive to 'well-living'. In other words, under this reading of natural law, flourishing for the full human being insofar as she participates in God's intention for her becomes the goal of moral action, just as the moral ontology defended in this book has also argued.[50]

Germain Grisez and 'New' Natural Law Theory

The link between this reading of a Thomist natural law ethic and a postmodern theistic ethic of response is the mutual focus on the particularity of the moral situation and the centrality of human flourishing as the aim of moral action. The primacy of flourishing is reflected in the work of a number of contemporary natural law theorists. Germain Grisez, one of the 'new' natural law moral theorists, develops a revised version of the natural law theory in which "the fulfillment of persons [rather than a premoral set of absolute norms] has to settle what is morally right."[51] Grisez is critical of scholastic moral theory for being more interested in promulgating prohibitions on human behavior than in moving people toward growth and flourishing. He denies, for example, that there is an objective hierarchy among the primary or basic human goods by reference to which moral choice can be absolutely determined in each and every instance.

Each moral agent has, in what Grisez calls the first principle of practical reason (fppr), an innate capacity to grasp goods as "possibilities" of human fulfillment "in existential reality".[52] What is crucial to this part of Grisez's argument is that the basic goods cannot be ranked, compared, or hierarchialized. They are, in the words of postmodern moral philosophy, incommensurate. This has the open-ended quality of giving the practical reason a multitude of different starting points for the development of the self's basic interests. This is quite the opposite of the traditional reading of natural law in which there is a clear hierarchical devolution of goods and values (from a single hypergood) to which the moral self is subject and which determine the self's moral choices. For Grisez "there is no objective standard by which one can say that any of the human goods immanent in a particular intelligible possibility is definitely a greater good than another."[53]

The goods to which we are oriented, or naturally inclined (to use Aquinas' formulation), are variously called by Grisez possibilities, purposes, values, basic human needs, tendencies, and basic inclinations. "A basic human good is an aspect of 'what one might call human "full-being"' ... definite possibilities of the fulfillment of human persons."[54] The reflexive goods are self-integration, practical reasonableness or authenticity, justice and friendship, and religion or holiness. The substantive goods are life, knowledge, and the activities of skillful work and play.[55]

If the primary goods are incommensurable and do not determine moral choice in a hierarchialized or lexically ordered way, there is need for a principle by which some moral norms can help the moral agent to make moral choices in a given situation. This principle is called by Grisez the first principle of morality (fpm). It says that one ought to choose "those possibilities whose willing is compatible with a will toward integral human fulfillment."[56] (It should be noted that Grisez feels that one important aspect of that fulfillment is communal: "The ideal of integral human fulfillment is that of a single system in which all the goods of human persons would contribute to the fulfillment of the whole community of persons." He rejects individualism as "not consistent with a will toward integral human fulfillment, which requires a fellowship of persons sharing in goods."[57])

There are difficulties in the full development of Grizez' moral philosophy which need not overly detain us here. (For example, how to choose between goods that cannot be evaluated *vis-à-vis* each other, and why he maintains that procreation is an irreducible good not to be overridden by any other good, such as community, or mutuality.) His commitment to the incommensurability of the basic goods becomes a straightjacket on human choice, even when that choice is made by the conscientious moral agent who believes that it will be for integral human fulfillment.

Russell Hittinger summarizes the problem with Grisez in the following way: he lacks a "teleology of the moral self." Each basic good has an end that the self must acknowledge, but the moral self, as such, has no end. Incommensurable values seem more basic and preeminent than persons. The individual is a *homo absconditus* in Grisez's philosophy.[58] Like many of the postmodernists, Grisez winds up not being able to suggest why one choice of life rather than another is better. The choice is ultimately left to "the vagaries of subjective temperament and cultural conditioning."[59]

If Hittinger is correct in his evaluation (and there are further complexities and qualifications both in his analysis and in Grisez that I do not take into account here), then despite Grisez's attempt to make natural law more open-ended and integral to human flourishing in concrete situations, he fails to find a place for the overarching good of mutuality in an objective relationship with a supreme historical agent whose acts work to establish the reality of that relationship.

Natural Law and Human Flourishing

Grisez's reformulation of the scholastic natural law theory (despite its failure to avoid some of its pitfalls), echoes persistent and common themes among a number of contemporary moral theologians who stand in the natural law tradition but who believe that they have identified elements in that tradition that do not commit them to buying the whole scholastic package in which it has usually been wrapped. At the heart of these common themes is the focus on the fulfillment and flourishing of the unique human person in accordance with God's intention. This focus obviously coheres nicely with the moral ontology I am developing. The significance of the natural law theory, they believe, is to remind moral theology that it is subordinate and responsive to the overarching reality of God's intention for human nature as God created it.

As John Macquarrie, who stands in the Anglo-Catholic natural law tradition, sees it, the natural law, rather than being a set of precise and specific prohibitions on any human actions that violate or frustrate the natural inclinations of human nature, should be taken as a norm of responsible conduct, a fundamental guideline that comes prior to rules and precise formulations of law.[60] In Macquarrie's view all moral striving is oriented to the enhancement and protection of the 'true humanity' of persons.[61] Therefore, what natural law prohibits is any action "fundamentally destructive of human relationships" because such relationships are of the very essence of true humanity (as a relational ethic is always at pains to point out). But relationships are essentially open-ended and permit a wide variety of forms of expression.

This means for Macquarrie that human nature is open, always calling the person beyond herself at any particular stage of her becoming. Natural law must be "on the move and cannot have the immutability once ascribed to it." The historical and evolutionary development of persons has in no way frustrated the well-being of human persons. In fact, it has enhanced it.

The natural law, for Macquarrie, is a created inner orientation toward responsible self-development and fuller existence. He argues, in a way that seems congruent with our reading of Aquinas, that "natural law changes, in the sense that the precepts we may derive from it change as human nature itself changes, and also in the sense that man's self-understanding changes as he sharpens his image of mature manhood. But through the changes there remains the constancy of direction."[62]

While Macquarrie does not use these terms, I would argue that the constancy of direction is another way of pointing to the constancy of the overarching reality of God's intention as it is continually enacted in the contingencies of human history. That intention does not (substantially) change and its fulfillment will be the complete and actual flourishing of all human persons in communal relation in and through mutual love. While averse to the language of Macquarrie's Heideggerian metaphysics, the way I have put the point is, I believe, faithful to his conviction that there is an ontological foundation for all human fulfillment, theist and non-theist. Natural law "allows us to see moral obligation in a new depth, as ontologically founded. It safeguards against moral subjectivism and encourages moral seriousness by locating the demand of moral obligation in the very way things are."[63] In this regard, Macquarrie reminds us of the importance of grounding our morality in an ontological reality that is more than what our imaginations have cooked up.

Josef Fuchs

One of the most persistent and informative interpreters of the natural law tradition within Roman Catholicism has been the Jesuit moral philosopher Josef Fuchs. He echoes Macquarrie's commitment to the ontological foundations of natural law. The Church's teaching on natural law assumes that the nature of man is the norm of moral behavior. Natural law defines the objective order of reality and is "ontologically rooted in human nature."[64] But at this level natural law is very general and abstract. It needs to be specified, as our reading of Aquinas suggests he also believed, by the concrete realities of the historical, and historically evolving, human being.

But the 'concrete' forms of abstract natural law, when applied to different historical situations, can be called, according to Fuchs, a 'relative' natural law inasmuch as they are its application to particular situations in salvation history.[65] The principles of absolute natural law "are changed materially according to the accidental changes of the various modes of being in human nature."[66]

This means, in particular, as Fuchs admits, that morality 'demands' that we consider the "historical peculiarities of society."[67] Moral truth must correspond to the concreteness of a specific personal situation that will always be 'richer' than the reality that is judged by more abstract principles.[68] No anti-theorist could have expressed the point more forcefully or clearly. What the anti-theorist misses, of course, is that the sensitivity to the particular situation is due, ultimately, to the ontological reality of God's will as it touches upon the contingencies of history in all their particularity, which rather than annulling the particularities of human historicity, intends them and undergirds them as necessary contributors to the fullness of life in mutual loving community as it is experienced in the ongoing vicissitudes of history.

If Fuchs' reading of natural law is indicative of one school of thought within natural law theory, one that is clearly open to the historical peculiarities of the human situation, then the postmodern critics have been woefully remiss in rejecting theistic moral ontology as expressed in these more sophisticated interpretations. They have also created straw men when they assert that religious ethics requires a timeless application of immutable laws without regard for unique situations, historical contingencies, and the well-being, development, and flourishing of particular individuals. Anti-theorists remain stuck with an outdated, inflexible, immutable concept of God, a concept that vitiates the dynamism, flexibility, and growth that only a living, acting, personal God can bring to life in the world.

Fuchs insists that only by grasping the 'concrete' reality of persons can we find a way through contemporary social problems.[69] He also insists on the strong element of creativity we must exhibit toward that end. This means using our insights and judgments to do the most effective planning and acting that we can.[70] This clearly makes the goal of morality to be human flourishing and the human contribution to that flourishing. Fuchs even suggests that ethics is one of the great cultural achievements of humanity,[71] and, as such accessible to Christian and non-Christian alike.

Roman Catholic scholar Columba Ryan, developing his own interpretation of natural law, echoes this last point of Fuchs'. Determining what is truly human and what will bring about human flourishing is a matter of human discovery.[72] It is not something that simply comes down from above to abstract rational thinkers regardless of historical, existential context. It is part of human flourishing to be an active participant in the determination of what truly constitutes one's further flourishing. And, of course, such participation works best only in community with others. To discover what is human, account must be taken not just of human biology but also of our relationships with others at the human level. What is natural to the person is what constitutes him in relation to others and to the world.[73] Once again, we find confirmation of our claim that community is the context of flourishing and flourishing serves the mutuality that constitutes community.

As Eric Loewy observes, without community, personal freedom and fulfillment are meaningless concepts. "Community is the necessary condition of freedom and fulfillment, the soil in which individual life is rooted and without which it inevitably dies."[74] Within community, what is distinct and particular to each individual is given the resources and support to grow, develop, and reach the fullest possible expression of its potential.

If, as Stephen Layman has argued, "the ways of promoting the fulfillment of others are exceedingly numerous,"[75] then only in a community can one enjoy the plurality and diversity of such ways. But the community remains one (rather than breaking into radically different parts) because the plurality of ways of promoting fulfillment need not be fundamentally at odds with each other. Instead, they can complement and supplement each other: they bring variety to what is, at bottom, a universal need: to help others to become more fully human. It is insane to believe that the various ways of doing this will fundamentally conflict with each other, especially if God has created us all and intends us all to flourish in mutual relations with each other. Some may flourish by exercising their talent for poetry, others by building houses, others by teaching, others by raising children: the list is virtually endless. But they all have one thing in common: they are attempting to bring to fruition what is genuinely human in those persons within their reach. Acts of torture, murder, betrayal, cheating, abuse, neglect, indifference, callousness, denigration, and arbitrary exclusion cannot be made to fit into the category of acts that build up the human. They are, therefore, ruled out of any community whose telos is the flourishing of human beings. As Margaret Farley has argued, there must be a sense of

> commonality in human experience – in the experience of what it means as a human person to rejoice and to be sorrowful, to be protected or violated, nurtured or stifled, understood or misjudged, respected or used. Whatever the differences in human lives, however minimal the actuality of the world community, however unique the social arrangements of diverse peoples, it is nonetheless possible for human persons to weep over commonly felt tragedies, laugh over commonly perceived incongruities, yearn for common hopes. And across time and place, it is possible to condemn commonly recognized injustices and act for commonly desired goals ... The content of universal morality may be modest and in many ways provisional, but it is not empty.[76]

On the other hand, Layman argues, there are many areas of life in which no one way is to be taken as absolutely essential for all persons. "Humanity is remarkably and gloriously complex, with different peoples establishing differing conventions.''[77] Who can count the number of different ways in which people can show affection for each other, or sacrifice for each other, or create bonds of trust between each other? If postmodern ethics is looking to preserve the pluralism of human life, it can do no better than to look to a theistic ethic in which 'remarkably and gloriously complex' forms of humanity are manifested, but always under the guiding intention of bringing persons to their fullest possible flourishing in and through mutual love.

The Limits of Contractual Association: The Case of Marxism

Contenders for the morality that claims to fulfill persons include, in today's world, some forms of association that privilege the individual and others that seem, on the surface, to privilege the social group. Among these are the social forms of capitalism and Marxist socialism. Both, ironically, share a common concern with the development of the individual self though they advocate rather different economic and political structures for fulfilling that concern. In human associations in which the primary and overriding value is the development of the individual self, relations with others generally become contractual forms through which each individual seeks her own good. Neither needs to think about or value the interests of the other for the other's own sake. As Adam Smith pointed out, in defending the contractual basis of atomistic capitalism, ''it is not from the benevolence of the butcher, the brewer, or the baker that we expect our dinner, but from their regard to their self-interest. We address ourselves, not to their humanity, but to their self-love, and never talk to them of our necessities, but of their advantages.''[78] This means that we do not have to concern ourselves with their interests or with the interests of the common good. In Smith's logic, an invisible hand has seen to it that if each pursues his own self-interest, each will be (without directly intending it) promoting the interest of the contractual association as a whole ''more effectually than when he really intends to promote it.''[79]

Even forms of human association that are critical of capitalistic atomism and propose more cooperative forms of relationship tend to see the cooperative association essentially as a means to the end of private flourishing. Karl Marx, who is often hailed not only as the most incisive critic of capitalism's atomistic view of the individual self, but as a strong proponent of an organic view of human relatedness, also winds up with a curious tendency toward viewing others as springboards for the individual's own self-fulfillment. He talks of cooperative activity with others ''as an organ for *expressing* my own life. ... My object [the other person] can only be the confirmation of one of my essential powers.''[80] Bertell Ollman, one of Marx's most astute contemporary interpreters, puts it this way: ''human beings possess those necessary attributes which enable others to achieve complete fulfillment through them.''[81] For Marx, self-determination seems to be a more basic value than mutuality or love. In fact, he seems decidedly hostile to any sense of dependence upon others (such as would be true in any mutual community). As he says in defense of independence, ''a *being* only considers himself independent when he stands on his own feet; and he only stands on his own feet when he owes his *existence* to himself. A man who lives by the grace of another regards himself as a dependent being."[82]

Eugene Kamenka nicely summarizes Marx's underlying attitude toward relations with others when he observes that for Marx (as well as Hegel from whom he drew much of his organic imagery), the logic of the organic model is that the self-determined individual "must become ... the single, all-embracing substance."[83] There is precious little room in this understanding of human relations for the sheer joy of being in the presence of others, of agape love in which one sacrifices one's own interests for the sake of the other, of mutuality, in which one enters into relationship bound to the other in bonds of mutual dependence (or, more accurately, interdependence). Instead, one finds in Marx a tendency to regard human relationships of a cooperative, functional, and organic sort as simply more effective in helping the individual achieve self-determination than are relationships of an atomistic, competitive, and individualistic sort.[84]

This is quite different, despite the apparent overlap in rhetoric about co-operation, from the core notion of a religious community in which the motivating force is communion with others and love for them for their own sakes, not for their ability to serve my needs. The 'other' is received and encountered in her genuine otherness, just as she is encountering me in my genuine otherness to her. In community, the other person is a gift to the self: a person who freely and lovingly seeks the other's good before its own (and whom the self did not create nor from whom the self can demand love as a matter of 'right' – it remains always a gift).[85] "The primacy of the other as gift in the moral situation precludes the understanding of morality or of the other as burden. The first reaction called for [in the presence of the other person] is one of thanksgiving for the gift, of celebrating its presence."[86]

But since we meet in mutuality, each of us seeks the full flourishing and well-being of the other. Flourishing requires mutuality. A fully self-determined person, either in Marx's or Smith's vision, does not need mutuality, but in the Biblically-based moral ontology she does. She needs mutuality for full flourishing, and the structures of reality, as created by God, see to it that if she gives herself fully to others in love, and they to her, then this mutuality will enhance her flourishing. That is the necessary ontological foundation on which a theistic religious community must be built. And its reality and trustworthiness is ultimately due to God's continuing and reliable intention and action to make it so.

Moral Rules and Relational Ethics

It is clear that the theistic ethic I have been defending is one that is highly contextual in nature. It avoids relativism, of course, by insisting that the source of ethics is the non-relative historically enacted will of God. It also holds that human beings attain the fullest possible flourishing and well-being only because they have been given non-relative God-created natures and the underlying structures of reality congruent with the fulfillment of those natures. The content of human flourishing is not completely open-ended because at a deep ontological level human beings have a common nature fulfilled in some ways and not in others. These non-relative ways of flourishing include mutual, intimate, compassionate love, trust, and care, as well as the opportunity to exercise one's gifts and talents as fully as possible in the presence and with the aid of other persons.

In such an ethic, it seems reasonable to find a place for rules of moral action, if not moral absolutes. Generally, rules are norms to which people playing the same game can appeal and by which their actions can be guided so as to play the game successfully; to achieve, in an effective manner, the goal of the game. If the game is how to flourish, then the rules, when adhered to, can help to accomplish that end. Rules work when they can reliably assume a steady, unchanging field of play and some constancy in the goal to be reached. 'Always cut with the grain of the wood' if the purpose of cutting is to get an undamaged and strong piece of wood. This rule, or rule of thumb, works as long as the wood conforms to the general characteristics found in wood and if one wants to cut as straight as possible. If the wood is defective in some serious way, the rule of thumb will be less helpful. Rules work because they prove reliable guides to action with respect to the realities of a particular field of action.

If God's will for flourishing remains essentially unchanged throughout history, and if the core content of flourishing remains essentially the same for all persons, then some universal moral rules designed to guide human behavior toward flourishing in conformity with God's will would seem to be indicated. A theist can invoke one of the most important insights of Kant at just this point: it ought to be a moral rule never to treat another person as a means only, but always as an end. Never exploit persons (and in the process deny them the integrity and dignity of their personhood) in order to achieve some objective that is other than or does not contribute to their flourishing.

The *application* of this rule may become extremely tricky in certain cases. A dying (and comatose) person (who has left a living will), with six hours to live (given every reliable medical estimate), has organs that could be 'harvested' just prior to the official termination of life. Let us assume that these organs, when transplanted, can bring health to at least three additional persons. Their flourishing will certainly be enhanced indirectly by the dying patient's death, since it will make her organs available to them. If his death is hastened by just three hours (by withdrawing life support), so as to increase the likelihood of a successful transplant without rejection by the recipients, is it moral to intervene in this way if the result is a somewhat earlier death than would be the case if he survived all six hours without medical intervention?

Clearly some form of sanctioning of 'pulling of the plug' is based upon an attitude toward the dying person as a means toward an end: his body is the organic field from which a successful, and hopefully beneficial, harvest will be made. Does a hastening of his biological death entail treating him as a means only? Does this violate the moral rule in question?

We cannot resolve the question with absolute certainty. But clearly the notion of flourishing would have to be factored in. The purpose of a Kantian rule is to ensure that we do not treat persons as things, as objects devoid of the capacity to flourish. And the flourishing of the would-be recipients is also morally relevant. What might be central to the practical resolution of the problem is whether the dying patient's flourishing would in any way be affected by a somewhat earlier 'harvest' brought about by an intervention. If he is comatose, it could well be argued that he is not now and (given his prognosis) will never be capable of flourishing. If so, then it is not clear what moral goal is being advanced by keeping his biological body alive any longer when his 'spirit' or consciousness may well be dead and beyond retrieval.

But the point of the moral rule is to remind us of certain important realities before we make a moral decision and act upon it. It does not mean that in every instance setting aside the rule is morally wrong. But we have to have strong and compelling reasons, justified by an appeal to flourishing for all persons, including the dying man, for doing so.

Another Kantian moral maxim, never lie, is a good moral rule that keeps us from easily slipping into the habit of telling falsehoods just because they are more convenient, less troublesome, more immediately advantageous, than telling the truth. Lying may be one of the most easily rationalized acts we perform. A moral rule against lying (especially given the Kantian justification that we would not want to permit others to lie to us) seems both reasonable and useful.

Nevertheless there are circumstances where the flourishing of all relevant parties would be severely diminished by telling the truth. The famous example of whether someone hiding Jews from the Nazis ought to lie when the Gestapo comes to the door inquiring where the Jews are, makes the point well. Clearly the flourishing of those being hidden can only be advanced by lying to the Gestapo. And almost as clearly, the flourishing of the human beings functioning as agents of the Gestapo (in the deepest human sense) is not advanced by participating in or colluding with their inhuman actions. To collude with people who are engaged in actions that demean not only other people's humanity, but in the process their own as well, is not to contribute to their flourishing, no matter how misinformed they are about what is truly in their essential best interests.

It might also be argued that the Nazi, in his capacity as an officer of an evil policy, has lost the status of a moral being who deserves the kind of moral respect that normally would entitle him to be told the truth. To treat him as someone with the same moral rights as his intended victim is to diminish the meaning of morality and, in the process, undermine his potential for becoming what he now is not, namely, a responsible moral being accountable to moral principles that he consciously shares with his fellow human beings.

Casuistry

Moral laws and maxims need always to be subjected to the test of whether they, in practice, advance, retard, or undermine the flourishing of human beings in and through communities of mutual love. This is one of the great virtues of a rule-oriented moral approach known as casuistry. Casuistry seeks to provide individuals with specific, but *case-sensitive* rules and moral guidance. It assumes the existence of moral norms but accepts the fact that in some moral situations these norms are not sufficient to provide definitive resolution of a moral problem. It takes moral rules that are general and applies them specifically.

One of the most articulate modern defenders of casuistry, the Anglican moral theologian Kenneth Kirk, has argued that the purpose of an ''ordered self-discipline" is not to penalize immoral behavior but to "strengthen the weak and restore the falling."[87] This suggests strongly that the application of moral rules of thumb is always oriented toward the flourishing of others, especially those who have difficulty in acting effectively toward their own fulfillment for reasons of impairment. Given this way of understanding casuistry, it loses some of its traditional connotation of being a rule-inflexible, person-insensitive, cold calculus procedure for moral decision-making. As moral philosopher Edward LeRoy Long puts it, casuistry "acknowledges that standards of good conduct must be applied in shifting circumstances, and that definitions of morality that seem altogether permanent are frequently more valuable if expressed in one manner under one set of conditions and in another manner under another set of conditions."[88] Describing casuistry this way makes it difficult to distinguish it from the revised version of natural law that we discussed earlier or from a neo-pragmatic reading of a contextualized understanding of how God's will is manifested in historically contingent situations.

The same family of resemblances can be found in the notion of 'middle axioms', first introduced into moral discussion by J.H. Oldham in 1937. These 'rules' exist "between purely general statements of the ethical demands of the gospel and the decisions that have to be made in concrete situations ... They are attempts to define the directions in which ... Christian faith must express itself. They are not binding for all time, but are provisional definitions of the type of behavior required of Christians at a given period and in given circumstances."[89] Long says that these middle axioms are helpful just to the degree that they are provisional, flexible, and subject to revision in particular, unique circumstances. As time-bound and historical, they make it possible for the general moral norm to make contact with and be informed by the "empirical realities of the present."[90] The terms 'direction', 'provisional', and 'time bound' certainly suggest the contextualized nature of this dimension of theistic ethics without abandoning the implicit notion that there is an unchanging divine will or intention to which responsible moral action is always an historically conditioned response.

In a way, James Gustafson put an end to the debate between the 'contextualists' and the 'principalists' nearly 30 years ago. In his now classic article 'Context Versus Principles: A Misplaced Debate in Christian Ethics', Gustafson pointed out that a contextualist is simply someone who is trying to make moral conduct realistic and responsible, that is, practically effective with respect to the actual conditions obtaining at the time he is acting. He wants to be 'realistic' about what is actually going on, so that he can draw reliable ideas about how to achieve the desired outcome of his moral act.[91] In a theological framework (congruent with that of H. Richard Niebuhr's ethics of the responsible self) Gustafson says that the primary questions for Christian ethics are 'What does God do?'[92] and what are we expected to do in response? Gustafson ties this aspect of contextualism directly to a relational ethic because persons live in relationships which make moral responsibility a particular response to persons or events in the context of a shared or common experience. There is, Gustafson argues, a commonality of moral experience that makes relational ethics entirely appropriate to all persons.[93]

But it is a mistake to think that principles, or moral rules, have no place in this relational, contextual setting. Principles can both illuminate and/or prescribe proposed moral actions in particular settings. Principles can help interpret a situation as falling under moral consideration, guided by a prior notion of the good and the right. But without concrete and changing situations in which to be applied, principles and rules become abstract and vacuous. It is obvious, to Gustafson, "that contextualists find some moral principles or generalizations that give guidance to existential decisions, and that the defenders of principles find some ways to proceed from generalizations to particular situations."[94]

In the end Gustafson argues for what he calls four base points for Christian moral discourse. These include theological affirmations, moral principles, contexts, and the nature of the Christian's moral life. These points are all perfectly congruent with the moral ontology I have been defending. It clearly has theological affirmations: God is at work in the world enacting the divine intention for human flourishing in and through mutual love in community. It has moral principles as those rules of thumb learned through experience and an increasingly sophisticated knowledge of human nature about what does and does not work for human fulfillment. It clearly has contexts as the locale for the actual living out of the human response to God's intention in particular and historically contingent settings. And, finally, it understands that in mutual love, each person's life must embody those intentions and ways of being that lead to the flourishing and fulfillment of others.

What I have been emphasizing is the centrality to these four base points of the reality of God's intention to empower human agents to cooperate with God in bringing the divine intention for them to realization. But since the locus of realization is the historically contingent reality of human life, context is crucial. Nevertheless, the divine intention both reshapes human life and gives its flourishing substantive content, and provides the guidelines for determining what will be realistic and effective in advancing that content at particular times and places. The pivot on which all this turns, therefore, is the reality of God's work in the world and our historical response to it. And this pivot, as should by now be obvious, is the one that defines and locates the moral ontology of flourishing in the lives of those persons who claim to stand within the historic Biblical traditions of belief, experience, and responsible moral action.

Virtue Ethics

Among many contemporary theistic ethicists a great deal is being said today about the importance of what has been called 'virtue ethics'. Developed in opposition to what Edmund Pincoffs calls 'quandary ethics',[95] virtue ethics stresses the centrality of the full moral character of the person-in-relation. The essential issue, for the virtue ethicist, is not what I ought to *do*, but rather *who* I ought to *be*. As Robert Johann puts it, "actions are good only in relation to the goodness of persons."[96] What really matters, according to Stanley Hauerwas, "is not the act itself, but the kind of person we will be."[97]

Virtues, as we have seen, are dispositions by which the individual "translates her general knowledge of that in which her good consists into specific actions."[98] A virtue "involves the exercise of judgment and leads to a recognizable human excellence or instance of human flourishing. Moreover, virtuous activity involves choosing virtue for itself and in light of some justifiable life plan."[99] The truly virtuous person is "one who has succeeded in integrating the multitude of desires and aversion into a unified character, who is able, therefore, to perceive the world clearly from the standpoint to her central commitments, and to act accordingly … Unity of character is the bedrock of a fully virtuous life."[100]

Virtues are an essential part of flourishing, and flourishing is what God intends for each person. Thus, it follows that the ultimate test of any moral theory, rule, principle, axiom, or practice is whether it fosters or retards the development of the *life* of the individual moral agent. The true test of morality is the flourishing person herself. "The flourishing person provides us with the ultimate criterion for deciding what characterizes human flourishing in all specific situations."[101]

But any virtue ethic, according to both Hauerwas and MacIntyre, two of its most prominent defenders, will necessarily be "context-dependent" involving the "particular traditions and history" of a community or society.[102] This puts it at odds with the 'false' universalism of the liberal project of finding an autonomous self, free from the accidents of particular (and limiting) historical traditions, especially those associated with religious communities. From a virtue perspective, virtues help the participating individual to live in fidelity to a particular tradition's moral goal.[103]

As such, virtue ethics fits quite well into a relational picture of Christian ethics. If the purpose of relationship is, in part, to enable the partners in mutuality to flourish as God has intended them to do, then clearly what is at stake, morally, is the full development of the whole person who lives in relation to others. Virtues are simply those dispositions, tendencies, traits, and habits that enable the person to flourish, and in the process to express, as part of her deepest character, her capacity to love, hope, trust, and be responsible for others as well as for herself.

This recalls, of course, Aristotle's understanding that "what constitutes the good for man is a complete human life lived at its best."[104] This means that a virtue ethic is founded on a concept of the good life for human persons. And, in the ontological context of theism, some visions of the good life are more congruent with God's will than others. There is, according to MacIntyre, 'a telos' which defines what is ultimately the good for human life.[105] Such a *telos* suggests an ontological objectivity that transcends the radical relativism of many postmodern versions of human nature. We may be able, MacIntyre concedes, to "disentangle from [the] rival and various claims [of the many different traditions and communities] a unitary core concept of the virtues of which we can give a more compelling account than any of the other accounts."[106] This concession radically qualifies the tendency among some virtue ethicists to relativize the claims of particular communities in which, alone, virtues can be lived out or practiced.[107] It is not necessary to abandon ontological claims about what constitutes the fullness of the flourishing life (grounded in the will and actions of God), in order to defend the historical truth that flourishing life always takes place in and through specific, historically situated communities. And in those communities, virtues are a necessary ingredient in the full life of each flourishing human person and must, consequently, be part of any religious understanding of the goal and purpose of both ethical theory and moral action.

Virtue and Community

But if our argument to this point has been credible, it is equally crucial that such flourishing occurs only within the context of a communal, personal, mutual relationship. The inextricable link between the virtuous person and her community has been stressed by all virtue theorists, including especially those who link virtue theory to a Christian understanding of ethics.[108] Only in the context of community, especially one that is oriented toward the mutual development and flourishing of all its members, can an individual find the concrete embodiment, in both individual lives as well as in traditions and teachings, of what the virtuous, flourishing life looks like.[109]

No person exists outside some kind of relational context. And that context, whether it be that of a purely self-interested contractual arrangement with other persons, a church, or a family, will necessarily create the conditions for and point persons toward a particular kind of life. (In the following chapter, we will take up the thorny political issue of how a 'communitarian' understanding of persons-in-relation relates to a more liberal, individualistic understanding. The issue has important implications for how a religious ethic of community works itself out in a political and social world that does not (or cannot) fully embody a specifically religious commitment to a fellowship of heterocentric and mutual love).

If communities (or associations) of some kind are the soil within which the seeds of flourishing are to grow, then all virtues must be developed and nurtured in and through the relationships persons develop with each other. A theistic ethic, therefore, has to have a special place for the distinctive nature of religious community as the necessary basis for the development of the full person of virtue. And what is distinctive about a religious community responding to the actions of God is its commitment to a belief that its understanding of human life is true.

But the argument of this study is that truth is ultimately 'proven' in the practice of human lives. And that practice must be toward the flourishing of persons-in-relation. As Hauerwas puts it, "the mark of a truthful community is partly seen in how it enables the diversity of gifts and virtues to flourish".[110] Among those virtues, trust and mutual love are paramount. The Biblical theist's moral ontology holds that these virtues are essential parts of the full and true life and that they are part of God's intention for God's human community.

Given the reality of the sin of pride and self-seeking (and its consequence, the inability to truly trust others in their otherness because they are assumed to be a threat to the interests of the self), the theistic moral ontology witnesses to the necessity for divine intervention to help break the stranglehold of sin. At the heart of the religious community is the bold affirmation that God has, in fact, acted in history (both in the life of nations and in the individual lives of persons) to annul the power of sin to block our ability to trust both God and other persons. And that redeemed and renewed ability can be lived out only in a community of other persons who are willing to commit their lives to its truth. For Hauerwas Christian community "is formed by a story that enables its members to trust the otherness of the other as the very sign of the forgiving character of God's Kingdom. ... In a community that has no fear of the truth, the otherness of the other can be welcomed as a gift rather than a threat."[111]

Hauerwas goes on to argue that the 'politics' or social ethic of a Christian should be that of developing virtue among other Christians who are committed to the same moral ontology. True politics is concerned with the development of virtue. The polity of the Church, he argues, is the "truest possible for human community."[112]

The question that now confronts us is whether Hauerwas has judged correctly that the 'politics' of a Christian ethic is essentially 'inner directed' toward the Christian community itself, or whether, as I will argue, a Biblically grounded community has an equally strong obligation to speak to and work with persons whose lives are shaped by other forms of association and visions of the good. Is a religious ethic in the Biblical tradition required to work at gathering the nations to act together in conformity to the one God's will, or to set the nations against each other so that the life of the religious community will shine the brighter by contrast? This is the question of politics and it leads us to our final set of considerations. How does a theistic ethic address the problems of contemporary political philosophy without either betraying its fundamental commitment to the development of full persons in their flourishing (which requires constant reference to the reality and action of God), or betraying its belief that God's intention ultimately includes all persons in all the dimensions of their lives, including the political and the economic?

Notes

1 Beverly Wildung Harrison, *Making the Connections: Essays in Feminist Social Ethics*, (Boston: Beacon Press, 1985). Christian ethicist Beverly Harrison has said emphatically that "mutuality, rather than control, ownership, or paternalism, is a major norm for social ... communication" (p. xix). Harrison has said that she has found Macmurray's notion of mutuality in relationship extremely useful in her moral thinking.
2 Rita Manning, *Speaking From the Heart: A Feminist Perspective on Ethics*, (Lanham, MD: Rowman and Littlefield, 1992), p. 28.
3 She does not use the term 'feminist' and is gently chided for failing to do so by feminist philosopher Marilyn Friedman. (See her *What Are Friends For?*, p. 83, n. 43.)
4 Nel Noddings, *Caring: A Feminine Approach to Ethics and Moral Education*, p. 2.
5 "Women have no need of a conceptualized God, one wrought in the image of man. All the love and goodness commanded by such a God can be generated from the love and goodness found in the warmest and best human relations" (*ibid.*, p. 97). This severely impoverished and false view of God ultimately undermines the ontological foundation of Noddings' ethics. However, it does not diminish the importance of her insights into the nature and dynamics of human love. It only qualifies her belief that such love is possible without the power of divine love to support it.
6 The philosophy of Rawls and the debate over community between liberalism and communitarianism follows in Chapter 9.
7 Noddings, *Caring*, p. 83.
8 *Ibid.*, pp. 4–5. Making such a claim, of course, is quite consistent with Charles Taylor's insistence that we cannot help but affirm some hypergoods as superior to others.
9 *Ibid.*, p. 33.
10 *Ibid.*, p. 99.
11 *Ibid.*, p. 14.
12 *Ibid.*, p. 33.

13 *Ibid.*, p. 36.
14 Joan Tronto, *Moral Boundaries: A Political Argument for an Ethic of Care*, (New York: Routledge, 1993), pp. 161, 163.
15 Carol Gilligan, 'Remapping the Moral Domain: New Images of the Self in Relationship', in Thomas C. Heller, Morton Sosna, and David E. Wellbery, eds., *Reconstructing Individualism: Autonomy, Individuality, and the Self in Western Thought*, (Stanford: Stanford University Press, 1986), p. 249.
16 Manning, *Speaking From the Heart*, p. 28.
17 This theme will be explored more fully later in a section on the relation between community and political/economic society.
18 Susan Frank Parsons, *Feminism and Christian Ethics*, (Cambridge: Cambridge University Press, 1996), p. 219.
19 *Ibid.*, p. 192.
20 *Ibid.*, pp. 197–198.
21 *Ibid.*, p. 198.
22 *Ibid.*, p. 199.
23 Carol Gilligan, *In a Different Voice: Psychological Theory and Women's Development*, (Cambridge: Harvard University Press, 1982), p. 73.
24 It is not clear that men cannot be as relational as women provided they live in and are influenced by a different societal structuring.
25 Gilligan, *In a Different Voice*, p. 164.
26 Gilligan, 'Remapping the Moral Domain', p. 242.
27 Marilyn Friedman, 'Beyond Caring', in Mary Jeanne Larrabee, *An Ethic of Care: Feminist and Interdisciplinary Perspectives*, (New York: Routledge, 1992), p. 263.
28 *Ibid.*, p. 267. John Macmurray, I believe, can provide the proper balance between justice and care and I will develop his argument subsequently in Chapter 9.
29 'The Vatican Declaration on Sexual Ethics', in Jacob Needleman, A.K. Bierman, James A. Gould, *Religion for a New Generation*, second edition, pp. 294–295. The second quotation is from *Dignitatis Humanae*.
30 *Ibid.*, p. 295. Quoting from the Second Vatican Council's Pastoral Constitution on the Modern World, *Gaudium et Spes*.
31 Thomas Aquinas, *The Summa Theologica*, First Part of the Second Part, XIII, Law, Question 91, Articles 1 and 2, in Anton C. Pegis, *Basic Writings of Saint Thomas Aquinas*, Vol. 2 (New York: Random House, 1945).
32 *Ibid.*, Question 94, Article 2.
33 *Ibid.*, Question 94, Article 2.
34 *Ibid.*, Question 94, Article 3.
35 *Ibid.*, Question 94, Article 4.
36 *Ibid.*, Question 94, Article 5.
37 Daniel Mark Nelson, *The Priority of Prudence: Virtue and Natural Law in Thomas Aquinas and the Implications for Modern Ethics*, (University Park, PA: The Pennsylvania State Press), p. 46.
38 Gilbert Meilaender, quoted *ibid.*, who in turn is quoting Josef Pieper, p. 72.
39 Jean Porter, *The Recovery of Virtue*, p. 40.
40 *Ibid.*, p. 48.
41 *Ibid.*, p. 81.
42 See my critique of Hauerwas, Introduction, pp. 10–11.
43 Porter, *The Recovery of Virtue*, p. 81.
44 *Ibid.*, p. 83.
45 Thomas Aquinas, *The Summa Theologica*, Habits, Virtues, and Vices, Question 58, Article 5.

46 Nelson, *The Priority of Prudence*, p. 102.

47 *Ibid.*, pp. 114–115.

48 Thomas Aquinas, *The Summa Theologica*, Law, Question 95, Article 2, Reply Obj. 3.

49 Nelson, *The Priority of Prudence*, p. 121.

50 One could ask, of course, why, if this is an accurate rendering of Aquinas' own understanding of natural law, he has been read, especially by the Roman Catholic Church, as rather absolute on particular matters, most tellingly in the area of sexual behavior? Nelson confesses that in this area Aquinas often slips into a "crude kind of physical naturalism" that is at odds with a fuller understanding of human fulfillment. Nelson inclines to the view that Aquinas formed his views on sexual matters early in his theological career and "never got around to revising [them] to cohere with his mature doctrine of natural law."

51 Quoted in Russell Hittinger, *A Critique of the New Natural Law Theory*, (Notre Dame: University of Notre Dame Press, 1987), p. 22. I draw much of my understanding of Grisez from Hittinger's detailed analysis and evaluation.

52 *Ibid.*, p. 31.

53 Quoted in *ibid.*, p. 75.

54 *Ibid.*, p. 41.

55 *Ibid.*, pp. 41–42.

56 *Ibid.*, p. 50.

57 *Ibid.*, pp. 50, 57.

58 *Ibid.*, p. 74.

59 *Ibid.*, p. 78.

60 John Macquarrie, 'Rethinking Natural Law', in Charles E. Curran and Richard A. McCormick, SJ, eds., *Readings in Moral Theology No. 2: The Distinctiveness of Christian Ethics*, p. 129.

61 *Ibid.*, p. 126.

62 *Ibid.*, pp. 140, 142.

63 *Ibid.*, p. 143.

64 Josef Fuchs, SJ, *Natural Law: A Theological Investigation*, translated by Helmut Reckter, SJ and John A. Dowling (New York: Sheed and Ward, 1965), p. 7.

65 *Ibid.*, p. 91.

66 *Ibid.*, p. 92.

67 *Ibid.*, p. 94.

68 Josef Fuchs, *Christian Ethics in a Secular Arena*, translated by Bernard Hoose and Brian McNeil (Washington: Georgetown University Press, 1984), p. 29.

69 *Ibid.*, p. 6.

70 *Ibid.*, p. 7.

71 *Ibid.*, p. 7.

72 Columba Ryan, 'The Traditional Concept of Natural Law: An Interpretation', in Ronald P. Hamel and Kenneth R. Himes, ed., *Introduction to Christian Ethics*, (Mahurah, NJ: Paulist Press, 1989), p. 418.

73 *Ibid.*, p. 419.

74 Eric Loewy, *Suffering and the Beneficient Community*, p. xvi.

75 C. Stephen Layman, *The Shape of the Good: Christian Reflections on the Foundations of Ethics*, (Notre Dame: University of Notre Dame Press, 1991), pp. 143–144.

76 Margaret Farley, 'Feminism and Universal Morality', in Outka and Reeder, eds., *Prospects for a Common Morality*, pp. 178–179.

77 Layman, *The Shape of the Good*, p. 135.

78 Adam Smith, *An Inquiry into the Nature and Causes of the Wealth of Nations*, edited, with an introduction, notes, marginal summary and an enlarged index by Edwin

Cannan, with an introduction by Max Lerner (New York: Modern Library, 1937), p. 14.

79 *Ibid.*, p. 423.
80 Karl Marx, *Economic and Philosophic Manuscripts.* Edited with an introduction by Dirk J. Struik. Translated by Martin Milligan. (New York: International Publishers, 1964), p. 140.
81 Bertel Ollman, *Alienation*, second edition, (Cambridge: Cambridge University Press, 1976), p. 107.
82 Marx, *Economic and Philosophic Manuscripts*, p. 146.
83 Eugene Kamenka, *The Ethical Foundations of Marxism*, (New York: Frederick A. Praeger, 1962), p. 83.
84 For a fuller examination of Marx's views on human community, including some counter-tendencies within his own work, see Frank G. Kirkpatrick, *Community: A Trinity of Models*, (Washington, DC: Georgetown University Press, 1986), pp. 79–95, and Frank G. Kirkpatrick, 'Macmurray's PostMarxist Vision of Community', in Harry Carson, ed., *The Primacy of Persons As Agents in Relationship: Essays on the Post Modern Philosophy of John Macmurray* (in press).
85 For a fuller development of the logic of what I have called 'mutual heterocentrism', see my article 'The Logic of Mutual Heterocentrism: The Self as Gift', in *Philosophy and Theology*, 6, 4, Summer, 1992, pp. 353–368.
86 Enda McDonagh, 'The Structure and Basis of Moral Experience', in Hamel and Himes, *Introduction to Christian Ethics*, p. 117.
87 Kenneth E. Kirk, *The Vision of God: The Christian Doctrine of the Summum Bonum*, (London: Longman's Green, 1931), pp. 6f, 147.
88 Edward LeRoy Long, *A Survey of Christian Ethics*, p. 104.
89 Quoted, *ibid.*, p. 108. I am indebted to Long's treatment of these forms of what he calls 'modified forms of prescription.'
90 *Ibid.*, pp. 108–109.
91 James Gustafson, 'Context Versus Principles: A Misplaced Debate in Christian Ethics', in Martin E. Marty and Dean G. Peerman, *New Theology No. 3*, (New York: The Macmillan Co., 1966), p. 73.
92 *Ibid.*, p. 78.
93 *Ibid.*, pp. 80–81.
94 *Ibid.*, p. 89.
95 Edmund Pincoffs, *Quandaries and Virtues: Against Reductivism in Ethics*, (Lawrence: University of Kansas Press, 1986), p. 14.
96 Robert Johann, *Building the Human* (New York: Herder and Herder, 1968), p. 145.
97 Stanley Hauerwas, *Character and the Christian Life: A Study in Theological Ethics*, (San Antonio: Trinity University Press, 1985), 8.
98 Porter, *Moral Action and Christian Ethics*, (Cambridge: Cambridge University Press, 1995), p. 141.
99 Lee Yearley, *Mencius and Aquinas*, (Albany, NY: State University of New York Press, c.1990), p. 14.
100 Porter, *Moral Action and Christian Ethics*, p. 173.
101 Yearley, *Mencius and Aquinas*, p. 202.
102 Hauerwas, *A Community of Character*, p. 112.
103 *Ibid.*, p. 115. As I have already indicated, Hauerwas avoids the complete relativism of contextuality by claiming that "our capacity to be virtuous depends on the existence of communities which have been formed by narratives *faithful to the character of reality*" (p. 116). See my additional comments on Hauerwas' often difficult dance between claiming the universality of Christian truth and the particularity of Christian living, as found in the Introduction.

104 See Alasdair MacIntyre, *After Virtue: A Study in Moral Theory*, (Notre Dame: University of Notre Dame Press, 1984), p. 140.
105 *Ibid.*, p. 203.
106 *Ibid.*, p. 186.
107 *Ibid.*, pp. 194–195.
108 Stanley Hauerwas, *Character and the Christian Life: A Study in Theological Ethics*, p. 33.
109 Edward LeRoy Long, commenting on Hauerwas' view of virtue ethics, notes that "the idea of character involves not only qualities in the moral agent but also the communities to which the moral agent has been related and from which he draws norms, values, and directions." Edward LeRoy Long, *A Survey of Recent Christian Ethics*, p. 108.
110 Hauerwas, *A Community of Character*, p. 3.
111 *Ibid.*, pp. 50–51.
112 *Ibid.*, p. 2.

Chapter 9

Theistic Ethics and Contemporary Political Philosophies

Varieties of Communities

A theistic ethic will be inclusive of all nations and peoples if, as I have argued, the core of human flourishing remains substantially the same across all historical periods and forms of human culture. But life in a community of mutual love is not possible in the abstract. It requires both the proper historical conditions as well as the provision of a sufficiently rich, and justly administered, society through which the material goods necessary for a life of well-being and flourishing are made possible. This societal base, with all its cultural, political, and economic dimensions, is not identical with a fully formed mutual community but it is a necessary precondition for it. Because we are embodied people, an adequate ethic of community must find a way to speak to the multiple social, political, cultural, and economic forms of life in which our lives are presently embedded. Whether at the end of history the Kingdom of God will have a politics and an economics is another question. Economic and political life, as such, do not constitute the fullness of mutuality but without them such fullness remains a naive dream as long as we live under the conditions of time, space, and materiality. Biblically-informed theists live in a world of political and economic associations while also aspiring to actualize their vision of God's calling to a different and higher kind of community, one that is not exhaustively fulfilled in political forms of association. Nevertheless, theology and political philosophy must find a way to talk to each other under the conditions of social life that now prevail since both speak to and about what it means to live together in the world.

Two of the most important contemporary forms of political philosophy are democratic liberalism and communitarianism. Both offer important insights and (partial) alternatives to a theistic social ethic. In its response to these philosophies a theistic ethic will, ideally, contribute to the flourishing of the associations they prescribe while at the same time standing firm on what it believes are the differences between its vision of mutual love and their understanding of justice and material well-being. Political associations need a richer vision of life lived beyond politics: life in mutual love needs a more realistic understanding of the political and economic conditions that provide its material foundation.

In speaking of political and social life, it is common to refer to them loosely and inclusively as 'communities'. But this indiscriminate use of the word 'community' obscures for the theistic ethicist some of the crucial differences between her understanding of what God intends for persons in mutual personal community and what persons intend for themselves in such social groupings as the 'State', professional organizations, neighborhoods, and interest groups, among others in which relations between persons are primarily indirect and impersonal. Community has come to mean any association of persons sharing a common goal, task, profession, genetic inheritance, geographical region, government, family, or an intimate, mutual love.[1] At stake is the question of whether the Christian ethicist must defend a particular, and specific and normative form of community, and if so, how that community is to be differentiated in concept, without completely isolating itself in practice from, the other forms of sociality that are currently being advanced and defended by liberals and communitarians. The issue is, in part, whether theists are to work to gather all nations to see the truth of God's intention by working within the structures of justice that could apply internationally, or whether they are to stand against the nations by creating alternative forms of community in which love alone characterizes personal relationships. Or, perhaps, there is a third way that can bridge the gap between these alternatives.

The term 'community' has particular resonance for those who wish to decry the poverty of individualism's truncated view of the human person and to espouse instead the riches of sociality. The modern "celebration of community," Elizabeth Fox-Genovese argues, "must be recognized as primarily a defense against the actual social, economic, political, and legal conditions of modern life"[2] as they have been defined by individualism's overriding pursuit of self-interest. Often the rhetoric of community falls short of providing concrete prescriptions for the 'community-in-general' that it extols. Whether such prescriptions are necessary is part of what the debate between communitarians and liberals is all about. Many non-theistic postmodern philosophers, despairing of any transcendent, ahistorical vantage point from which to adjudicate differences among rival views of human flourishing, have retreated into ethnocentric communities of discourse (for example, Richard Rorty) or into vague forms of association, often without any specific content. Given their ontological and epistemological skepticism, most postmodern moral thinkers are loath to argue that, except at the thinnest level, there are any cross-communal, or universal forms of human flourishing. The debate between liberals and communitarians is also, in part, over whether human social relationships need ontological foundations and justification.

I believe that the disjunction often suggested between communitarianism and liberalism unjustly dislocates the place a Christian moral ontology's notion of community can rightfully claim. I want to develop this suggestion by proposing the following:

- that the differences between liberalism and communitarianism are not as great as often portrayed in the literature
- that a way through the debate for the religious ethicist within a theistic tradition can be provided by a moral ontology grounded in the intention and actions of a Divine Agent
- that, in particular, the moral philosopher John Macmurray's understanding of both religious community and political society provides a way of linking that moral ontology with the work (or as Macmurray puts it, the 'devices') of politics
- that Macmurray's notion of community both goes beyond and incorporates key provisions in both the liberal and communitarian notions, and

- that the moral ontology on which his notion of community rests has the potential for contributing to an ethical resolution of many of the issues now facing the democratic, pluralist, and liberal societies in the world without sacrificing the key insights of the religious vision of a community of mutual love.

In the process crucial differences between society and community will be drawn, and the emptiness of many notions of community-in-general can be replaced by the substance of a particular and specific normative form of community derived from a Biblically-informed moral ontology.

A theistic moral ontology is metaphysically committed to the importance of community as the divinely intended substance of and locus for human flourishing. Its ethic proclaims a thick vision of human flourishing that transcends and links otherwise limited and incommensurate communities of discourse by specifying mutual heterocentric love and trust as the very substance of the fulfillment of human life for all persons, regardless of the very real, historically contingent realities of the particular communities that religious people create and sustain in their daily lives and visions.

The religious appeal to community is neither as vague or thin as the abstract notion of 'situatedness' or 'communities of discourse' in general, nor as limited and incommensurate as these communities often are in practice. The linchpin for keeping the reality of God from falling prey to postmodern epistemological skepticism is the development of a pragmatically reliable construal (expressed in narrative form) of God's acts in history. The outlines of this construal have already been sketched in Chapters 3 and 4. It does not depend on ahistorical, transcendent, or absolutist theories of knowledge expressed in timeless principles or bloodless abstractions.

Abandoning a Metaphysical Basis for a Liberal Community

For most philosophers of political liberalism the creation of a liberal, pluralistic society of individual autonomous moral agents requires a robust rejection of both theism and metaphysics in general. Both Richard Rorty and John Rawls, the latter at least in his earlier work beginning with *A Theory of Justice*, are insistent that a liberal community has no need for a metaphysical foundation nor do its values require any ultimate ontological grounding. Rawls insists that philosophy ("the search for truth about an independent metaphysical and moral order,") cannot "provide a workable and shared basis for a political conception of justice in a democratic society."[3] There is simply too much diversity in religious, philosophical, and ethical conceptions to countenance the imposition of one of them on the others.

Rorty goes even further than Rawls in rejecting a metaphysical foundation for the liberal society. In fact, his defense of society requires, for him, a clear break with any notion of God.[4] For Rorty, an "enlightened, secular" liberal society would have no need for the notion of non-human forces and would drop not only the idea of devotion to the truth but also of the "fulfillment of the deepest needs of the spirit."[5] The only beings from whom we might derive any sense of meaning for our lives would be other finite entities. Rorty wants to abandon once and for all theological accounts of "a suprahistorical ground or an end-of-history convergence."[6] The only grounding for ethnocentric solidarity is the narratives of how a given community came to be. At its best this solidarity is a loyalty to those who are 'like us.'[7] Since there is no objective view of how things really are and no divine ground from which to evaluate one community in comparison with another, we must, in the end, privilege our own group and there is no way to do so non-circularly or objectively.[8]

There is, Rorty confesses, a kind of tragic heroism in this kind of solidarity and loyalty that has no ontological foundation. In the end, he says, what matters is our "loyalty to other human beings clinging together against the dark, not our hope of getting things right."[9] Whatever loyalty to each other we can eke out, it will always be in tension with and against the "background of an increasing sense of the radical diversity of private purposes".[10] There is no ground for believing that we can ever unify our private ways of dealing with our finitude or with our sense of moral obligation to other human beings.

The most that a community can be, for Rorty, is a "band of eccentrics collaborating for purposes of mutual protection rather than as a band of fellow spirits united by a common goal."[11] There is no purpose to the historically contingent liberal society beyond freedom itself. Its morality does not "approximate the will of God or the nature of man."[12] The government of a liberal society, at its best devotes itself "to optimizing the balance between leaving people's private lives alone and preventing suffering".[13]

John Rawls and the Liberal Position

Assuming then the non-theistic, non-metaphysical character of political liberalism, we now need to examine its classic development in the work of its chief exponent, John Rawls, whose seminal book *A Theory of Justice* (1971) has spawned an entire industry of scholarly studies.[14] Rawls begins with the assumption that society is "a system of cooperation designed to advance the good of those taking part in it. [It] is a cooperative venture for mutual advantage."[15]

To generate the principles of social justice that will assign rights and duties to all the members and institutions of society, as well as to articulate the just distribution of the benefits and responsibilities of social cooperation, Rawls engages in a thought-experiment. He calls this purely theoretical situation the 'original position' in which the participants are to determine what is fair and just in the arrangements of society to which they will give their consent. We are to imagine that the parties in this position (behind a veil of ignorance as to their actual situations in real life) are driven primarily by self-interest, that they have conflicting claims to the division of social advantages, that they may have no extensive ties of natural sentiment, and that they take no interest in one another's interests.[16] None of these assumptions may turn out to be true once the parties emerge from the original position, but the original position has to assume them in order for the participants to reach consensus on the most basic procedural principles for determining what everyone will ultimately agree is just once they 're-enter' society and 'discover' what their actual interests and situations are, in fact.

No one in the original position knows what her advantages or disadvantages in the real world are or what vision of the good she will hold. But, given the reality of self-interest, no one, Rawls claims, has a moral reason to accept any loss to herself in order that someone else might have greater satisfaction.[17] (A Rawlsian society, at this level, has no place for altruism or heterocentricity.)

From the 'original position' behind the 'veil of ignorance', Rawls argues, rational people would emerge having accepted two fundamental principles of justice: the first principle is that "each person is to have an equal right to the most extensive basic liberty compatible with a similar liberty for others."[18] The second, or difference principle, holds that: "social and economic inequalities are to be arranged so that they are both (a) to the greatest benefit of the least advantaged ... and (b) attached to positions and offices open to all under conditions of fair equality and opportunity."[19]

There is no presumption that there will be any agreement as to the good to be pursued by individuals, or that there will be any harmony between individual life-plans. In fact, Rawls' individualism is sufficiently strong to lead him to believe that there will be "conflicting and incommensurable conceptions of the good."[20] Individuals in liberal cultures have many different comprehensive religious, philosophical, and moral commitments. These differences require that agreement on social principles must be made solely on the basis of individual rights. This is particularly true of the right to choose freely one's own life-plan according to one's own lights, not on the basis of a common notion of the good (that is, a life-plan similar for everyone) imposed on all without their consent. No one life-plan for everyone can be expected to emerge under these conditions.

This leads to Rawls' insistence that "justice as fairness [is] the concept of right prior to that of the good."[21] It is based on the idea that persons must first agree to the principles for organizing their life together before they can begin to contemplate what is good for each of them individually. We must first define the social principles that will "govern the background conditions under which" our individually chosen aims "are to be formed and the manner in which they are to be pursued. For the self is prior to the ends which are affirmed by it."[22] The most we can hope for in a liberal, morally diverse society, is an "overlapping consensus" in the political realm as to what the rules of engagement are as persons are given the greatest possible latitude to pursue their individual life-plans as they see fit. This has the important implication, as we have already indicated, that the political conception of justice does not require acceptance of any particular religious or metaphysical doctrine.[23]

What Rawls has described is the form of a just *society*. It is the form of impersonal (or less than fully personal) and usually indirect associations among persons each seeking his or her good under the conditions of the greatest possible degree of freedom and in accord with an overlapping consensus of general social principles. This form of life together is best referred to as a society rather than as a community since the latter presupposes a greater degree of direct personal relations, intimacy, mutual love, and a sense of being bound together by a common commitment to seeking the good of all. Societies may provide the necessary material means and political conditions for smaller, more basic, more personally direct communities that can bring out in their members more fully those qualities that lead to greater flourishing and fulfillment through love. Nevertheless, societies are not communities, and communities do not have all the elements of societies. Communities, being more intense, intentional, and intimate, are not the same as but cannot exist in the absence of more formal, impersonal, and just forms of human association. Communities, however, must build upon the fundamental insight of the communitarian critics of liberalism: namely, that persons are constituted (though *not wholly*) by their historical and cultural traditions, including visions of the good and the true.

For the liberal, carrying forward the individualistic dimension of liberal political philosophy, the purpose of the state (the governmental dimension of society) is simply to ensure that all citizens have equal opportunity to advance whatever conception of the good they might individually happen to hold provided only that they do so without violating the initial two principles of justice. The only conception of the person in the liberal society is a political one at the heart of which is the primacy of the individual's freedom to choose his or her own life-plan without unfair coercion by others.

What is left unexamined, given the assumptions and self-limitations of liberalism, is the possibility that there is a religious (metaphysical) option that locates the good of all persons in a divine intention that, *by its very content*, underwrites and empowers human freedom as essential to flourishing but believes that ultimately the exercise of freedom and all visions of the good can find fulfillment only if persons choose to live in certain (broadly conceived) forms of community characterized essentially, though not solely, by mutual love in addition to justice.

The Communitarian Critique

A step in the direction of this notion of community is found in the communitarian critique of liberalism. This criticism of liberalism objects that it leaves the human self in a naked, isolated, and radically untenable individualistic posture, cut off from the very others whose relationships with the self enable it to flourish. Such a view of the self, the communitarian critics argue, is not true to the fact of the self's actual historical embeddedness in a particular culture's or community's traditions, language, and views of the good. Michael Sandel was one of the first to dissect Rawls' assumption of what Sandel called liberalism's 'unencumbered self'. For the liberal, Sandel argues, my essential identity can be distinguished from the ends that I choose. I am, essentially, a chooser who is not 'constituted' by his choices. There are no 'constitutive ends' that define the self prior to its choosing of any ends.

Sandel argues that this unencumbered self is capable of joining a 'community', but what is denied to such a self "is the possibility of membership in any community bound by moral ties antecedent to choice; he cannot belong to any community where the self *itself* could be at stake. Such a community – call it constitutive as against merely co-operative – would engage the identity as well as the interests of the participants, and so implicate its members in a citizenship more thorough-going than the unencumbered self can know."[24] While acknowledging that the liberal view of the self has a liberating quality to it, Sandel denies that it is true. We cannot, he argues, view ourselves as so independent that our identity is separated from those "loyalties and convictions whose moral force consists partly in the fact that living by them is inseparable from understanding ourselves as the particular persons we are – as members of this family or community or nation or people, as bearers of that history, as citizens of this republic."[25]

The liberal self that exists prior to her choice of attachments is a self without character or moral depth. To have character is to "move in a history I neither summon nor command, which carries consequences none the less for my choices and conduct." Whatever distance I can get on my encumberedness is always "precarious and provisional, [and] the point of reflection never finally secured outside [my contextual] history itself." The liberal self, however, is "beyond the reach of its experience, beyond deliberation and reflection. Denied the expansive self-understandings that could shape a common life, the liberal self is left to lurch between detachment on the one hand, and entanglement on the other."[26]

Communitarians such as Alasdair McIntyre insist that we cannot escape being the "bearers of a particular social identity. I am someone's son or daughter, someone else's cousin or uncle; ... The story of my life is always embedded in the story of those communities from which I derive my identity."[27]

Macmurray and Rawls

Now on first reading, it would seem that the communitarian claims of Sandel and MacIntyre track much more closely to John Macmurray's view of community (which has deeply informed my construal of the theistic moral ontology) as the ontological condition for and the constitutive substance of the fulfillment of persons whose essential nature has been created by God as profoundly interpersonal. But a closer reading suggests that Macmurray actually has the ability to accommodate much in the Rawlsian liberal tradition as well as to provide a basis for an 'internal' critique of some of communitarianism's claims. This critique centers, in particular, on an unguarded flank in communitarianism: namely its difficulty in establishing a basis on which to reject certain constitutive forms of embeddedness as being ontologically 'wrong' for persons. In the process, Macmurray's moral ontology, especially in its understanding of how a society is to be distinguished from while intimately related to a community, provides him with some clear criteria for determining what particular political and economic policies are more conducive to human flourishing (more in conformity with God's intention for all humankind) than others. And with this determination, Macmurray can give a theistic moral ontology a way through the political philosophical debates about how societies can best serve the needs of their members, especially the disadvantaged, without diminishing the genuine, authentic flourishing of all, including the most advantaged. In the process, Macmurray provides a moral ontology in which the reality of God's intention can become a decisive factor in a social ethic that does not betray the principles of justice but goes beyond them to a common vision of the common good and thus reconciles the concerns of both the liberals and the communitarians. As a result Macmurray's work helps to situate a religiously-based ethics squarely in the center of the political philosophical debate between liberalism and communitarianism.

I will not develop the full notion of community in Macmurray since that has been the subject of another work.[28] Instead I want to direct attention to Macmurray's treatment of society. Suffice it to say that for Macmurray a true or genuine community is one in which the members stand in direct, personal, intimate, face-to-face relations to each other, characterized ultimately by the experience of mutual love. This vision of community is quite close to that of the Biblical tradition within which I have placed the moral ontology I have been defending in this book. It is a vision that is not uniquely Christian (though certainly it conforms to what Christians generally take genuine community to be), but it is rooted for Macmurray in the intentions and empowering actions of a personal, historically engaged divine Being, actions which both Jews and Christians believe have been reflected in the Biblical narrative.

The bridge from a Biblically-based understanding of life together under the divine intention to political philosophy is built over their respective understandings of society. For without a societal base it is rare for genuine communities to exist.

Society

The cooperative indirect relations relative to the material foundation of community and the political structures that express them are what constitute a society. For Macmurray, like Rawls, the basis of any human society is the "intention to maintain the personal relation which makes the individual a person, and his life a common life."[29] This intention does not, however, constitute a community. Many societies are based on a personal relation motivated by fear: fear for the self and fear of the other, when the other is seen as a threat to the freedom of the self to acquire unlimited material possessions and social status by which the self believes, falsely, it will be able to give itself both fundamental identity and worth. The unity of this kind of individualistic, or atomistic society is intended, for example, to advance the interests of "aggressively egocentric individuals" (as in Hobbes' conception). Society is the necessary evil that permits these "inherently isolated or unrelated" atomic units to live together. Their unity is imposed on them by the heteronomous power of the State maintained through the sanctions of the Law which counteracts the tendency of each member to resist and repel the others.[30]

In this kind of society, because the self fears the other, its freedom to express itself fully is inhibited. It is afraid to open itself to others, to share its goods, to sacrifice some of its narrow interests for the sake of others because it fears that everything it gives away will diminish it and will entail a loss of its identity and meaning. Because it is motivated by fear of others, it assumes that they are also fearful of it and wish it harm. In this kind of society, any basic trust that persons will lovingly look after each other's interests is absent, and its absence eliminates the necessary conditions for supporting other-regarding behavior. The result can only be the further disintegration and alienation of the society and its members in relation to each other.[31]

In Macmurray's philosophy, a community is distinguished from a society by the positive apperception of its members toward each other. If a society is held together by a unity of fear and distrust, the unity of a community is a personal and positive one. The members of a community in its fullest possible sense (as understood within a theistic moral ontology) have overcome (or have been empowered by God to overcome) the fear *for* the self and its correlative fear *of* the other. And in so doing it has opened up the possibilities of freedom *for* the other.

> A community is for the sake of friendship and presupposes love. But it is only in friendship that persons are free in relation; if the relation is based on fear we are constrained in it and not free. Society is maintained by a common constraint, that is to say by acting in obedience to law. This secures the appearance of freedom, for it secures me from the expression of the other's animosity. But it does so by suppression of the motive which constitutes the relation.[32]

In society, in short, I cannot act upon the positive motive to love the other, but must suppress it out of fear that my love will be betrayed or exploited by those others who fundamentally mistrust me as much as they think I mistrust them and who will therefore use my love for them to take advantage of me.

Macmurray does not believe that the negative (fearful or egocentric) motive can, in societies of indirect impersonal relations, ever be entirely replaced by the positive (or heterocentric) motive of direct personal love for all the others. It is utopian fantasy to believe that a society, especially one of the enormous size and complexity of a modern nation-state, can be turned into a mutual community by the devices of politics appropriate for societal relations based primarily on fear. Avoiding this fantasy is crucial to any realistic understanding of politics and economics. Societies cannot provide in and of themselves the full substance of mutuality that constitutes the heart of authentic communities of mutual flourishing. Built as they are on indirect relations between persons, societies are only 'potentially' communities. And because of this fact, the limitations of politics must be recognized as persons struggle to develop the conditions for full human flourishing, both for themselves and for others. But if we know what those conditions are, at least in a general kind of way (given the particular moral ontology in which the will of God plays a central role), then we have a fulcrum by which to critique and reform the structures and institutions of society so as to best serve the purposes of community without replacing or becoming identified with them. Without this crucial distinction between society and mutual community, non-theistic moral philosophers have no way to argue the superiority of the latter. They become, generally, unable to do more than Richard Rorty who defends his version of 'community' solely because it is his by the contingency of history with no deeper ontological foundation or justification.

Within a theistic moral ontology, the crucial function of a society is to provide the material conditions and the principles of justice through which they can be appropriated fairly. Without these necessary but not sufficient conditions and principles the flourishing of individuals within communities is not possible. Macmurray is fully in accord with both liberals and communitarians in regarding what Rawls calls the primary social goods as essential to a full, even spiritual life.

These goods include individual rights and liberties, powers and opportunities, income and wealth, and self-respect.[33] The basic moral question for any society is not, however, whether it serves a 'metaphysically superior' vision of community, but whether these social goods are fairly distributed in ways that permit all persons to flourish as fully as possible. This is, both for Macmurray and for Rawls, the question of justice.[34]

Justice and Politics

Justice is inseparable from politics and the State. Politics, for Macmurray, is the "maintaining, improving and adjusting [of] the indirect or economic relations of persons."[35] The institutional expression of politics is the State whose central function is to maintain justice. Justice, in this context, is the minimum of reciprocity and interest in the other in the personal relation: it is a "kind of zero or lower limit of moral behavior."[36] It keeps relationships from disintegrating under the centrifugal force of suspicion and animosity. Justice is a necessary, but never a sufficient condition of the mutual personal relationship.[37]

Even the deepest friendships cannot pretend to have transcended the need for justice. To allow friends to be immune from the standards of justice is a sure way to open the gates to abuse and exploitation. In any relationship, one partner may bear a greater burden and derive less immediate benefit for her efforts than the other partner. "Justice," Marilyn Friedman notes, "sets a constraint on such relationships by calling for an appropriate sharing, among the participants, of the benefits and burdens that constitute their relationship."[38]

Friedman also observes that the trust and intimacy that are part of deeply personal relationships also make their partners vulnerable to harm. And when someone is harmed because of this vulnerability in a personal relationship she can rightfully demand rectification.[39] Justice in personal relationships does not conflict with care or love, but does, among sinners or (using secular vocabulary, fallible persons) living in a world not yet fully redeemed, provide love with the necessary constraints, conditions, and resources to do its work without falling into exploitation and effete sentimentalism. Justice is part of the way in which we can truly care for other persons. The bare minimum of that care is to "respect their rights and accord them their due, both in the distribution of the burdens and benefits of social cooperation and in the rectification of wrongs done."[40]

This view of justice does not fundamentally conflict with Rawls' notion that the original position does not require the parties to be positively motivated toward the others. But it does require enough common interest among them so that they can all agree on a set of principles that will bind them together in various forms of less than fully personal mutual association, transaction, and exchange. These forms constitute society.

As subordinate to mutuality, justice insists that the others with whom I am in social relation remain differentiated from me and from each other. One danger in 'pure' mutual love is that each partner will seek to submerge her identity in the interests and identities of the others for whom she cares.[41] Justice keeps morality from becoming sentimental or lapsing into what Macmurray calls "a minor mutuality'' which is hostile to the interests of the larger society. Persons who focus exclusively upon the intimacy of their relationship can easily block out the needs of others with whom they are not in such intimate relationship. And if those others are impaired in their ability to flourish because the conditions under which they live are stifling and unjust, then the intimate lovers focused exclusively upon themselves in their 'minor mutuality' can contribute nothing to the pursuit of social justice. The other must remain other, both in society and in community, and justice attempts to see to it that this will be the case in both.

Justice also stands as a safeguard against a larger organic whole absorbing individuals into its embrace without granting them the respect they are due because of their unique individualities. An organic form of social relationship, in which there is a single common good and a single set of approved moral practices runs the risk of totalitarianism. Situating justice firmly within a communitarian 'community', as a reminder that it is not yet the fullness of mutuality, keeps the latter from degenerating into a purely sentimental, or totalitarian whole in which the rights of the individual get swamped by the imperatives of group solidarity. Justice acts as a block on forms of organic social unity that privilege ethnic, gender, class, racial, or other types of identity to the exclusion of individual rights.

Preserving Particularity and Otherness

Iris Marion Young has been particularly clear about the danger of abusing the notion of community to nullify the distinctiveness of individual persons in relation and to privilege the prevailing subordination of one group to another.[42] Like the communitarians, she appreciates that living in community requires paying particular attention to the 'particularity' of others' needs and interests.[43] But she argues that the 'ideal' of community (she fails throughout to distinguish various conceptions of community) desires a "*fusion of subjects* [emphasis mine] with one another which in practice operates to exclude those with whom the group does not identify. The ideal of community denies and represses social difference ... in its privileging of face-to-face relations.''[44] Its ideal is social relations as the "*copresence of subjects*, that is, the transparency of subjects to one another.''[45] But this ideal of copresence, she argues, is a metaphysical illusion.[46] And in the process the ideal of community winds up denying the 'ontological difference' between its members.[47]

Young counters this ideal by arguing that true sharing between people can never be complete mutual understanding because persons always 'transcend' one another. At one level, the other person is always objectified. As such that uniqueness that characterizes each individual can never be completely comprehended.[48] Privileging face to face relations, she believes, winds up avoiding the political question of justice between the various units of relationship.[49] The liberals, she points out, deny difference by understanding the self as completely autonomous and self-sufficient, separated and undefined by others. Communitarians deny difference by fusing the self with others in a single totality.[50]

Young does not want to deny the value of small group personal relationships: she simply refuses to privilege them. Conditions for nurturing the experience of mutual friendship should be part of any good society. But these experiences cannot fundamentally define or model that society if we are to take justice seriously.[51]

Even what she calls a 'wildly utopian' view of the good society in which small self-sufficient 'face-to-face' communities function as autonomous political units, winds up avoiding politics as well. In so doing, the crucial political question of how to nourish justice while minimizing oppression among these units remains unasked and unresolved.[52]

Young's arguments are quite telling against visions of community that reduce the individual to an organ in an organism, or that fail to appreciate difference and otherness. But she completely fails to grasp the vision of community in the theistic moral ontology precisely because she assumes it requires 'fusion' between partners. Such fusion flies in the face of the centrality in a theistic ethic of respecting the 'otherness' and distinctive particularities of the other persons whom one wishes to flourish precisely because they were created as unique persons by God. Nevertheless, Young's insistence on justice in close relationships is a helpful antidote to too much emphasis on communion without proper regard for the practicalities of life together in the world as it is. Like Macmurray, she wants to avoid minor mutualities that obscure the need for major structures of social justice. As long as lovers live in a larger social world in which indirect relations will be necessary, justice will be essential.

Justice will also be necessary even when genuine fellowship has been attained. For even then, Macmurray argues, "there must be no self-identification of the one with the other, or the reciprocity will be lost and the heterocentricity of the relation will be only apparent."[53] The equality of persons, with respect to their functioning within society, is necessary and it is one of the ends of justice. I can genuinely care for you only if I am concerned about and intend your freedom as an agent, a freedom that is the basis of your independence from me.[54] Your decisions must remain under your control, even if they can be ultimately fulfilled only in communal interdependence with me. Whether in community or in society, therefore,

> I can hope to secure justice in my dealings with [others] by limiting my activities for the sake of their interests, provided they will do the same in their dealings with me ... We can consult together and come to an agreement about what is fair to each of us, so far as our separate courses of action affect one another and impinge on one another. This can be achieved by a common consent to general principles by reference to which each of us can determine what would or would not be fair to the other person if we did it. Such agreement is a contract between us, which ... determines reciprocal rights and obligations which we engage ourselves to respect. It is a pragmatic device to secure justice in co-operation and to eliminate injustice.[55]

There is much in this lengthy statement by Macmurray from his 1954 Gifford Lecture (published as *Persons in Relation*) that stands in close relation to (even anticipates) Rawls' development of the principles of justice. It assumes society is a cooperative endeavor; that it is based on a contract; and that it protects the rights of individuals by limiting the activities of all for the sake of each. The parties to the contract must reach common consent (which is the purpose of the original position). Macmurray does not presume the veil of ignorance, but there is no reason to assume that he would be opposed to it as a heuristic device (which is the use to which Rawls puts it – given an important qualification taken up below) because it does ensure that the common consent that emerges will not unfairly privilege some at the expense of others because they are not allowed to know their actual situation beforehand and thus will be unable to take steps to ensure the security of their contingent and accidental advantages.

Interactive Communicative Ethics

Macmurray would, however, also agree with much of what has been called the communicative ethics position, in particular its criticism that Rawls' original position runs the risk of obscuring the uniqueness of the concrete other, the individual person who cannot be reduced to a general, purely rational self. Seyla Benhabib, a feminist moral philosopher drawing on the discourse ethics of Jurgen Habermas, calls this position "interactive universalism."[56] Like Macmurray, she holds out for some form of ontologically based universal moral principles. Her stance is pragmatic, based on the actual discourse of persons in interactive communication with each other in any particular form of human association. She agrees with the communitarians that the self is "embodied and embedded" with an identity that is narratively constituted. She also agrees with liberalism that the moral point of view is a contingent achievement, not a "timeless standpoint of a legislative reason [the Kantian factor]."[57] An interactive discourse ethic asks what principles of action can participants engaged in practical discourse agree upon.[58] This clearly tracks with both Rawls' and Macmurray's notion of persons consulting together to reach common consent about the principles of justice in a social (if not fully communal) order.

Consistent with her search for the universalization of moral principles, Benhabib rejects the extreme claims of the cultural relativists like Richard Rorty. She denies, for example, their conviction that there is nothing beyond the incommensurability of moral frameworks. There is no reason, she argues, why we cannot engage other frameworks in dialogue, provided one is truly prepared to hear a different voice from one's own and to reformulate one's views as a result if the arguments are persuasive. Cultural relativists, she argues, are simply too quick to assume no kind of conversation at all is possible with people in different cultures. But this assumption rests on poor sociology and history. There has been much more interaction (and not always of the imperialist kind) between cultures than the "armchair philosophers of cultural relativism" have been willing to acknowledge. In the process they ignore the real, though incredibly complex, ways in which a common humanity can move from being an abstract ideal to becoming a concrete reality.[59] This last claim from a secular moral philosopher echoes Macmurray's theological claim in *The Clue to History* that God's intention for the unity of humankind is increasingly becoming an historical reality because it is the ontological basis for abiding and ultimately fruitful moral principles.[60]

Unlike the strict liberal proceduralists who insist that procedures determining the right are more basic and universal than any particular conceptions of the good chosen by individuals, Benhabib insists that communicative ethics entails strong normative assumptions about the moral status of persons within the communicative community. Among these are the "principle of universal moral respect" and the "principle of egalitarian reciprocity."[61] Both of these principles accord with Macmurray's notion of equality and the differentiation of the other as truly other in any genuine personal relationship. "We ought to *respect* each other as beings whose standpoint is worthy of equal consideration", and "we ought to treat each other as concrete human beings whose capacity to express this standpoint we ought to enhance by creating, whenever possible, social practices embodying the discursive ideal (the principle of egalitarian reciprocity)."[62]

The second principle requires us to engage in what Benhabib calls the reversal of perspectives. We should be able to think from the other person's point of view and see how she judges others. Only if we do this can we avoid consigning others to a diminished status of otherness that can be neglected or treated with indifference in the interactive communicative conversation that constitutes the good society.

Benhabib also insists that discourse requires the participants to make sure that they have genuinely heard the voices of those others who have traditionally been excluded from the conversation, namely women and minorities. Benhabib criticizes Rawls on just this point. She points out that Rawls' argument, by ignoring the standpoint of the *concrete* other[63] tends to assume the point of view of "the disembedded and disembodied *generalized* other."[64] Behind the veil of ignorance "the *other as different from the self* disappears." The particular self is abstracted from her concrete and specific identity within the complex of human social relationships and treated simply as one of many indistinguishable selves. As a result her 'voice' as this different and unique other is effectively silenced. What remains is the Kantian noumenal self that is, abstractly, everyone in general and no one in particular. To create the conditions for real community in which real persons are real contributors, the concrete, embedded lives of different concrete others must be included (what Macmurray calls the heterocentric dimension of relationship).

The inclusion of traditionally excluded particular others also undercuts or deconstructs the privileging of certain individualistic moral ideals, such as the abstract 'economic' or the 'political man' as rational chooser, both of which seem to predicate the superiority of the male autonomous morality free from the constitutive bonds of family, personal and communal interdependence. Benhabib, echoing themes found in feminist thought, argues that there is no reason, once the voices of women are brought into the conversation, why morality should be understood primarily as the rational actions of impersonal agents in a field of indirect relations, such as economics and politics. Self-consciously employing the term that has come to characterize the theistic vision of community (but apparently without any intent to link it to that vision), communicative ethics "projects a utopian way of life in which *mutuality* [emphasis added], respect and reciprocity become the norm among humans as concrete selves and not just as juridical agents."[65] Macmurray's insistence that a heterocentric ethic focus, as a necessary part of any mutual relationship, on the uniqueness of the other, and not on her usefulness for the egocentric self, suggests a similar support for treating others as concrete, and not simply as generalized others.

Empowering Positive Liberty

One important implication of the communicative ethics view, as well as of Macmurray's social ethic, is that a society has a special obligation to empower all persons with the necessary material means to engage in the reasoned conversation from which a mutual consensus will be reached about the principles by which all those participating in the conversation agree to be governed. These conditions of empowerment, or positive liberty, go far beyond the negative liberty that conservatives and libertarians are so interested in, a liberty simply to be left alone by others in order to pursue one's private life-plan with as little interference as possible.

Carol Gould has argued (echoing Isaiah Berlin) that positive liberty is the right to be provided with the means, economic, social, and personal, necessary for the full exercise of one's personhood; the right, in short, to have "access to enabling conditions." Positive freedom presumes the importance of social relations in providing the "fundamental context" for the self-development that each person intends for herself and for others. This context requires that a wide range of actual life options be made available to people. And they require, in turn, "the availability of the objective conditions – both material and social – without which the purposes [of the self] could not be achieved." Among these conditions are the means for daily subsistence, the means for labor and for leisure activity, and access to training and education.[66] I would add that any Biblically-informed social ethic that is incarnational and non-dualistic (that is, does not believe that full flourishing can exist solely at a spiritual level) must also embrace this kind of positive social freedom and justice as indispensable conditions for genuine community and a just society.

Out of the experience of positive freedom, Gould goes on to suggest, a sense of reciprocity or mutuality may begin to develop among persons. In the process of securing the conditions of positive freedom the individual may come to share and adopt as her own the social or common purposes of the groups to which she belongs. She requires the recognition by others of her freedom. She also is positively affected by the kind of mutual support that individuals may give to each other in the self-development of each.[67] She calls this relationship of mutual support 'full reciprocity' or *mutuality*, and distinguishes it from customary, formal, instrumental, and social forms of reciprocity. Mutuality

> is a relation in which (a) each agent recognizes the other as free and as capable of self-development, (b) each acts with regard to the other in ways that enhance the other's self-development on the basis of a consideration of the other's needs, and (c) both agents take such mutual enhancement of each other's agency as a conscious aim.[68]

Gould suggests that there is a complementary kind of mutuality which is also essential to the self-development at which positive freedom aims.

> It consists in the contribution that is made ... by all those individuals who, in the development of their own capacities, have enriched the range of possible human actions, intentions, skills, and practices. This cultivation of human capacities provides an individual with options or models for his or her own development.[69]

Gould is clear, however, that the mutual forms of full reciprocity are not necessary for political democracy. Only social reciprocity is required at that level.[70] Mutuality presumes "an altruism that is supererogatory" in a political context.[71] So far, this sounds as if it would fit nicely into the moral ontology of community within a theistic ethic, especially Gould's stress on each member in the mutual relationship taking the enhancement of the other's self-development as a conscious aim, that is, what Macmurray calls heterocentricity.

But Gould draws back from a full development of the implications of her ideas for relationships of agape and heterocentric love. While acknowledging the social nature of the self and the importance of mutuality, her understanding of it is essentially one of reciprocity in which each self uses the social bond with the other as a means to self-development. In a strong echo of Marx's view of the relation between society and the individual, she says "sociality is one of the conditions of freedom as self-development."[72] The "reciprocal recognition" of persons is a necessary means for providing each other the resources and support that each needs for the achievement of his or her personal purposes.

What is significant about these observations is, despite her reliance upon *a* concept of mutuality, Gould's utter avoidance of any reference to a community in which mutual love is an end in itself and her studious avoidance of any consideration of a metaphysical concept of a divine being whose actions and intentions might underwrite, as ultimately realistic, the kind of mutuality that she considers "supererogatory" in a political context. The theist's claim is that such a metaphysical concept is a true construal of the nature and direction of human history and cannot, therefore, be dismissed or relegated to the status of the historically impossible. It is significant, therefore, that the examples Gould gives of mutuality all seem to fall into the category of instrumental means for the development of the individual self. The sheer intrinsic delight of fellowship and agape love is simply not considered by her to have any particular significance or even reality.

It is significant as well that she fails to suggest any ranking of the various forms of mutuality in terms of which ones are more conducive to the full flourishing of the human person. She prizes shared common activity, but does not discuss activities in which the mutual joy of personal relationship is itself the goal.

Nevertheless, Gould is right about the importance of providing the material means of support for human self-development. Alan Gewirth has argued, in a complementary vein, that all moral action requires the freedom and well-being of the moral agent. Freedom presumes not only unforced choice but also relevant contextual knowledge of the situation. Substantive well-being includes the abilities and conditions one needs for achieving one's purposes and additive well-being requires those abilities and conditions one needs for increasing one's capabilities for acting so as to fulfill one's purposes. These include such things as self-esteem, education, and opportunities to earn one's economic sustenance.[73]

Economic Empowerment and Justice

Human rights are, like positive liberty, the minimum conditions for life in community. They include not only civil and political rights but economic rights as well. The provision of a just economy is part of the functions of what Macmurray calls 'positive government'.

Positive government, in Macmurray's political philosophy, is one that exercises a "positive control of the material life of its citizens, [and] determines what use shall be made of the material resources of the nation."[74] Macmurray's basic point (one that survives the failures of many socialist governments in practice) is that we cannot separate the spiritual life (the life of love and mutuality) from its material base. "Without adequate material resources, the personal life must remain stunted and undeveloped ... The means of life are also the means of a good life."[75] These means include the equitable provision of economic goods.

> The means of *exercising* the freedoms that democracy assures to its members are distributed by the chances of economic success or failure in free competition. This means, in effect, that the realization of the good life depends upon relative wealth. Whoever controls wealth controls the means of cultural development and personal freedom.[76]

Positive government sees its duty as providing the material resources necessary for achieving the welfare of the people who comprise the society.[77]

A social ethic flowing from Macmurray's moral ontology that takes the provision of the material and political conditions of moral agency, well-being, and self-development that Gould and Gewirth have advanced seriously would resonate with the recent *Pastoral Letter* of the Roman Catholic Bishops in the United States dealing with economic justice.[78] The Bishops argue that an economic system must be judged "by what it does *for* and *to* people and by how it permits all to *participate* in it."[79] This requires that the social and economic conditions of community be socially protected, that all persons have a right to participate in the economic life of society, that all members of the society have a special obligation to the poor, and that Christians are to make a fundamental 'option for the poor' to strengthen the whole society by assisting those who are most vulnerable to economic exploitation. The Bishops' letter is a fine example of how a religiously informed social ethic can draw upon and contribute to a secular philosophical concern for the minimal conditions of human freedom, well-being, moral agency, and self-development, regardless of the various 'communities of discourse' that may exist within the society.

This does not mean that government or society engulfs the individual to such an extent that she has no privacy or life outside the constraints of government. It is vitally important that persons retain a degree of transcendence over even the most powerful and well-entrenched conditions of social life in order to be able to critique and reform them. In this sense, Macmurray would be hesitant to accept a communitarian view of the self's embeddedness that is so total and exhaustive that it negates her freedom to stand outside that social context in order to subject it to critical scrutiny and transformation.

The transcendence to which he refers is found primarily in the religious life and Macmurray denies the government any right to interfere with it.[80] The State's power ought to be limited to the provision of the material goods necessary for freedom and well-being. On the foundation these goods provide, the person can use her freedom to reflect critically upon how her political, legal, and cultural traditions might be altered (or better defended) in the light of the overarching purposes of genuine community to which they ought to be the means.

The Limits of Communitarianism

The critical distance between the self and her societal base is made possible because, if she is a theist, she can appeal to the will of God as that which transcends all particular and historically contingent forms of society even while she is embedded and 'constituted' in large part by belonging to one of them. This fact suggests some limits on extreme forms of communitarianism. The element of transcendence required for critical distance does not seem nearly as well developed in Hauerwas' and MacIntyre's notion of the Christian community as virtually and completely inclusive of the essential identity of its members. They seem particularly vulnerable to Gould's, Young's, and Benhabib's concern that persons not 'fuse' with each other, or become indistinguishable within an organic soup of communitarian common identity. Being able to retain one's individuality, even against the community in which one is embedded is essential to the full flourishing of the human self.

As political philosopher Will Kymlicka argues in defense of liberalism and against some its more extreme communitarian critics, "we *can* be mistaken about even our most fundamental interests, and because some goals *are* more worthy than others. Liberty is needed precisely to find out what is valuable in life – to question, re-examine, and revise our beliefs about value."[81] It is because our life-plans are so important that "we should be free to revise and reject them, should we come to believe that they are not fulfilling or worthwhile ... Freedom of choice [is] a precondition for pursuing those projects and tasks that *are* valued for their own sake."[82]

This is also what I take to be the heart of Macmurray's defense of religious and spiritual freedom from interference by the political sphere. It is within our religious lives that we discover the truly worthwhile form of life that is ultimately brought to completion in mutual community. And that form of life, for most religious people, presupposes an ontology that has a place for the intentions and actions of a divine agent both in establishing the ontological conditions of community and in moving history toward its fullest realization. Therefore, Macmurray, like Kymlicka, would reject the more extreme communitarian claim that our identity is fully or completely determined by our embeddedness in an historically contingent culture or tradition. There must be a sense in which the liberal is right that there is a self prior to its ends. It need not be a totally denuded or abstractly general self: it can be, as Benhabib has argued, a concrete and particular self in continual ongoing conversation and communion with others open to change in and through that relationship.

It is impossible to view ourselves as totally without social embeddedness, but we can envisage ourselves without our *present form* of embeddedness. As long as we have the possibility of interactive conversation among and between equal partners in relation, and the social bonds that make it possible, we can enter the process of ethical reflection and compare one 'encumbered' potential self with another. We can continually expose ourselves to other views of the good and in the process keep open our right to re-examine "even our most deeply held convictions about the nature of the good life."[83]

There must be a vantage point from which even the most rock-hard of such cultures can be viewed from beyond itself by a reasoned conversation that opens up the vision of a human community that goes beyond (while remaining dependent upon) both society and its devices of politics. Only within the context of that reasoned conversation can the religious philosopher hope to ground her conviction that belief in the overarching intention for universal community of a divine agent makes the best sense (gives what Charles Taylor calls the best account) out of life in comparison with other construals of the source and means of fulfillment. But until that vision can be fully effected, law and the devices of politics remain indispensable instruments for life in a just society.

This is precisely where Rawls' two liberal principles of justice have their significance. They ensure that each person has an equal right to the most extensive basic liberty compatible with a similar liberty for others, and, in accord with the difference principle, that social and economic inequalities must work for the greatest benefit of the least advantaged.

Macmurray essentially agrees: a society is ultimately to be judged by how far it succeeds in "achieving and maintaining justice in the indirect or economic relations of men ... The appeal must be to a sense of justice of all those affected, and the pragmatic evidence of this is a common consent."[84] And a common consent is best reached in a democratic society by an inclusive conversation among all the members, including those who have been historically disenfranchised by the unjust exercise of disproportionate power on behalf of economic, gender, and political elites. Thus Macmurray's commitment to justice is congruent with Rawls' principles of justice, Rorty's notion of conversation among those who constitute 'our' culture, and Benhabib's discourse ethics of communicative interaction.

Yet none of this denies the ontological and moral primacy of a community (that includes but is more than a society) as the context in which persons truly achieve their flourishing in accordance with God's purpose for them. The society that is maintained by common consent to the principles of justice is still, ultimately, in service to the community that is maintained by common consent to and ongoing practice of the principles of love and mutuality in direct, intimate, personal relationships.

Communities Within Liberalism

It is extremely significant that at the end of the day even Rawls, the arch-liberal, has room for such communities within his liberal society of social cooperation. Critics and defenders have so focused on the priority of the right in Rawls' theory of society that they have overlooked the importance he places on the possibility of the practice of life in community. But, as Roberto Alejandro has pointed out, Rawls also has a strong sense of an encumbered self (quite at odds with what the communitarians criticize him for) who actually lives fully only in one form of community or another.[85] Rawls admits that "there should be for each person at least one community of shared interests to which he belongs and where he finds his endeavors confirmed by his associates.''[86] This notion of communal confirmation (what Gould would call 'mutual support') suggests that, even for Rawls (who eschews a metaphysical view of the self) selves, ontologically and empirically, do not fully flourish until and unless they are affirmed and appreciated by others. This has parallels to Macmurray's claim that because it is "natural for human beings to share their experience, to understand one another, to find joy and satisfaction in living together; in expressing and revealing themselves to one another,"[87] it is necessary to enter a social union, or community. Thus for both Macmurray's theistic moral ontology and Rawls' liberal social philosophy, a goal of radical self-sufficiency is neither possible nor desirable. One depends upon others "to confirm his sense of his own worth."[88]

Rawls concedes that some form of social union is necessary for the individual's powers to reach fruition. "Only in social union is the individual complete."[89] This suggests that Rawls understands that society (the cooperative association) is not sufficient for the completion of the deepest aspirations of human beings. They require a closer, more direct and personal form of community and this fact opens Rawls up to a consideration of communal relationships that go beyond, without replacing, societal principles of justice.

If this is true, Alejandro is right in claiming that "for a Rawlsian community is far from being a mere attribute ... it is *constitutive* (emphasis added) of the individual's identity," just as the communitarians claim.[90] What Rawls does not do is argue that any *one particular kind* of community or social union is better than another. But Macmurray and the Biblical theist would make just such an argument, drawing on their construal of God's intention for the fulfillment of human persons in and through mutual love. In this respect, Macmurray keeps alive the importance of a moral ontology grounded in the will of God as the basis for a full understanding of the relationship between society and its devices of politics, and community with its mutuality of love.

Notes

1 In keeping with my attempt to distinguish community from society, I will try to use the term 'society' to refer to what liberalism and communitarianism often have in mind. However, since they frequently use the term 'community' to refer to what I call 'society' there may be an initial confusion. I will, of course, retain the term 'community' in direct quotes from liberals and communitarians, but try to use 'society' when paraphrasing or discussing their views.

2 Elizabeth Fox-Genovese, 'Women and Community', in *Feminism Without Illusions: A Critique of Individualism*, (Chapel Hill: University of North Carolina Press, 1991), pp. 37–38.

3 John Rawls, 'Justice as Fairness: Political not Metaphysical', *Philosophy and Public Affairs*, 14, 1985, p. 230.

4 The epistemological reasons for that break were dealt with in Chapter 1. Here I want to explore further how his abandonment of God plays itself out in his political philosophy of a liberal democratic community.

5 Richard Rorty, 'The Contingency of a Liberal Community', in *Contingency, Irony, and*

Solidarity, (Cambridge: Cambridge University Press, 1989), p. 45.

6 *Ibid.*, p. 68.

7 Richard Rorty, 'Solidarity or Objectivity?', *Objectivity, Relativism, and Truth*, p. 23.

8 *Ibid.*, p. 29.

9 Richard Rorty, 'Pragmatism, Relativism, and Irrationalism', *Proceedings and Addresses of the American Philosophical Association* 53 (1980), p. 736. Quoted in Richard J. Bernstein, *Beyond Objectivism and Relativism: Science, Hermeneutics, and Praxis*, pp. 203–204.

10 Rorty, 'The Contingency of a Liberal Community', pp. 67–68.

11 *Ibid.*, p. 59.

12 *Ibid.*, pp. 60–61.

13 *Ibid.*, p. 63.

14 Rawls' notion of a liberal community parallels much in Rorty's conception as well.

15 John Rawls, *A Theory of Justice*, (Cambridge, MA: Harvard University Press, 1971), p. 4.

16 Rawls, *A Theory of Justice*, pp. 127–129.

17 *Ibid.*, p. 14. In this respect Rawls qualifies traditional utilitarian theory.

18 *Ibid.*, pp. 60–61.

19 *Ibid.*, p. 302.

20 John Rawls, 'Justice as Fairness: Political not Metaphysical', *Philosophy and Public Affairs*, p. 245.

21 Rawls, *A Theory of Justice*, p. 31.

22 *Ibid.*, p. 560.

23 John Rawls, 'The Priority of Rights and Ideas of the Good', *Philosophy and Public Affairs*, 17 (1988), p. 252.

24 Sandel, 'The Procedural Republic and the Unencumbered Self', in Shlomo Avineri and Avner De-Shalit, eds., *Communitarianism and Individualism*, (New York: Oxford University Press, 1992), p. 19.

25 *Ibid.*, p. 23. (Rorty seems to split the difference between this communitarian attack and the liberalism against which it is directed. He, too, accepts the ethnocentric preconditions of the self's 'community', but as a liberal democratic wants to emphasize the right of the individual within that community to question its values and self-understanding. Whether this gives Rorty a completely coherent and consistent political philosophy is an open question.)

26 *Ibid.*, p. 24.

27 Alasdair MacIntyre, *After Virtue*, (South Bend: University of Notre Dame Press, 1981), p. 205.

28 See Frank G. Kirkpatrick, *The Ethics of Community*, (Blackwell, 2001).

29 John Macmurray, *Persons in Relation*, (New York: Harper and Brothers, 1961), p. 128.

30 *Ibid.*, p. 137.

31 This is the thrust of recent work being done by the African-American philosopher, Laurence Thomas. See especially Laurence Thomas, *Living Morally*. See my comments on his work earlier in this book.

32 John Macmurray, *Persons in Relation*, p. 151.

33 Macmurray does not question whether these goods carry over into non-democratic, non-liberal societies. Like Rawls, he seems to be working within the given framework of western liberal society and assuming that its basic goods are those that, for the most part, constitute the foundation, if not the full meaning, of human flourishing.

34 Rawls, *A Theory of Justice*, p. 62.

35 John Macmurray, *Persons in Relation*, p. 188.

36 *Ibid.*, p. 188.

37 Macmurray argues that even in family relations, there must be some differentiation and

resistance among the members. Otherwise the individual's own identity will be submerged (and thus disappear) in the identities of others, including those most inclined to care for her. Genuinely mutual relations require the relative autonomy of each partner so that her individual uniqueness can emerge. In these relations of differentiation and resistance principles of justice must always condition the practices of love and mutuality.

38 Marilyn Friedman, 'Gendered Morality', in *What Are Friends For? Feminist Perspectives on Personal Relationships and Moral Theory*, p. 129.

39 *Ibid.*, p. 130.

40 *Ibid.*, p. 135.

41 This is the fear that philosophers like Marilyn Friedman have about too much emphasis on care as a basis for morality. See, for example, her 'Care and Context in Moral Reasoning', in *What Are Friends For?*.

42 Iris Marion Young, 'City Life and Difference', *Justice and the Politics of Difference*, (Princeton: Princeton University Press, 1990).

43 *Ibid.*, p. 228.

44 *Ibid.*, p. 227.

45 *Ibid.*, p. 231.

46 *Ibid.*, p. 233. (Obviously Young has not taken in Rorty's and Rawls' contention that no metaphysical judgments about the human self and its relation to others can be made.)

47 *Ibid.*, p. 231.

48 *Ibid.*, p. 232.

49 *Ibid.*, p. 233.

50 *Ibid.*, p. 229.

51 *Ibid.*, p. 233.

52 *Ibid.*, p. 234.

53 John Macmurray, *Persons in Relation*, p. 189.

54 *Ibid.*, p. 190.

55 *Ibid.*, p. 191.

56 Seyla Benhabib, *Situating the Self*, (New York: Routledge, 1992), passim. Benhabib's notion of universalism has strong parallels with Susan Frank Parson's work referred to earlier under a consideration of feminist ethics.

57 *Ibid.*, p. 6. The bracketed words are my addition to her quotation.

58 *Ibid.*, p. 28.

59 *Ibid.*, footnote 48, pp. 62–63.

60 Macmurray argues in *The Clue to History* (London: SCM, 1938) that if history is both the act(s) of God in the world and the acts of human beings, and if God's intention for the world and human beings will be accomplished, then "human intentions which are opposed to the intention of God for man are necessarily self-frustrating" (pp. 94–95). Human persons are themselves God's act, and "his intention is embodied in their nature. To act in defiance of the will of God is to intend the impossible ... Thus, whether our intention conforms to the purpose of God or opposes it, we cannot *achieve* anything but the purpose of God" (pp. 95–96). This means that "there are limits to the length that men can go on frustrating their own nature. There is a point at which a false purpose *must* be given up, because the impossibility of achieving it reveals itself and destroys the motive for persisting in it" (p. 96). Macmurray believed in the late 1930s that fascism which denies the individual in the name of a collective individualism to which the individual person, and her freedom, are subordinated had revealed its own impossibility and would necessarily be defeated by an intention toward community. Whether the radical individualism of contemporary contractual, self-interested forms of association has equally proved itself impossible is the major question of our time.

61 Benhabib, *Situating the Self*, p. 29.

62 *Ibid.*, p. 31.
63 *Ibid.*, p. 161.
64 *Ibid.*, p. 160.
65 *Ibid.*, footnote 34, p. 60.
66 See Carol Gould, *Rethinking Democracy: Freedom and Social Cooperation in Politics, Economy, and Society*, (Cambridge: Cambridge University Press, 1988), pp. 39–41.
67 *Ibid.*, p. 50.
68 *Ibid.*, p. 77.
69 *Ibid.*, p. 50.
70 *Ibid.*, p. 77.
71 *Ibid.*, p. 292.
72 *Ibid.*, p. 72.
73 Alan Gewirth, 'Common Morality and the Community of Rights', in Gene Outka and John Reeder, Jr., *Prospects for a Common Morality*, (Princeton: Princeton University Press, 1993), p. 36.
74 John Macmurray, *Constructive Democracy*, (London: Faber and Faber, 1943), p. 8.
75 *Ibid.*, pp. 21–22.
76 *Ibid.*
77 *Ibid.*, p. 28. While Macmurray goes on to argue that the government "would plan and administer the economic life of the community" (p. 29), I do not believe that he would necessarily subscribe to all the details of a communist or socialist command economy. In fact, his whole argument on behalf of positive government is couched in the context of a defense of political democracy and the prohibition on government from entering into the spiritual and personal lives of its subjects.
78 See *Economic Justice for All: Pastoral Letter on Catholic Social Teaching and the U.S. Economy*, (National Conference of Catholic Bishops: Washington, DC, 1986), passim.
79 *Ibid.*, p. ix.
80 John Macmurray, *Constructive Democracy*, p. 11.
81 Will Kymlicka, 'Liberalism and Communitarianism', *Canadian Journal of Philosophy*, 18, 2, June 1988, p. 185.
82 *Ibid.*, p. 187.
83 *Ibid.*, p. 189.
84 John Macmurray, *Persons in Relation*, p. 203.
85 See Roberto Alejandro, 'Rawls's Communitarianism', *Canadian Journal of Philosophy*, 23, 1, March, 1993, pp. 75–100.
86 John Rawls, *A Theory of Justice*, p. 442.
87 John Macmurray, *Reason and Emotion*, p. 98.
88 John Rawls, *A Theory of Justice*, 445. This also echos Marx's notion that in a truly human society, through your enjoyment of the product of my labor, "I would have had the direct enjoyment of realizing that I had both satisfied a human need by my work ... and would have been for you the mediator between you and the species and thus been acknowledged and felt by you as a completion of your own essence and a necessary part of yourself and have thus realized that I am confirmed both in your thought and in your love [and] in my expression of my life I would have fashioned your expression of your life, and thus in my own activity have realized my own essence, my human, my communal essence.' Karl Marx, 'On James Mill', in *Karl Marx: Selected Writings*, edited by David McLellan (Oxford: Oxford University Press, 1977), p. 122.
89 John Rawls, *A Theory of Justice*, p. 525.
90 Alejandro, 'Rawls's Communitarianism', p. 94.

Summary and Conclusion

A theistic ethic is one that is rooted in an ontology of God's acts in history. At the heart of those acts is a divine intention for human flourishing and well-being. A precondition for (though not the substance of) such flourishing is social justice in the societies within the context of whose political and economic structures more intentional communities can emerge and develop. Full flourishing is possible only in mutual loving relationship with others and, thus, a religious ethic forged in the theistic traditions of Judaism and Christianity is necessarily an ethic of flourishing in and through mutual love in community sustained materially and politically in the context of less than mutual societal associations.

The ontology on which this ethic rests is, ultimately, a reasoned construal, drawn from the narrative memory and ongoing experiences of a people (Jews and Christians) who believe that there is a supreme power bearing down on them and providing them life-transforming experiences, especially in the religious communities that constitute the essential meaning of their lives. These communities are historical experiments, subject to the same contingencies, contradictions, confusions, and ambiguities as any human forms of association. Nevertheless, as constituting communities of faith, they are committed to a set of reasoned and well-informed inferences that out of this web of contingent and interlocking threads, an overarching and unifying purpose can be discerned. They have concluded that this divine purpose will ultimately be realized in, or at the end of, history and will bring to fulfillment the basic aspirations and yearnings of all human persons. In the meantime those persons who have acted, responsively to the divine intention as they have construed it, will be graciously permitted to experience in the present a foretaste of what that greater fulfillment will bring.

In agreement with the deconstructionists, this theistic construal of 'what is going on' does not claim exemption from contingent and conditioning forces, nor absolute finality, nor immunity from 'getting it wrong' (which it could only get by appeal to a trans-rational faith). It also commits itself to an essentially pragmatic and ultimately historical 'proof' of the correctness of its construal. This is the case precisely because its construal is based on the ontological primacy of the actions of a divine personal Agent. As such its construal is dependent on the future actions of this Agent for validation of its current reading of God's intentions. It thus lives with a degree of uncertainty in the present. It is committed, however, to a belief that the divine Agent's intentions are ultimately friendly and supportive of human well-being (as they may also be of the whole non-human created order). It is equally committed to a belief that some significant acts in history have decisively advanced God's intention. But it does not claim to have ahistorical proof of or certainty for its belief in God or of God's intention. Therefore its commitment to its construal about God has a profoundly practical dimension: to 'know' God is to do what God intends, to align or conform one's own actions with the intention one believes God is enacting in establishing the conditions of fulfillment and the direction of history. It thinks it knows what is going on in the world through the powerful acts of God and it believes that God is faithful to God's promises. And so it awaits the future in hope. But it waits actively, not passively, fully engaged in responsible action in conformity with the divine intention.

Because it believes that God's overarching intention is for the fulfillment of human persons (as well as of the creation as a whole), a theistic ethic has much in common with secular emphases on human 'flourishing'. God intends persons to flourish. The postmodern non-theist makes no reference to a divine intention but often expresses an understanding of the core of human flourishing that has striking parallels with the theistic construal. For a theist this fact should not be remarkable because part of her understanding of reality (her moral ontology) is a belief that the truth about human beings is not a uniquely religious truth but a truth embedded in the structures of reality as such and therefore accessible to human understanding. Theism is not a truth 'in' the empirical facts but an inference drawn from them. Therefore, theists and non-theists alike should be able to agree as to what 'is the case' about nature without having to adopt the other's theism or non-theism. They will differ over a reading of where history 'is going', whether there is a divine force at work in it, and whether the common nature of human beings they both discern is stable and continuous over the course of this history.

Unlike some postmodern views, however, a theistic ethic holds that the basic elements of flourishing in accordance with God's intention do not take radically incommensurate forms for different persons and peoples. There is a common core to all human flourishing and that core is mutual love, otherwise known as agape love, fellowship, friendship, in a community of mutuality. The initially paradoxical character of mutual love, however, is that it must necessarily nurture and protect what is genuinely unique to each person's own particular form of flourishing. Thus, a theistic ethic can accept the secular emphasis on enhancing the uniqueness of the particular 'other'. The secret of mutual love is that it unites particular and unique selves in a bond of care in which each partner seeks the other's flourishing in ways that are unique to that other. But such other-regarding heterocentric love (altruism) requires and produces a relationship of deep intimacy, trust, and interdependence. In short, the character of mutual love is that the more each person seeks the other's well-being the more the partners are brought together in bonds of mutuality that constitute the core of human flourishing.

One consequence of this commitment to human flourishing is a strong affirmation of the human freedom to choose. But a second apparent paradox emerges and is resolved by the fact of mutual love. To truly flourish, one must be free to choose the other and the particular modes of relationship one will have with him or her. But full flourishing, if it is to be truly possible, also requires that freedom find its completion in choices that intend mutual love, not self-sufficiency, radical independence, or alienating autonomy. When freedom is not directed toward and *for* mutuality it is ultimately alienating and self-stultifying.

Mutuality is essential to the community that makes flourishing possible, but not all forms of association are mutual communities. Nevertheless, the religious believer lives in a variety of communities, associations, and societies simultaneously. Until all nations are gathered into what Martin Buber calls a community of communities, and there is genuine reconciliation and unity among its many members, religious people will live in and at the intersection of multiple political societies and religious communities. The former will provide the material conditions, and their just allocation and access to the basic social goods necessary for flourishing, but the latter will provide much more of the substance and fullness of flourishing, especially those forms of communion that emphasize intimacy, trust, care, compassion, and spiritual sharing. Thus a theistic ethic will have much to say about the appropriate forms for providing and giving access to those material goods that contribute directly to people's well being in areas from education, housing, nourishment, recreation, to meaningful labor and participation in the governing structures of social life.

A theistic ethic, however, must ultimately be about more than the rectifying of unjust economic and political conditions. To be faithful to its construal of God's intention and God's ongoing relationship with God's human creation, a theistic ethic must constantly remind itself of human sin. Part of the need for God's ongoing intervention into human history is the ever-present fact of human opposition to both God's will and its own best interests. A theistic ethic must avoid sliding into unwarranted optimism or naivety about the purity of any particular political, economic, or social program that seems to forward the intention of God. Human pride, arrogance, and self-interest have an insidious way of never entirely leaving the stage of even the best-laid plans of the best-intentioned religious people.

At the same time a theistic ethic must avoid completely identifying or equating the flourishing that is possible even in the best of empirical conditions with the flourishing that it believes awaits us in the fullness of life in God. The Scylla and Charybdis between which the theistic ethic must sail are the temptation to radical dualism on one side and a full-body embrace of the world on the other. A dualism in which life in this world is treated as radically and utterly unlike life in the fullness of God is Biblically unfounded and philosophically untenable. But so is an uncritical affirmation of the world as if the world is now already beyond sin and imperfection.

Such imperfection need not be related to finitude or history as such. The Kingdom of God might well turn out to be a fully historical community. But life in the Kingdom may be so radically superior to life in our present historical condition as to be virtually unrecognizable. What the religious believer can say is that in an historical life with God, in which God's will and ours are perfectly conformed, we will experience love, mutuality, and joy to such a degree that the foretaste we have of them in the present will seem anemic by comparison. But if the Biblical theist's construal of history is correct, there will be a core to the experience of love, mutuality, and joy in our life together now that will not be abolished but, as Aquinas so boldly claimed, completed in God.

Bibliography

Adams, Robert M. 'A Modified Divine Command Theory of Ethical Wrongness', in Paul Helm, ed. *Divine Commands and Morality*. New York: Oxford University Press, 1981.

Adams, Robert M. 'Common Projects and Moral Virtue', in Peter French, Theodore Uehling, and Howard Wettstein, eds. *Midwest Studies in Philosophy: Volume XIII Ethical Theory: Character and Virtue*. Notre Dame, IN: University of Notre Dame Press, 1988.

Adams, Robert Merrihew 'Religious Ethics in a Pluralistic Society', in Gene Outka and John P. Reeder, Jr., eds. *Prospects for a Common Morality*. Princeton: Princeton University Press, 1993.

'Agape', in John Macquarrie, ed. *Dictionary of Christian Ethics*. Philadelphia: Westminster Press, 1967.

Alejandro, Roberto. 'Rawls's Communitarianism', *Canadian Journal of Philosophy*, 23, 1, March, 1993.

Alston, William P. *Epistemic Justification*. Ithaca: Cornell University Press, 1989.

Alston, William P. *Perceiving God: The Epistemology of Religious Experience*. Ithaca: Cornell University Press, 1991.

Alston, William P. *A Realist Conception of Truth*. Ithaca: Cornell University Press, 1996.

Aquinas, Thomas. *The Summa Theologica*, in Anton C. Pegis, *Basic Writings of Saint Thomas Aquinas*, Vol. 2. New York: Random House, 1945.

Avineri, Shlomo and Avner De-Shalit, eds. *Communitarianism and Individualism*. New York: Oxford University Press, 1992.

Baier, Annette. 'Doing Without Moral Theory?', in Stanley G. Clarke and Evan Simpson, eds. *Anti-Theory in Ethics and Moral Conservatism*. Albany: State University of New York Press, 1989.

Baier, Annette. 'Trust and Antitrust', in Joram Graf Haber, ed. *Doing and Being: Selected Readings in Moral Philosophy*, New York: Macmillan, 1993.

Banks, Robert. *Paul's Idea of Community*. Grand Rapids: Wm. B. Eerdmans, 1980.

Bauman, Zygmunt. *Postmodern Ethics*. Oxford: Blackwell, 1993.

Benhabib, Seyla. *Situating the Self*. New York: Routledge, 1992.

Bernstein, Richard J., *Beyond Objectivism and Relativism: Science, Hermeneutics, and Praxis*. Philadelphia: University of Pennsylvania Press, 1983.

Bhaskar, Roy. *A Realist Theory of Science*. Atlantic Highlands, NJ: Humanities Press, 1978.

Boff, Leonardo. *Trinity and Society*. Trans. Paul Burns. Maryknoll, NY: Orbis Books, 1988.

Bonhoeffer, Dietrich. *Ethics*. Trans. Eberhard Bethge. New York: Macmillan, 1965.

Brueggemann, Walter. *Theology of the Old Testament*. Minneapolis: Fortress Press, 1997.

Capaldi, Nicholas. 'Copernican Metaphysics', in Robert Neville, ed. *New Essays in Metaphysics*. Albany: State University of New York Press, 1987.

Caputo, John C. *Against Ethics*. Bloomington: Indiana University Press, 1993.

Clarke, Stanley G. 'Anti-Theory in Ethics'. *American Philosophical Quarterly*, 24, 3, July 1987.

Clarke, Stanley G. and Evan Simpson, eds. *Anti-Theory in Ethics and Moral Conservatism* Albany: State University of New York Press, 1989.

Curran, Charles and Richard A. McCormick, eds. *Readings in Moral Theology, No. 2: The Distinctiveness of Christian Ethics*. Ramsay, NJ: Paulist Press, 1980.

Davidson, Donald. 'On the Very Idea of a Conceptual Scheme', in *Inquiries into Truth and Interpretation*. Oxford: Clarendon Press, 1984.

de Rivera, Joseph. 'Choice of Emotion and Ideal Development', in L. Cirillo, B. Kaplan and S. Wapner, eds. *Emotion and Ideal Human Development*. Hillsdale, NJ: Erlbaum, n.d.

de Sousa, Ronald. *The Rationality of Emotion*. Cambridge: MIT Press, 1987.

Dean, William. *History Making History*. Albany: State University of New York Press, 1988.

Diggins, John Patrick. *The Promise of Pragmatism*. Chicago: University of Chicago Press, 1994.

Eliot, T. S. *The Complete Poems and Plays, 1909–1950*. New York: Harcourt, Brace, 1952.

Economic Justice for All: Pastoral Letter on Catholic Social Teaching and the U.S. Economy. National Conference of Catholic Bishops: Washington, DC, 1986.

Farley, Margaret. 'Feminism and Universal Morality'. in Gene Outka and John P. Reeder, eds. *Prospects for a Common Morality*. Princeton: Princeton University Press, 1993.

Farrell, Frank B. *Subjectivity, Realism, and Postmodernism – the Recovery of the World*. Cambridge: Cambridge University Press, 1994.

Finkelstein, Israel and Neil Asher Silberman, *The Bible Unearthed*. New York: Free Press, 2001.

Florovsky, Georges. 'The Predicament of the Christian Historian'. C.T. McIntire, ed. *God, History, and Historians*. New York: Oxford University Press, 1977.

Fox-Genovese, Elizabeth. 'Women and Community'. *Feminism Without Illusions: A Critique of Individualism*. Chapel Hill: University of North Carolina Press, 1991.

French, Peter, Theo. Uehling and Howard Wettstein, eds. *Midwest Studies in Philosophy: Volume XIII Ethical Theory: Character and Virtue*. Notre Dame, IN: University of Notre Dame Press, 1988.

Freud, Sigmund. *The Future of an Illusion*. Garden City: Doubleday, 1964.

Friedman, Marilyn. 'Beyond Caring', in Mary Jeanne Larrabee, ed. *An Ethic of Care: Feminist and Interdisciplinary Perspectives*. New York: Routledge, 1992.

Friedman, Marilyn. *What Are Friends For? Feminist Perspectives on Personal Relationships and Moral Theory*. Ithaca: Cornell University Press, 1993.

Fuchs, Josef, SJ. *Natural Law: A Theological Investigation*. Trans. Helmut Reckter, SJ and John A. Dowling. New York: Sheed and Ward, 1965.

Fuchs, Josef, SJ. 'Is There a Specifically Christian Morality?' in Charles Curran and Richard A. McCormick, eds. *Readings in Moral Theology, No. 2: The Distinctiveness of Christian Ethics*. Ramsay, NJ: Paulist Press, 1980.

Fuchs, Josef, SJ. *Christian Ethics in a Secular Arena*. Trans. Bernard Hoose and Brian McNeil. Washington: Georgetown University Press, 1984.

Fuchs, Josef, SJ. 'The Absoluteness of Behavioral Moral Norms', in Ronald P. Hamel and Kenneth R. Himes, eds. *Introduction to Christian Ethics*. Mahwah, NJ: Paulist Press, 1989.

Gewirth, Alan. 'Common Morality and the Community of Rights', in Gene Outka and John Reeder, Jr., eds. *Prospects for a Common Morality*. Princeton: Princeton University Press, 1993.

Gilligan, Carol. *In a Different Voice: Psychological Theory and Women's Development*. Cambridge: Harvard University Press, 1982.

Gilligan, Carol. 'Remapping the Moral Domain: New Images of the Self in Relationship', in Thomas C. Heller, Morton Sosna, and David E. Wellbery, eds. *Reconstructing Individualism: Autonomy, Individuality, and the Self in Western Thought*. Stanford: Stanford University Press, 1986.

Gould, Carol. *Rethinking Democracy: Freedom and Social Cooperation in Politics, Economy, and Society*. Cambridge: Cambridge University Press, 1988.

Graham, George and Hugh Lafollette, eds. *Person to Person*. Philadelphia: Temple University Press, 1989.

Grant, C. David. *God the Center of Value: Value Theory in the Theology of H. Richard Niebuhr*. Fort Worth: Texas Christian University Press, 1984.

Greenberg, Jay R. and Stephen A. Mitchell. *Object Relations in Psychoanalytic Theory*. Cambridge: Harvard University Press, 1983.

Greenson, R. *The Technique and Practice of Psychoanalysis*. Vol. 1. New York: International Universities Press, 1967.

Griffin, James. 'How We Do Ethics Now', in A. Phillips Griffiths, ed. *Ethics*. (Royal Institute of Philosophy Supplement: 35). Cambridge University Press, 1993.

Griffiths, A. Phillips. *Ethics*. (Royal Institute of Philosophy Supplement: 35). Cambridge University Press, 1993.

Gunton, Colin. *The One, the Three and the Many. God, Creation and the Culture of Modernity*. The Bampton Lectures 1992. Cambridge: Cambridge University Press, 1993.

Gustafson, James M. 'Context Versus Principles: A Misplaced Debate in Christian Ethics', in Martin E. Marty and Dean G. Peerman, eds. *New Theology No. 3*. New York: The Macmillan Co., 1966.

Gustafson, James M. *Ethics From a Theocentric Perspective: Theology and Ethics*. Vol. Two. Chicago: University of Chicago Press, 1984.

Gustafson, James M. 'Moral Discernment in the Christian Life'. Ronald P. Hamel and Kenneth R. Himes, eds. *Introduction to Christian Ethics*. Mahwah, NJ: Paulist Press, 1989.

Hamel, Ronald P. and Kenneth R. Himes, eds. *Introduction to Christian Ethics*. Mahwah, NJ: Paulist Press, 1989.

Hampshire, Stuart. *Morality and Conflict*. Cambridge: Harvard University Press, 1983.

Hampshire, Stuart. 'Morality and Conflict', in Stanley G. Clarke and Evan Simpson, eds. *Anti-Theory in Ethics and Moral Conservatism*. Albany: State University of New York Press, 1989.

Hanson, Paul D. *The People Called: The Growth of Community in the Bible*. San Francisco: Harper and Row, 1986.

Hardwig, John. 'In Search of an Ethics of Personal Relationships', in George Graham and Hugh Lafollette, eds. *Person to Person*. Philadelphia: Temple University Press, 1989.

Harrison, Beverly Wildung. *Making the Connections: Essays in Feminist Social Ethics*. Boston: Beacon Press, 1985.

Harvey, Van. *The Historian and the Believer*. New York: The Macmillan Company, 1966.

Hauerwas, Stanley. *A Community of Character*. Notre Dame: University of Notre Dame Press, 1981.

Hauerwas, Stanley. *Against the Nations*. Minneapolis: Winston Press, 1985.

Hauerwas, Stanley. *Character and the Christian Life: A Study in Theological Ethics*. San Antonio: Trinity University Press, 1985.

Hauerwas, Stanley and Alisdair MacIntyre, eds. *Revisions*. Notre Dame: University of Notre Dame Press, 1983.

Heilbroner, Robert L. *The Worldly Philosophers*. New York: Simon and Schuster, 1961.

Hittinger, Russell. *A Critique of the New Natural Law Theory*. Notre Dame: University of Notre Dame Press, 1987.

Irenaeus. 'Against Heresies'. *The Apostolic Fathers With Justin Martyr and Irenaeus*. American edition, arranged by A. Cleveland Coxe, in Alexander Roberts and James Donaldson, eds. *The Ante-Nicene Fathers*, Vol. I. Grand Rapids: Wm. B. Eerdmans, 1885.

Johann, Robert. *The Pragmatic Meaning of God*. Milwaukee: Marquette University Press, 1966.

Johann, Robert. *Building the Human*. New York: Herder and Herder, 1968.

Jones, James W. *Contemporary Psychoanalysis and Religion: Transference and Transcendence*. New Haven: Yale University Press, 1991.

Jones, James W. *Religion and Psychology in Transition: Psychoanalysis, Feminism, and Theology*. New Haven: Yale University Press, 1996.

Kamenka, Eugene. *The Ethical Foundations of Marxism*. New York: Frederick A. Praeger, 1962.

Kekes, John. *The Morality of Pluralism*. Princeton: Princeton University Press, 1993.

Kirk, Kenneth E. *The Vision of God: The Christian Doctrine of the Summum Bonum*. London: Longman's Green, 1931.

Kirkpatrick, Frank G. *Community: A Trinity of Models*. Washington, DC: Georgetown University Press, 1986.

Kirkpatrick, Frank G. 'The Logic of Mutual Heterocentrism: The Self as Gift'. *Philosophy and Theology*, 6, 4, Summer 1992.

Kirkpatrick, Frank G. *Together Bound: God, History, and the Religious Community*. New York: Oxford University Press, 1994.

Kirkpatrick, Frank G. *The Ethics of Community*. Oxford: Blackwell, 2001.

Kirkpatrick, Frank G. 'Macmurray's PostMarxist Vision of Community'. Harry Carson, ed. *The Primacy of Persons As Agents in Relationship: Essays on the Post Modern Philosophy of John Macmurray* (in press).

Kymlicka, Will. 'Liberalism and Communitarianism'. *Canadian Journal of Philosophy*, 18, 2, June 1988.

LaCugna, Catherine Mowry *God For Us: The Trinity and Christian Life*. San Francisco: Harper San Francisco, 1991.

Lakoff, George and Mark Johnson. *Metaphors We Live By*. Chicago: University of Chicago Press, 1980.

Layman, C. Stephen. *The Shape of the Good: Christian Reflections on the Foundations of Ethics*. Notre Dame: University of Notre Dame Press, 1991.

Loewy, Eric. *Suffering and the Beneficient Community*. Albany: State University of New York Press, 1991.

Lohfink, Gerhard. *Jesus and Community: The Social Dimension of Christian Faith*. New York: Paulist Press, 1984.

Long, Edward LeRoy Jr. *A Survey of Christian Ethics*. New York: Oxford University Press, 1967.

Louden, Robert B. *Morality and Moral Theory*. New York: Oxford University Press, 1992.

McConnell, Terrance. 'Metaethical Principles, Meta-Prescriptions, and Moral Theories'. *American Philosophical Quarterly*, 22, 4, October 1985.

McCormick, Richard A. 'Does Religious Faith Add to Ethical Perception?', in Ronald P. Hamel and Kenneth R. Himes, eds. *Introduction to Christian Ethics*. Mahwah, NJ: Paulist Press, 1989.

McDargh, John. *Psychoanalytic Object Relations Theory and the Study of Religion*. Lanham, MD: University Press of America, 1983.

McDonagh, Enda. 'The Structure and Basis of Moral Experience' in Ronald P. Hamel and Kenneth R. Himes, eds. *Introduction to Christian Ethics*. Mahwah, NJ: Paulist Press, 1989.

McDowell, John. 'Virtue and Reason', in Stanley G.Clarke and Evan Simpson, eds. *Anti-Theory in Ethics and Moral Conservatism*. Albany: State University of New York Press, 1989.

MacIntire, C.T., ed. *God, History, and Historians*. New York: Oxford University Press, 1977.

MacIntyre, Alasdair. *After Virtue: A Study in Moral Theory*. Notre Dame: University of Notre Dame Press, 1984.

MacIntyre, Alasdair. *Whose Justice? Which Rationality?* Notre Dame: University of Notre Dame Press, 1988.

Mackie, J.L. 'The Subjectivity of Values', in Geoffrey Sayre-McCord, ed. *Essays on Moral Realism*. Ithaca: Cornell University Press, 1988.

Macmurray, John. *The Clue to History*. London: SCM Press, 1938.

Macmurray, John. *Constructive Democracy*. London: Faber and Faber, 1943.

Macmurray, John. *The Self as Agent*. Introduction by Stanley M. Harrison. Atlantic Heights: Humanities Press, c. 1991. Originally published by Faber and Faber, 1957.

Macmurray, John. *Persons in Relation*. Introduction by Frank G. Kirkpatrick. Atlantic Heights: Humanities Press, c. 1991. Originally published by Harper and Brothers, 1961.

Macmurray, John. 'Reason in the Emotional Life'. *Reason and Emotion*. New York: Barnes and Noble, 1962.

Macquarrie, John. 'Rethinking Natural Law', in Charles Curran and Richard A.

McCormick, eds. *Readings in Moral Theology, No. 2: The Distinctiveness of Christian Ethics*, Ramsay, NJ: Paulist Press, 1980

Manning, Rita. *Speaking From the Heart: A Feminist Perspective on Ethics.* Lanham, MD: Rowman and Littlefield, 1992.

Markham, Ian S. *Plurality and Christian Ethics.* Cambridge: Cambridge University Press, 1994.

Marx, Karl. *Economic and Philosophic Manuscripts.* Edited with an introduction by Dirk J. Struik. Trans. Martin Milligan. New York: International Publishers, 1964.

Marx, Karl. 'On James Mill'. *Karl Marx: Selected Writings.* Edited by David McLellan. Oxford: Oxford University Press, 1977.

Meeks, Wayne. *The First Urban Christians.* New Haven: Yale University Press, 1983.

Meeks, Wayne. *The Moral World of the First Christians.* Philadelphia: Westminster Press, 1986.

Meeks, Wayne. *The Origins of Christian Morality: The First Two Centuries* New Haven: Yale University Press, 1993.

Morgan, Michael L. 'Religion, History, and Moral Discourse', in James Tully, ed. *Philosophy in an Age of Pluralism: The Philosophy of Charles Taylor in Question.* Cambridge: Cambridge University Press, 1994.

Mouw, Richard J. 'Biblical Revelation and Medical Decisions', in Stanley Hauerwas and Alisdair MacIntyre, eds. *Revisions.* Notre Dame: University of Notre Dame Press, 1983.

Nagel, Thomas. *The View From Nowhere.* New York: Oxford University Press, 1986.

Needleman, Jacob, A. K. Bierman and James A. Gould. *Religion for a New Generation*, 2nd edn., New York: Macmillan, 1977.

Nelson, Daniel Mark. *The Priority of Prudence: Virtue and Natural Law in Thomas Aquinas and the Implications for Modern Ethics.* University Park, PA: The Pennsylvania State University Press, 1991.

Neville, Robert C., ed. *New Essays in Metaphysics.* Albany: State University of New York Press, 1987.

Niebuhr, H. Richard. *The Responsible Self.* New York: Harper and Row, 1963.

Noble, Cheryl. 'Normative Ethical Theories', in Stanley G. Clarke and Evan Simpson, eds. *Anti-Theory in Ethics and Moral Conservatism.* Albany: State University of New York Press, 1979.

Noddings, Nel. *Caring: A Feminine Approach to Ethics and Moral Education.* Berkeley: University of California Press, 1984.

Norris, Christopher. *What's Wrong with Postmodernism?* Baltimore: Johns Hopkins Press, 1990.

Nussbaum, Martha. *The Fragility of Goodness.* Cambridge: Cambridge University Press, 1986.

Nussbaum, Martha. 'Non-Relative Virtues: An Aristotelian Approach', in Peter French, Theo. Uehling, Howard Wettstein, eds. *Midwest Studies in Philosophy: Volume XIII Ethical Theory: Character and Virtue*, Notre Dame, IN: University of Notre Dame Press, 1988.

Oakeshott, Michael. 'The Tower of Babel', in Stanley G. Clarke and Evan Simpson eds. *Anti-Theory in Ethics and Moral Conservatism*. Albany: State University of New York Press, 1979.

Olds, Linda. *Metaphors of Interrelatedness: Toward A Systems Theory of Psychology*. Albany: State University of New York Press, 1992.

Ollman, Bertel. *Alienation*. 2nd edn. Cambridge: Cambridge University Press, 1976.

Outka, Gene. 'Universal Love and Impartiality', in Edmund N. Santurri and William Werpehowski, eds. *The Love Commandments*. Washington: Georgetown University Press, 1992.

Outka, Gene and John P. Reeder, Jr. eds. *Prospects for a Common Morality*. Princeton: Princeton University Press, 1993.

Pannenberg, Wolfhart. 'Revelation as History', in C.T. MacIntire, ed. *God, History, and Historians*. New York: Oxford University Press, 1977.

Parsons, Susan Frank. *Feminism and Christian Ethics*. Cambridge: Cambridge University Press, 1996.

Perry, Michael J. *Love and Power*. New York: Oxford University Press, 1991.

Pincoffs, Edmund. *Quandaries and Virtues: Against Reductivism in Ethics*. Lawrence: University of Kansas Press, 1986.

Pols, Edward. *Radical Realism*. Ithaca: Cornell University Press, 1992.

Porter, Jean. *The Recovery of Virtue: The Relevance of Aquinas for Christian Ethics*. Louisville: Westminster/John Knox Press, 1990.

Post, Stephen. *A Theory of Agape*. Lewisburg: Bucknell University Press, 1990.

Rawls, John. *A Theory of Justice*. Cambridge, MA: Harvard University Press, 1971.

Rawls, John. 'Justice as Fairness: Political not Metaphysical'. *Philosophy and Public Affairs*, 14, 1985.

Rawls, John. 'The Priority of Rights and Ideas of the Good'. *Philosophy and Public Affairs*, 17, 1988.

Reeder, John P. Jr. 'Assenting to Agape'. *Journal of Religion*, 60, 1, 1980.

Reeder, John P. Jr. 'Analogues to Justice', in Edmund N. Santurri and William Werpehowski, eds. *The Love Commandments*. Washington: Georgetown University Press, 1992.

Rorty, Richard. *Consequences of Pragmatism*. Minneapolis: University of Minnesota Press, 1982.

Rorty, Richard. 'Pragmatism, Relativism, and Irrationalism', *Proceedings and Addresses of the American Philosophical Association* 53, 1980.

Rorty, Richard. 'The Contingency of a Liberal Community'. *Contingency, Irony, and Solidarity*. Cambridge: Cambridge University Press, 1989.

Rorty, Richard. 'Solidarity or Objectivity?' *Objectivity, Relativism, and Truth*. Cambridge: Cambridge University Press, 1991.

Rorty, Richard. 'Trotsky and the Wild Orchids'. *Common Knowledge* 1, 1 Spring 1992.

Ross, James F. 'Rational Reliance'. *Journal of the American Academy of Religion*, 42, 3, Fall, 1994.

Ryan, Columba. 'The Traditional Concept of Natural Law: An Interpretation', in Ronald P. Hamel and Kenneth R. Himes, eds. *Introduction to Christian Ethics*. Mahrah, NJ: Paulist Press, 1989.

Sandel, Michael. 'The Procedural Republic and the Unencumbered Self'. Shlomo

Avineri and Avner De-Shalit, eds. *Communitarianism and Individualism*. New York: Oxford University Press, 1992.

Santurri, Edmund N. and William Werpehowski, eds. *The Love Commandments*. Washington: Georgetown University Press, 1992.

Sayre-McCord, Geoffrey, ed. *Essays on Moral Realism*. Ithaca: Cornell University Press, 1988.

Schuller, Bruno, SJ. 'Can Moral Theology Ignore Natural Law?', in Ronald P. Hamel and Kenneth R. Himes, eds. *Introduction to Christian Ethics*. Mahrah, NJ: Paulist Press, 1989.

Schwartz, Barry. *The Battle for Human Nature*. New York: W.W. Norton, 1986.

Sherover, Charles M. 'Toward Experiential Metaphysics: Radical Temporalism', in Robert C. Neville, ed. *New Essays in Metaphysics*. Albany: State University of New York Press, 1987.

Skinner, Quentin. 'Who Are "We"? Ambiguities of the Modern Self', *Inquiry*, 34, 1992, p. 148.

Smith, Adam. *An Inquiry into the Nature and Causes of the Wealth of Nations*. Edited, with an introduction, notes, marginal summary and an enlarged index by Edwin Cannan, with an introduction by Max Lerner. New York: Modern Library, 1937.

Soskice, Janet Martin. *Metaphor and Religious Language*. Oxford: Clarendon Press, 1985.

Taylor, Charles. 'What is Human Agency?', in Theodore Mischel, ed. *The Self: Psychological and Philosophical Issues*, Oxford: Oxford University Press, 1977.

Taylor, Charles. *Sources of the Self: The Making of the Modern Identity*. Cambridge: Harvard University Press, 1989.

Taylor, Charles. 'Comments and Replies'. *Inquiry*, 34, 1991.

Taylor, Mark C. *Erring: A Postmodern A/theology*. Chicago: University of Chicago Press, 1984.

Thomas, Laurence. 'Moral Motivation: Kantians Vs. Humeans', in French *et al.* eds. *Midwest Studies in Philosophy XIII Ethical Theory: Character and Virtue*, Notre Dame, IN: University of Notre Dame Press, 1988.

Thomas, Laurence. *Living Morally*. Philadelphia: Temple University Press, 1989.

Tillich, Paul. *Dynamics of Faith*. New York: Harper Torchbooks, 1957.

Tronto, Joan. *Moral Boundaries: A Political Argument for an Ethic of Care*. New York: Routledge, 1993.

'The Vatican Declaration on Sexual Ethics', in Jacob Needleman, A.K. Bierman, James A. Gould, eds. *Religion for a New Generation*. 2nd edition. New York: Macmillan, 1977.

Walzer, Michael. *Spheres of Justice*. New York: Basic Books, 1983.

Whittaker, John. ''Agape' and Self-Love', in Edmund N. Santurri and William Werpehowski, eds. *The Love Commandments*. Washington: Georgetown University Press, 1992.

Wiggins, David. 'Truth, Invention, and the Meaning of Life', in Geoffrey Sayre-McCord, ed. *Essays on Moral Realism*. Ithaca: Cornell University Press, 1988.

Williams, Bernard. *Ethics and the Limits of Philosophy*. Cambridge: Harvard University Press, 1985.

Wong, David B. 'On Flourishing and Finding One's Identity', in French *et al.* eds.

Midwest Studies in Philosophy Volume XIII Ethical Theory: Character and Virtue. Notre Dame, IN: University of Notre Dame Press, 1988.

Wren, Thomas. *Caring About Morality*. Cambridge: MIT Press, 1991.

Wright, Paul H. 'The Essence of Personal Relationships and Their Value for the Individual', in George Graham and Hugh Lafollette, eds. *Person to Person*. Philadelphia: Temple University Press, 1989.

Yearley, Lee. *Mencius and Aquinas*. Albany, NY: State University of New York Press, c. 1990.

Young, Iris Marion. 'City Life and Difference', in *Justice and the Politics of Difference*. Princeton: Princeton University Press, 1990.

Index